Commercial Banks and Monetary Policy in India

Partha Ray is currently Adviser to the Executive Director (India, Bangladesh, Sri Lanka and Bhutan) at the International Monetary Fund, Washington D.C. For more than a decade he, as an economist at the Department of Economic Analysis and Policy, Reserve Bank of India, has been involved with applied economic research with policy content. He also has been associated with a number of official committees on policy matters. Educated in Kolkata, Mumbai and Oxford, he has published extensively on issues related to banking and monetary policy in professional journals in India and abroad. He taught economics to under-graduate students in RBC College, University of Kolkata during 1987-89.

PARTHA RAY

Commercial Banks and Monetary Policy in India

ACADEMIC FOUNDATION
NEW DELHI
www.academicfoundation.com

The views expressed in the book are of the author and not necessarily of the institution(s) to which he belongs.

First published in 2008
by

ACADEMIC FOUNDATION
4772-73 / 23 Bharat Ram Road, (23 Ansari Road),
Darya Ganj, New Delhi - 110 002 (India).
Phones : 23245001 / 02 / 03 / 04.
Fax : +91-11-23245005.
E-mail : academic@vsnl.com
www. academicfoundation.com

Cataloging in Publication Data--DK
Courtesy: D.K. Agencies (P) Ltd. <docinfo@dkagencies.com>

Ray, Partha.
Commercial banks and monetary policy in India / Partha Ray.
p. cm. Includes bibliographical references (p.)
Includes index.
ISBN 13: **9788171886357**
ISBN 10: 8171886355

1. Banks and banking--India. 2. Monetary policy--India. I. Title.

DDC 332.109 54 22

Typeset by Italics India, New Delhi.
Printed and bound in India.

10 9 8 7 6 5 4 3 2 1

To the memory of my parents

Indira
and
Nityananda

CONTENTS

List of Tables, Figures and Annexes

TABLES

FIGURES

ANNEXES

Foreword

Among the more interesting recent developments in economic policy in India is the resurgence of active and intense debate on the practice and effectiveness of monetary policy. Because of the long prevalence of administered interest rates and fiscal dominance of monetary policy in the 1970s and 1980s, theoretical and empirical work on monetary policy had declined significantly in the country. As the economy gets more developed and as financial markets develop further, the role of monetary policy in economic management will increase in importance. Hence, achieving better understanding of the monetary policy transmission process in India needs increased emphasis on research in this area.

While we know that monetary policy actions do influence economic activities, we do not know for certain the working of the channels through which such actions get transmitted. Even if one accepts such a fuzzy state of knowledge on monetary transmission channels as a whole, the importance of commercial banks in the transmission of monetary policy action is well-known. Thus, an understanding of the impact of central bank policy actions on commercial banks' behaviour is crucially important for the effective practice of monetary policy.

With the deregulation of interest rates in the 1990s, the credit channel of monetary policy transmission has assumed increased importance in recent years. Apart from the differential impact of monetary policy on different borrowers, a major question that has attracted some attention is: do all banks react uniformly to central bank's policy actions? Does size of banks matter in determining the nature and extent of monetary policy transmission? Are there are any other attributes of banks that can have a significant impact as well?

The theoretical predictions of the credit channel literature and the related role of banks has been subjected to extensive empirical verifications for developed economies. For India as well there is some evidence of the bank lending channel working in addition to the conventional interest rate channel. In view of the asymmetry in the resource base, access to non-deposit sources, asset allocation and liquidity, big and small banks are often found to respond in significantly different ways. In particular, small banks are more acutely affected by contractionary monetary policy shocks as compared to big banks, i.e., smaller banks curtail their lending more sharply *vis-à-vis* large banks. Available empirical evidence also indicates that prudential norms, as proxied by banks' capital adequacy ratios, exert a significant influence on bank lending.[1]

Seen in this context, the present book constitutes an important contribution to the extant literature. In the backdrop of the financial sector reforms process in India and the theoretical developments in analysing the credit channel of monetary transmission, the author has attempted to evaluate the impact of monetary policy on commercial banks. In specific terms, the book attempts to locate the impact of monetary policy on banks' balance sheets in India. It analyses the response to the Central Bank's policy actions on macro-portfolios of banks as well as portfolios of different type of banks (with respect to ownership, *i.e.*, private, public and foreign banks). This apart, the book examines the impact of the two basic constraints faced by banks in determining the nature of impact of monetary policy, *viz.*, liquidity constraints, and capital constraints. The important contribution of the book is perhaps its investigation of the micro evidence relating to the differential impact of monetary policy on different types of banks—be it from the standpoint of ownership or from capitalisation and put the econometric questions in the context of relevant theories and stylised facts for India.

Broadly speaking, the book finds some evidence favouring the differential effect of monetary policy on banks. Thus, while monetary

---

1. I have discussed some of these issues in detail in my lecture at the Bank for International Settlement, Basel; see Rakesh Mohan (2007). "Monetary Transmission in India", *RBI Bulletin*, April, pp.421- 472.

policy actions do influence commercial bank behaviour in general, not all the banks respond uniformly. In particular, attributes like ownership, size, liquidity of the balance sheet, or capitalisation play important roles in determining the nature of response. In conclusion, the author has investigated three interesting issues, *viz.* (a) consolidation in Indian banking, (b) changes in operating procedure of monetary policy, and (c) newer norms of bank capital, in a somewhat futuristic scenario and conjectured that the extent of differential impact of monetary policy is perhaps going to get exacerbated in the days to come.

The Indian banking sectors and the financial sector as a whole will undoubtedly go through significant change over the next decade and beyond. Financial markets will increase in importance as the purveyors of monetary policy transmission and the interaction of the credit channel with the debt market channel will become more complex. With fuller capital account convertibility, monetary policy transmission will be influenced increasingly by global monetary and financial developments. With increased exposure to markets, the behaviour of banks has already undergone considerable change and will presumably continue further transformation. Finally, the medium term objectives of reduction in CRR and SLR will also alter the channel of monetary policy transmission through banks.

Hence the study of monetary policy transmission needs continued attention and I hope that others will follow Partha Ray's example of careful empirical investigation for enhancing our understanding of these issues. We can then look forward to more informed debate on monetary policy issues in the country.

Rakesh Mohan
Deputy Governor
Reserve Bank of India
Mumbai

Preface

The monetary transmission mechanism is one of the cornerstones of monetary policy. The standard means through which monetary policy of the central banks influence prices or output in the macroeconomy is discussed in great detail along with their various ideological moorings of different schools of thought in any undergraduate text of macro-monetary economics. Despite such importance, the monetary transmission mechanism is often termed as a black box. That is to say we know that money influences the economy but we do not know for certain how does it influence.

It is in this context, that the response of the commercial banks to monetary policy actions had attracted attention in recent years. In fairly general terms, the present book looks into this issue within the broad framework of credit channel of monetary transmission. The analysis is done at three planes. First, at a theoretical plane, the literature on extended IS-LM model with banks is looked into. Second, trends in Indian macro-economy and regulatory regime are analysed so as to discern the broad stylised facts. Finally, at an empirical plane, econometric assessment of commercial banks' response to monetary policy actions is evaluated in the Indian context both at an aggregative as well as at a micro level.

Despite the fact that analysis is made at three different but inter-related levels, the present book is fundamentally empirical in nature and describes the Indian experience of impact of monetary policy on commercial bank behaviour. As someone not very generous to the discipline of Economics commented, "An economist is a trained professional paid to guess wrong about the economy and an econometrician is a trained professional paid to use computers to guess wrong about the economy." Seen from this standpoint, the present book is expected to suffer from both these two sources of possible follies of inference—human capital and information technology. Specifically, against the emerging theoretical literature on credit channel of monetary policy (Chapter 2) and regulatory and monetary policy environment within the broad framework of the financial sector reforms process in India (Chapter 3), the present book looks into the response of the commercial banks in general (and bank credit in particular) to central bank's policy actions (Chapters 4, 5 and 6).

What does the book say in the end? At the risk of broad generalisation, if the findings of the book are to be believed then it seems that while monetary policy actions do influence commercial bank behaviour, not all the banks respond uniformly. In particular, attributes like ownership, size, liquidity of balance sheet, and capitalisation play important roles in determining the nature of response. In specific terms, the commercial banks have the capability to cushion off its portfolio, at least partially, from the impact of a contractionary monetary policy, depending on these attributes.

My teachers (at various places) have been very supportive in my endeavour in writing the book. First and foremost, I am indebted to Professor D. M. Nachane for his intellectual contribution and constant encouragement over the long incubation period of the book. The book also owes a lot to Professor Veena Mishra who motivated me in the initial years to think into the various issues pursued in the book. Besides, Professor(s) L. Gambacorta, Gabe de Bondt, Pulapre Balakrishnan, Subroto Sarkar, Bibhas Saha, Anindya Sen and Kunal Sen were extremely supportive at different points of time.

The book owes a lot to my employer, the Reserve Bank of India (RBI), which exposed me to look at the realities of the financial sector and allowed me to take a sabbatical. In this effort various officials have been extremely helpful to me. In particular, I am indeed grateful to Dr. S.L. Shetty, Dr. Narendra Jadhav, Mr. M.R. Nair, Dr. G.S. Bhati, Dr. R.K. Pattnaik, and Dr. M.D. Patra for their encouragement and support. Dr. A. Vasudevan was very generous both intellectually and emotionally. It is entirely due to his encouragement and involvement that the book saw the light of the day. I am highly obliged to Deputy

Governor Dr. Rakesh Mohan for agreeing to write the Foreword to this book. My friends in the Reserve Bank have always been very supportive all through out. Mridul Saggar, Rajiv Ranjan, Muneesh Kapur, Abha Prasad and A Prasad—all were extremely helpful. Sanjay Hansda, Indranil Sen Gupta, Saibal Ghosh, Indranil Bhattacharya and Alpana Killawala had the misfortune of going through the draft at various stages and gave detailed comments and I learnt a lot from them. This book indeed owes a lot to the benevolence, support and kind considerations of various people of the RBI. Needless to say, the views expressed in the book are entirely my own and not to be ascribed to the Reserve Bank of India or to the International Monetary Fund.

My debt to Mr. Rituraj Kapila of the Academic Foundation is also immense. Over the recent period, my association with him exceeded the limit of the normal author-publisher relationship.

Following the Indian tradition let me not resist the temptation of thanking my wife Shyamali and daughter Ronjini, as also my brothers Rajat and Jayanta and sister-in-laws Shefali and Anusri. All of them bore the burnt of my labour of love.

Finally, this is a book about the interaction of monetary policy and banking behaviour in general and bank credit in particular. There is a story about the FIRST National Bank of Washington, who wanted to encourage business through billboard advertising and put the following ad: *"Loans make life easier, at FIRST."* I do hope the book does not suffer from such over-simplification related slips.

Partha Ray

Acronyms

AD	Aggregate Deposits
AFS	Available for Sale
AIC	Akaike Information Criterion
B-B Model	Bernanke-Blinder (1998) Model
BC	Bank Credit
BIS	Bank for International Settlements
BPLR	Benchmark Prime Lending Rate
BSE	The Stock Exchange, Mumbai
CBLO	Collateralised Borrowing and Lending Obligations
CCIL	Clearing Corporation of India Ltd
CDs	Certificates of Deposit
C-D Ratio	Credit-Deposit Ratio
CDR	Corporate Debt Recovery
CIBIL	Credit Information Bureau (India) Limited
CP	Commercial Paper
CPI	Consumer Price Index
CPI-IW	Consumer Price Index—Industrial Workers
CRAR	Capital to Risk-Weighted Assets Ratio
CRR	Cash Reserve Ratio
CSO	Central Statistical Organisation
DFHI	Discount and Finance House of India
EMEs	Emerging Market Economies
FCNR	Foreign Currency Non-Resident
FCNR(B)	Foreign Currency Non-Resident (Banks)
FEVD	Forecast Error Variance Decomposition
FI	Financial Institution
GAAP	Generally Accepted Accounting Principles
GRM	Growth of Reserve Money

G-S Model	Greenwald-Stiglitz (2003) Model
HQC	Hannan-Quinn Criterion
HTM	Held to Maturity
I-D Ratio	Investment-Deposit Ratio
IIP	Index of Industrial Production
INVA	Aggregate Investment
IRF	Impulse Response Function
LAF	Liquidity Adjustment Facility
MSS	Market Stabilisation Scheme
NDS	Negotiated Dealing System
NDTL	Net Demand and Time Liabilities
NFA	Net Foreign Exchange Assets
NPAs	Non Performing Assets
NSE	National Stock Exchange
PLR	Prime Lending Rate
PSU	Public Sector Undertaking
RBI	Reserve Bank of India
RIB	Resurgent India Bonds
RIDF	Rural Infrastructure Development Fund
RM	Reserve Money
s.d.	Standard Deviation
Sensex	BSE (The Stock Exchange, Mumbai) Sensitive Index, BSE 30
SBI	State Bank of India
SBIC	Schwartz Bayesian Information Criterion
SCBs	Scheduled Commercial Banks
SIDBI	Small Industrial Development Bank of India
SLR	Statutory Liquidity Ratio
STCI	Securities Trading Corporation of India
VAR	Vector Autoregression
WPI	Wholesale Price Index

Note on Lakh and Crore

The book uses the Indian notions of lakh and crore. For ready reference it may be noted that:

- 1 lakh = 100,000 = 1/10 million
- 1 crore = 100,00,000 = 10 million.

1

Introduction and Overview

1.1 Banks and Monetary Policy

Central banks all over the world are entrusted with the responsibility of conducting monetary policy. The agents through which their action gets transmitted to the economy at large are primarily the commercial banks. However, unless it operates in an absolute command economy, the central bank tries to influence the behaviour of commercial banks through various monetary policy instruments. Thus, the very premise of effectiveness of monetary policy is that central banks can control the behaviour of commercial banks through operations of various instruments of monetary control.

Despite this, in the theoretical discussion of monetary policy, commercial banks are relegated to the backdrop. In fact, in the basic workhorse of the undergraduate macroeconomics, *viz.*, the IS-LM model, commercial banks are not explicitly modelled as the credit market plays the role of a hidden market. It is eliminated from the three commodity/asset (*viz.*, goods, money and bonds) world of IS-LM *via* the application of Walras law.

During the last decade and a half there has been a revival of interest in the role of banks in the transmission of monetary policy. While this is primarily due to a revival of the credit channel of monetary transmission, one can trace three factors responsible for such interest. First, there has been a major development in the literature on microeconomic information-asymmetry based credit rationing (Stiglitz and Weiss, 1981) and existence of banks (Diamond and Dybvig, 1983). Second, on a macro plane, Bernanke and Blinder (1988) reconstructed the standard IS-LM model with bank loans as another asset. Besides, the role of financial factors in business cycles has also emerged as a current topic of interest (*e.g.*, Greenwald and Stiglitz, 1993). Third, there have been a number of empirical and narrative studies highlighting the role of credit crunch in financial crisis and depression (Bernanke, 1983; Bernanke and Lown, 1992).

But how important are commercial banks in the transmission of monetary policy? Let us consider an illustration. In order to pursue a contractionary monetary policy, let the central bank increase the cash reserves ratio, so that commercial banks need to keep a higher proportion of their total liabilities as deposits with the central bank. Assuming default on account of reserve requirement is very expensive (on account of the fine and the reputation risk of the bank), banks have to adjust their portfolio. In the traditional textbook version of monetary policy, when banks are assumed to hold a single catch-all asset called 'bonds' the question is not interesting as bonds have to do the adjusting act. However, if this hypothetical bank has two assets, *viz.*, loans and investment in bonds (including Treasury bills), then the question arises which one of these assets (or both) bear the burnt?

The crucial issue is, however, the degree of substitutability of the two assets. If these two assets are perfectly substitutable, then the introduction of the second asset does not materially change the scenario. However, there could be many reasons for which the assets may not be perfectly substitutable. The liquidity of a bond could be more than a pre-negotiated loan. A recent resurgence of a strand of monetary economics in this context is the credit channel literature, which posits that it is also the bank loans that bear the resource crunch faced by the banks. However, there are at least two ways in which the banks can bypass the resources crunch caused by a contractionary monetary policy. First, if the banks can sell securities (like Treasury bills), then bank-dependent borrowers are not deprived of their credit needs. Second, they can take recourse to non-deposits resources like certificates of deposit, which could attract a lower reserves ratio.

1.2 Indian Context

How far are these postulates valid in an emerging market economy (EME) like that of India? The ability of the central bank to control money supply in a developing economy could be different from that in a developed country. It could be 'more' if instruments like certificates of deposit are nonexistent or marginally present. On the contrary, it could be 'less' if alternative sources of informal finance in the economy are present. In the Indian context, it can be argued that the stock of commercial bank credit to the private sector had significant effects on the interest rate in the informal credit market (Acharya and Madhur, 1983). In other words, official monetary policy could have substantial impact on informal credit markets as well.

At this juncture it may be noted that the issue of central banks' policy actions and commercial banks' portfolio behaviour will be less interesting in a controlled regime. After all, in a controlled regime much of the monetary policy actions are effected through administrative instructions. Illustratively, during the 1980s in India, when strict inventory and receivables norms and elaborate stipulations on priority sector lending existed, there was little leeway for the banks in having any innovative response to central bank's policy actions. Presence of high cash reserve (CRR) and statutory liquidity ratios (SLR) also provided little freedom for the commercial banks to make adjustments on the asset side of their balance sheet. After all, when CRR would go up, with SLR already at its statutory maximum, the only adjustment the banks could make on their asset side was to reduce their lending. The scenario changed radically since the initiation of the financial sector reform programme in the early 1990s, which brought about far-reaching changes in the Indian financial sector.

It may be noted that notwithstanding the spread of banking institutions, the Indian banking system as it emerged in the early 1990s suffered from three major structural bottlenecks. First, there were multiple restrictions on bank portfolios along with segmented financial markets. Second, a regime of administered interest rates blunted the process of price discovery. Third, bank profitability was affected by the need to compensate the depositor for the rising inflation, partly driven by the monetary expansion emanating from deficit financing, on the one hand, and the imperative to provide soft loans to spur industrial development, on the other.

India embarked upon a massive programme of stabilisation and structural reforms in the midst of the unprecedented balance of payments and fiscal crisis in mid-1991. A basic component of the reforms is the financial sector, initiated since 1992-93, aimed at providing a diversified, efficient and competitive operating environment with the ultimate objective of improving the allocative efficiency of available resources.

The Committee on the Financial System (Chairman: M. Narasimham), which laid down the blue print of financial sector reforms, recognised that a vibrant and competitive financial system was central to the wide-ranging structural reforms (RBI, 1992). In order to ensure that the financial system operates on the basis of operational flexibility and functional autonomy with a view to enhancing efficiency, productivity and profitability, the Committee recommended a series of measures. These measures aimed at according greater flexibility to bank operations (especially by lowering of statutory pre-emptions and broad-basing of the directed credit programmes), institution of prudential norms in line with international best practices, greater disclosures and better house-keeping, in terms of accounting practices. The period was also marked by a regime of deregulation of interest rates.

The period also witnessed the deregulation of bank operations and prudential regulation, including capital adequacy (Nachane, 1999). The Reserve Bank has prescribed banks capital to risk-weighted assets ratio (CRAR) since 1992-93. CRAR stipulations have been gradually increased, especially in case of domestic banks, from 4 per cent during 1992-93 to 9 per cent in 1999-2000. The notion of risk-weighted assets has been gradually expanded from credit risk to include market risks and has also been extended to government paper as well. In order to ensure a smooth transition, the Government has recapitalised a number of public sector banks and allowed foreign banks to bring capital from their parent bank abroad. Strict provisioning norms have been specified in case of the various categories of non-performing assets (NPAs).

To sum up, the noteworthy developments in the financial system over the period were as follows:

(a) Financial repression through statutory pre-emptions has been eased. Illustratively, at end-March 2006, the CRR stood at 5 per cent (legal minimum is 3 per cent) and SLR at 25 per cent (legal minimum).

(b) The administered interest rate regime has been mostly dismantled, allowing banks the freedom to choose their deposit and lending rates.

(c) Competition has been infused by allowing more liberal entry of foreign banks and permitting functioning of new private banks.

(d) A set of micro-prudential measures (capital adequacy requirements, income recognition, asset classification and provisioning norms for loans, exposure norms, accounting norms) has been stipulated.

An analysis of the balance sheet of the commercial banks during this period reveals a number of interesting trends. First, there was a gradual decline in the share of balances held with the Reserve Bank reflecting the sharp reduction in reserve requirements. Second, banks were allowed to increasingly take exposures in foreign currencies as part of the liberalisation of the external account in the 1990s. Third, while it is true that the share of bank credit has not appreciably increased despite the cut in statutory pre-emptions, this has been in the backdrop of the weakening of credit demand in the latter half of the 1990s.[1] Finally, despite the progressive reduction of SLR, the share of government paper in the bank portfolio, climbed to 41 per cent of assets as at end-March 2004 from 26 per cent as at end-March 1993. There was, however, a major shift in the rationale of such investment. Unlike till the mid-1990s when gilt investment was largely on account of high SLR requirements, during the latter half of the 1990s, the persistent preference for government paper reflected the lack of alternative avenues of investments in the face of a lacklustre domestic credit demand. In such a situation, parking funds in government paper allowed them to augment their Treasury incomes in a scenario of falling interest rates during the downturn in economic activity in the later half of the 1990s.

---

1. As the time span of the present book stops at 2003-04 (i.e., March 2004), the later spurt in credit disbursals by commercial banks is beyond its scope.

Insofar as the relationship between the central bank's policy actions and commercial bank behaviour is concerned, it may be noted that to brand the whole experience of the 1990s as one of unbridled financial de-control would perhaps be misleading. After all, the liberalisation measures towards removal of interest rate regulation and reducing the extent of statutory pre-emption were accompanied by a concomitant imposition of income recognition, asset classification and provisioning norms. Illustratively, the impact of a contractionary monetary policy (say, as captured by an increase in CRR) may get magnified if accompanied by a simultaneous imposition of capital adequacy on the commercial banks. Take the recent behaviour of commercial banks, when it is widely known that commercial banks hold large volumes of government securities far in excess of the required SLR. While one may argue that this could be due to a depressed investment climate and that there is no pick-up in the credit demand, there are allegations of 'lazy banking' (Mohan, 2002) as well as 'missing monetary policy' (Balakrishnan, 2005).

1.3 Issues

In this context of theoretical developments and Indian economic reforms, the present book examines the response of commercial banks in terms of their portfolio behaviour (with particular emphasis on credit) to the central bank's policy actions in India. The story has been traced since the early 1990s and coincides with the initiation of the financial sector reform process in India. In particular, the following three issues are delved:

1. Analysis of the aggregative response of banks' portfolios in general, and credit in particular, to the central bank's policy actions.
2. Analysis of the response of different banks to the central bank's policy actions.
3. Examination of the impact of the two basic constraints faced by the banks, *viz.*, (a) liquidity constraints, and (b) capital constraints, in determining the nature of impact of monetary policy.

In examining the response of bank portfolios to monetary policy actions, a specific characteristic of banks, *viz.*, ownership was looked into. While the differential impact of monetary policy has been extensively dealt with in the literature with respect to bank size (e.g., Kashyap and Stein, 1995), the issue of ownership has an Indian perspective, where the public sector banks co-exist with sizeable number of private Indian and foreign banks. An attempt was made to see whether the behaviour of public, private and foreign banks differ with respect to monetary policy actions in terms of their credit, deposit and investment.

In the context of the third question, it may be noted that there is a recent literature that probes whether the lending behaviour of the capital-constrained and capital-unconstrained banks (Peek and Rosengren, 1995a) or of the liquidity-constrained and liquidity–unconstrained banks (de Bondt, 2000) are different. In particular, it has been pointed out that for in case of a capital constraint, the sensitiveness of loans to a change in monetary policy would be more for the capital-unconstrained banks than the capital-constrained banks. The role played by three attributes, *viz.*, capital, liquidity and size, in determining the nature of lending behaviour of commercial banks has been examined in this context.

1.4 Methodology

Since the book makes an endeavour to evaluate the impact of the central bank's policy action on commercial banks' behaviour in quantitative terms, a digression on the econometric methodology is in order. The domain of interest in the book has been the post reforms Indian economy, i.e., 1991-92 through 2003-04, i.e., 12 years. Hence, in order to evaluate the impact econometrically, there was the problem of paucity of observations. Thus, to solve the degree of freedom problem and to arrive at econometrically robust conclusions, two routes was adhered to—either, high frequency monthly data (Chapters 3 and 4) was used, or alternatively annual data for a panel of observations (Chapter 5) was utilised. In terms of techniques, the high frequency monthly data has been typically used for estimating the vector autoregression (VAR) models, and annual data for a panel of banks have been utilised to estimate the panel regressions.

1.5 Broad Findings

At the risk of broad generalisation, the finding of the present book may be summarised as follows. While monetary policy actions do influence commercial bank behaviour, not all banks respond uniformly. In particular, attributes like ownership, size, liquidity of balance sheet, or capitalisation play important roles in determining the nature of response. In specific terms, depending on these attributes the commercial banks have the capability to bypass, at least partially, the impact of a contractionary monetary policy.

The findings have been evaluated in the context of three major developments that are expected to come up in a futuristic scenario, *viz.*, (a) consolidation in Indian banking, (b) changed operating procedure of monetary policy, and (c) adoption of newer norms of bank capital (*viz.*, Basel II).

The conclusions are expected to shed light on the role of commercial banks in transmitting the monetary policy instruments as well as the role of various attributes like size, liquidity and capitalisation in determining the importance of bank credit channel in India.

The rest of the book proceeds as follows. Apart from surveying the theory and presenting some extensions on the role of banks in monetary policy (Chapter 2), the book presents a description of the stylised facts of Indian macro-economy, monetary and banking policy and commercial banks' balance sheet/portfolio behaviour (Chapter 3). Next three chapters are devoted to the empirical evaluation of the research questions raised earlier. In particular, while Chapter 4 looks into the aggregative response of banks' portfolios to central banks' policy actions, the ownership-wise disaggregated bahaviour of different bank groups are investigated in chapter 5. Chapter 6 probes into the influence of size, liquidity and capital on the credit behaviour of a panel of Indian commercial banks. Chapter 7 presents the epilogue and the way forward.

2

Commercial Banks and Monetary Policy

Some Theoretical Considerations

2.1 Introduction

In the theoretical discussion of monetary policy, commercial banks often take a backseat. In fact, in the IS-LM framework, commercial banks are not explicitly modelled and with the credit market playing the role of a hidden market, credit is eliminated from the three commodity/asset (*viz.*, goods, money and bonds) world of IS-LM from explicit consideration *via* the application of Walras law. Credit, in general, is subsumed under the catch-all financial assets called 'bonds.' This is most clearly brought out in Patinkin (1965) wherein aggregate demands for goods, money and other assets are functions of income, relative price and aggregate net wealth of the private sector. However, the role of credit has not been examined explicitly through the examination of an equivalent and off-setting liability within the private sector.[1]

Nevertheless, within the framework of standard macro theory, there is a class of models where bank credit traditionally plays an important role. These are models with an expanded financial sector (e.g., Tobin (1969) or Brainard and Tobin (1968)). In these models, the financial market is typically disaggregated into a number of sub-sectors, devoted to specific assets. While the present chapter makes no attempt in this direction, one may note an interesting implication in these models.[2] It has been shown that the degree of substitutability between money and other financial assets in these models is far from complete.[3] This really calls for a reconsideration of the IS-LM model

---

1. See Baltensperger (1989) for details.
2. See Sen *et al.* (1996) for an application for Brainard-Tobin model in India.
3. This result has also been independently arrived at by Brunner and Meltzer (1972).

with an explicit role of banks and consequent credit channel of monetary policy.

During the last 15 years or so, there has been a revival of interest in the role of banks in monetary policy. Broadly speaking, this happened due to the renewal of the credit channel of monetary transmission. In particular, one can trace three factors responsible for such revival. First, there has been a major development in microeconomic information-asymmetry based credit rationing (Stiglitz and Weiss, 1981) and existence of banks (Diamond and Dybvig, 1983). Second, on a macro plane, Bernanke and Blinder (1988) reconstructed the standard IS-LM model with bank loans as another asset. The role of financial factors in business cycles has also emerged as a current topic of interest (*e.g.*, Stiglitz and Greenwald, 2003). Third, there have been a number of empirical and narrative studies highlighting the role of credit crunch in financial crisis and depression (Bernanke, 1983 or Bernanke and Lown, 1992).

This chapter is in the nature of a theoretical introduction to the present book which is primarily empirical in nature. In this chapter, we will be concerned with the second development as described above. In doing so, we will look into the role of banks in monetary policy or the linkage between the central bank's policy actions and commercial bank behaviour within the broad confines of credit channel of monetary transmission. The basic thrust of the credit view of monetary policy is the idea that not only is the liability side of the banks' balance sheet (*i.e.*, deposits) important in understanding future economic activity, but a significant part of the asset side of the balance sheet also contains relevant valuable information. That is to say, commercial bank's decision to cut down loans, even with unchanged monetary policy and deposits, is capable of depressing economic activity (Hein and Mercado-Mendez, 1992). All these forge a new link between commercial bank behaviour and central bank's policy actions (Dimsdale, 1994).

At this point, it is important to recognise that the basis for such considerations can broadly be sought in what Stiglitz and Greenwald (2003) termed as a "new paradigm for monetary economics," which is fundamentally different from the traditional theory. Stiglitz and

Greenwald (2003) argue that the traditional approach to monetary economics is seriously flawed; it does not provide a persuasive explanation for why—or how—money matters. According to them, the key to understanding monetary economics is the demand and supply of loanable funds, which in turn is contingent on understanding the importance, and consequences, of imperfections of information and the role of banks. In particular, the market for loans is not identical to the market for commodities, which works through the principles of demand and supply with the price mechanism as the equilibrating factor. The supplier of loans, i.e., banks provide vital certification, monitoring and enforcement services, by ascertaining the default probability and credit worthiness of the buyer, i.e., the loan recipient. Thus, a central function of banks is to determine who is likely to default, and in doing so, banks determine the supply of loans. They point out that a theory of monetary policy that pays no attention to bankruptcy and default is likely to lead to drastically erroneous policies. Providing these certification, monitoring and enforcement services involves risk taking; thus, the key to understanding the behaviour of banks is in their ability and willingness to absorb risks and adapt to changes in economic circumstances and in government regulations. A closer look at these determinants of banks behaviour reveals why economic activity may depend on nominal interest as well as the real interest rate.

This paradigm has an important role for commercial banks. An important reason for focusing on the impact of banking institutions is the rapid pace at which these institutions are changing. Existing theoretical models, largely institutionally independent, provide little or no guidance for assessing the effect of these changes on monetary policy. For example, transactions based monetary theories that concentrate on money as a medium of exchange would tend to count money market accounts simply as an exogenous increase in the money supply and hence, of no particular significance for the incremental impact of central bank monetary operations. Yet, in the context of an institutional banking system that competes with money market accounts for deposits, their long-run impact on the efficacy of monetary policy may be a far more difficult matter to assess. For policy purposes, it is important to understand the forces involved.

In advocating the new paradigm, several fundamental differences between money and credit may be cited. First, the relationship between money and credit is by no means a firm one. There are other institutional arrangements by which credit can and is provided. Any attempt to restrict banks may simply divert more of the credit creation activities to non-bank sources of credit. Second, interest rate adjustments do not play the central role as in conventional monetary theories. Credit market is not cleared by the market mechanism; instead credit is allocated by the lender on the basis of risk profile and risk appraisal of potential borrowers. The credit market is inherently imperfectly competitive because of the sunk costs associated with the acquisition of information and only a few lenders will have the full information on riskiness of any borrower. Third, the allocation of credit by the process of credit certification tends to generate excess demand for credit, which does not get corrected by a rise in interest rates. Instead, it reduces the bankruptcy rate, increasing bank's willingness to lend and firms' willingness to borrow thereby exacerbating the problem. Finally, the credit-interest rate nexus is a complicated one with interdependence between borrowers and lenders, which leaves the financial system quite fragile to financial shocks. The default of one firm can cascade into the breakdown of the entire system. Such non-linearities and associated irreversibilities are the genesis of a financial crisis.

Stiglitz and Greenwald (2003) found that inherent in the new paradigm of monetary theory is a "new theory of monetary policy" derived from the credit channel. The new monetary policy is different from the standard one on several counts. While loan supply is more relevant than loan demand, loan rate is the relevant real interest rate for economic activity. Banks are indeed central in the provision of credit. Informational and organisational capital within the banking system is important from monetary policy angle. Credit is heterogeneous by nature i.e., loans are not perfect substitutes. Interestingly, in the new paradigm, regulatory policy can have an important impact on credit availability. Regulatory policy and monetary policy need to be based on the theory of bank behaviour. Monetary (and regulatory) policy imparts its effects not only through aggregate demand but also aggregate supply. There is a need to ensure adequate supply of credit at reasonable terms to certain sections who are particularly adversely affected by credit tightening. Monetary policy has to take cognizance of bankruptcy costs. While restructuring financial systems, government needs to ensure smooth flow of credit. Central banks have a role even in dollarised economies or countries experiencing currency substitution. Excessive reliance on monetary policy could be distortionary and induce institutional adjustments. Future changes in transaction and information technologies may have distinct effects on the efficacy of monetary policy.

While it is not possible to track down the implications of each of the above features in the current chapter, it is important to note that against this backdrop this chapter provides a selective survey and some extensions on the issues relating to commercial bank behaviour and central banks' policy actions in its conduct of monetary policy. In particular, we evaluate the comparative static derivatives of a change in monetary stock in all these models so as to examine the role of commercial banks in monetary transmission. The rest of the chapter is organised as follows. Section 2.2 delves into the basic issues relating to ability of central banks to constrain bank lending. Extended IS-LM models with a specific banking sector are discussed in Section 2.3. Section 2.4 looks into the relaxation of two specific assumptions in the model, *viz.*, existence of certificates of deposit and commercial paper. Section 2.5 looks into the microeconomics of bank behaviour in the context of information asymmetry, while concluding observations are presented in Section 2.6.

2.2 The Ability of Central Banks to Constrain Bank Lending

How do central banks constrain bank lending? Traditionally, the answer to this question was provided in the form of various transmission channels. Since a discussion of the various transmission channels is beyond the scope of the present book, Table 2.1 presents a synoptic overview of the various monetary transmission channels. It may be noted at the very outset that while the linkage between monetary policy and central bank takes different forms in various transmission channels, our focus is confined to the traditional interest rate (or the money view) and the credit channel, either in the form of bank lending or balance sheet channel.

Table 2.1

Monetary Transmission Channels

Channel	*Transmission Mechanism*
(1)	(2)
1. Interest-Rate	$M\uparrow \rightarrow i^R \downarrow \rightarrow I\uparrow \rightarrow Y\uparrow$ $M\uparrow \rightarrow P^e \uparrow \rightarrow \pi^e \uparrow \rightarrow i^R \downarrow \rightarrow I\uparrow \rightarrow Y\uparrow$
2a. Bank Lending	$M\uparrow \rightarrow$ Bank Deposits $\uparrow \rightarrow$ Bank Loans $\uparrow \rightarrow I\uparrow \rightarrow Y\uparrow$
2b. Balance-Sheet	$M\uparrow \rightarrow P^e \uparrow \rightarrow$ Adverse Selection $\downarrow$ and Moral Hazard $\uparrow \rightarrow$ Lending $\uparrow \rightarrow I\uparrow \rightarrow Y\uparrow$
3. Exchange Rate	$M\uparrow \rightarrow i^R \downarrow \rightarrow e\downarrow \rightarrow (X-M)\uparrow \rightarrow Y\uparrow$
4. Tobin's q	$M\uparrow \rightarrow P^e \uparrow \rightarrow q\uparrow \rightarrow I\uparrow \rightarrow Y\uparrow$
5. Wealth Effects	$M\uparrow \rightarrow P^e \uparrow \rightarrow W\uparrow \rightarrow C\uparrow \rightarrow Y\uparrow$
6. Cash Flow	$M\uparrow \rightarrow i\downarrow \rightarrow$ cash flow $\uparrow \rightarrow$ adverse selection $\downarrow$ and moral hazard $\downarrow \rightarrow$ lending $\uparrow \rightarrow I\uparrow \rightarrow Y\uparrow$
7. Unanticipated Price Level	$M\uparrow \rightarrow$ unanticipated $P\uparrow \rightarrow$ adverse selection $\downarrow$ and moral hazard $\downarrow \rightarrow$ lending $\uparrow \rightarrow I\uparrow \rightarrow Y\uparrow$
8. Liquidity Effects	$M\uparrow \rightarrow P^e \uparrow \rightarrow$ Value of financial assets $\uparrow \rightarrow$ likelihood of financial distress $\downarrow \rightarrow$ consumer durable and housing expenditure $\uparrow \rightarrow Y\uparrow$

Symbols: M: Money Supply; P^e: Expected price level; π^e: Expected inflation; i^R: Real interest rates; i: nominal interest rates; I: Investment; Y: Output; e: Exchange Rate; X: Exports; M: Imports; W: Wealth, C: Consumption.

Source: Adapted from Mishkin (1995) and Vasudevan (2003).

What is the role of banks in the operation of monetary policy or permeation of monetary transmission channels? The typical story runs as follows. When a central bank adopts a contractionary monetary policy, whether by a hike in the cash reserve ratio or by a hiking of the rate at which commercial banks get the refinance from central bank, commercial banks too will adopt a similar stance. But the transition of a contractionary monetary policy on the part of the central bank to a contractionary policy of the commercial banks is not automatic. After all, when, as a result of a contractionary monetary policy pursued by the central bank, banks are faced with a lower amount of investible resources, which item of their balance sheet bears the crunch? The adjustments are entirely dissimilar in the two standard forms of monetary transmission channels, *viz.*, (a) money view, and (b) credit view. Thus, there are at least two alternative ways in which this can happen.

- First, in the traditional money view of monetary policy, the adjustment occurs in the liability side of the balance sheet.
- Secondly, if the credit channel is operational, then it is bank loans that bear the crunch.

However, this may not be necessarily so and there are at least two ways in which the banks can bypass such a credit crunch.

- First, the banks can sell securities (like Treasury bills), so that bank-dependent borrowers are not deprived of their credit needs. Such reduction in investment happens when loans and securities are perfect substitutes as asset items of the bank's balance sheet.
- Secondly, they can take recourse to non-deposit resources like certificates of deposit, which attract a lower reserve ratio.

If either of these happens then the credit channel of monetary policy ceases to be valid.

Consider the possibility of selling securities like Treasury bills first. As Bernanke and Gertler (1987) have pointed out there is a significant difference between loans and securities as far as the extent of liquidity is concerned. Since securities are more liquid, in order to avoid any default on account of required reserves, banks will normally cut down loans in the event of a contractionary monetary policy, affecting their investible resources adversely. Extending the arguments, Stiglitz and Greenwald (1992) have shown that risk-neutral banks will reduce their lending as a result of increased reserve requirement so long as they do not go bankrupt and given a high cost of bankruptcy, they try to avoid it. This is because of the fact that, given the increased cost of borrowing, an increase in reserve requirement causes a rise in both marginal and average bankruptcy probabilities. Thus, as a result of a reduction in banks' investible surplus, the possibility of selling securities so as to maintain the loans to bank dependent borrowers cannot be ruled out.

The issue of raising non-deposit resources as a possible lacuna in the credit channel has attracted more attention in the literature.[4] Romer and Romer (1990) have pointed out that if banks view deposits and CDs as perfect substitutes, the link between open market operations and credit supply to bank dependent borrowers is broken and consequently, credit channel ceases to be operational. Nevertheless, as Hubbard (1994) notes, as long as banks have private information about a portion of their loan portfolio, the marginal cost of external finance will be rising due to the consequent adverse selection problem (*e.g.*, Myers and Majluf, 1984). This, coupled with the fact that some banks will be constrained in the CD market, will still make the credit channel operational. Furthermore, CDs are only one example of non-deposit resources mobilised by the banks; the existence of many other kinds of non-deposit resources like Eurodollar borrowing, rise of money market mutual funds, need to be taken into account. The issue is, thus, primarily empirical.[5]

How does the role of banks in the credit channel get modelled? What is the implication of the postulate of speciality of bank credit for monetary transmission mechanism? It is in this context that next sections look into some representative models.

2.3 Extended IS-LM Models with Explicit Role for Banks

We have already noted that the standard IS-LM model neglects the credit view and role of banks by subsuming all interest bearing securities under the catch-all term 'bonds.' However, if instead, we assume that there exists a single asset called 'bank loans', credit view

4. Section 2.4 takes up this argument in greater detail.

5. It may be noted in this connection that even for the money view of the monetary transmission to be valid some preconditions are needed, the important ones being: (i) the central bank must be able to affect the supply of bank deposits through a change in bank reserves, and (ii) money has no perfect substitutes, so that agents cannot offset the effects of monetary policy changes by switching to non-money substitutes. This apart, implicitly a third condition is needed for both the money and credit channel to be operational. This is the existence of some form of imperfect price adjustment that prevents monetary policy shocks from being neutral. Nevertheless, it is a prerequisite for any theory where monetary policy has real effect (Blanchard, 1995). This assumption is mostly implicit in the credit view.

is not necessarily established. After all, in such a situation, money and credit are, by definition, equal to each other, through the banking sector's balance sheet identity. An alternative way of expressing the above fact is to assume perfect substitutability between money and loans so that there is a single independent interest rate in the economy. In this section we consider two distinct classes of models, *viz.*, (a) those which can be broadly classified as extended IS-LM models with credit, but without any independent credit channel, and (b) those where banks are given a special role.

2.3.1 Extended IS-LM Models without an Independent Role of Banks

Modigliani and Papademos

One of the initial pioneering works incorporating the role of banks in monetary policy is that by Modigliani and Papademos (1980).[6] A simplified version of the Modigliani and Papademos (1980) model is presented below. Let us consider a simple financial structure without any debt instruments, where the non-bank public can hold three assets, *viz.*, physical capital (K), narrow money (M1, comprising currency and demand deposits) and time deposits (TD). The only type of loan available to the non-bank public is the bank loans (L). There are, thus, three rates of interest in the model, the borrowing rate on bank loans (r), and lending rates on DD and TD (denoted by r_{DD} and r_{TD}, respectively). The equilibrium conditions of the model along with the balance sheet identities and interest rate determination equations are given in Table 2.2 with + or – sign below a variable indicating the sign of its first derivative.[7]

Two salient features of the model deserve special mention. First, note that there are three kinds of financial assets in the model, *viz.*, demand deposits (DD), time deposits (TD), bank loans (L). Accordingly, as already indicated, there are three interest rates in the

6. This has been their concern in a number of papers; see also Modigliani and Papademos (1987, 1990).

7. Unlike Modigliani and Papademos (1980), we have assumed standard signs of the derivatives. They instead of distinguishing between household and firm, segregated the non-bank public into 'surplus' and 'deficit' units, and consequently got the signs of the a number of derivatives to be ambiguous. This simplifying assumption that we have adopted in the present context, however, does not materially change the conclusions of their model.

model, *viz.*, r_{DD}, r_{TD}, and r. However, Modigliani and Papademos (1980) assumed r_{DD} to be given, and related r_{TD} to r through a constant spread (d); hence the whole model is reduced in terms a single interest rate, *viz.*, the loan rate (r). Secondly, by the balance sheet identity of the banks, broad money (M2 = M1+TD) and bank loans (L) are equivalent.

Table 2.2

Structure of a Modified Modigliani and Papademos (1980) Model

Equation No.	*Items*	*Equation*
(1)	*(2)*	*(3)*
2.1	Commodity Market (IS)	$S(\underset{+}{Y}) = I(\underset{-}{r}, r_{TD})$
2.2	Narrow Money Market (LM1)	$M1 = M1(r, \underset{-}{r_{DD}}, r_{TD}, \underset{+}{Y})$
2.3	Broad Money (LM2)	$M2 = M2(\underset{-}{r}, r_{DD}, \underset{+}{r_{TD}}, Y)$
2.4	Bank Loan Market (LL)	$L = L(\underset{-}{r}, r_{DD}, \underset{+}{Y})$
2.5	Balance Sheet Identities	
	(a) Non-Bank Sector	$S + \Delta L = I + \Delta M2$
	(b) Bank Sector	$L = M2$
2.6	Interest rate Determination	
	(a) Interest Rate on DD	$r_{DD} = r$
	(b) Interest Rate on TD	$r_{TD} = r - d$

In what way does the model differ from the standard IS-LM model? As an alternative to the standard IS-LM, Modigliani and Papademos (1980) considered a variant, *viz.*, IS-LL model, and established the following proposition:

> The purpose of monetary mechanism—the determination and control of nominal income can be achieved without exogenous control of the money supply and requires instead only exogenous control of some financial aggregate or of a linear combination of such aggregate (Modigliani and Papademos, 1980: 129).

However, as we see below, since M2 = L by the balance sheet identity and since there is a single independent rate of interest, r, both these alternatives will yield equivalent transmission mechanism.

The IS-LL case can be comprehended more easily once we note that, the LL curve in the (r,Y) plane is positively sloped too.[8] Hence any credit expansion will lead to a higher Y and lower r. After all, in order to expand loans, banks must bid down the loan rate so that demand for credit, as well as investment, gets stimulated. Thus, in both the money mode and credit mode, the transmission channel remains unaltered. Hence, with a single rate of interest, mere incorporation of bank loans as an asset in the banks' portfolio does not yield an independent credit channel.

Brunner and Meltzer

Brunner and Meltzer (1993) considered three assets in their model —two financial assets, *viz.*, government debt and bank loans, and one real asset, *viz.*, real capital. However, instead of the loan rate, they preferred to work with the nominal price of real capital, and effectively ruled out any independent role of bank.

Let us consider a simplified version of Brunner and Meltzer's three asset economy, comprising money (M), government debt (S) and real capital (K). In this model, banks' credit (L) is defined as the sum of loans to public and banks' holding of government securities. There are two crucial asset prices in the economy, *viz.*, the rate of interest on government debt (i) and the price of real capital (P). All other rates of interest like the deposit rates or the loan rate are assumed to be functions of i. Thus through this assumption, any independent credit channel is ruled out in the monetary transmission mechanism. Though Brunner and Meltzer include a number of variables like price level, human and non-human wealth as determinants of credit and money demand function, they have neglected these variables while considering the transmission channel. In a simplified manner the commodity, credit and money market equilibrium conditions are given in Table 2.3.

Let us consider the asset markets specifically. Both the money and credit supply are expressed in terms of the money multiplier (β) and credit multiplier (α), respectively, and high powered money (H). L(•) and M(•) denote the credit and money demand, respectively.

8. Modigliani and Papademos consider a case where the LL curve is negatively sloped but flatter than the IS curve (in order to maintain local stability). Even in that case since LL shifts down as a result of credit expansion, r goes down and Y goes up (as in the usual IS-LM case).

Table 2.3

Equilibrium Conditions in a Simplified Brunner and Meltzer Model

Equation No.	*Items*	*Equation*
(1)	(2)	(3)
2.7	Equilibrium in the Commodity Market (IS)	$\underset{-\ +}{Y = Y(i,\ P)}$
2.8	Equilibrium in the Credit Market (LL)	$\underset{+\ +}{\alpha(i,\ P)}\ H = \underset{-\ -}{L(i,\ P)}$
2.9	Equilibrium in the Money Market (LM)	$\underset{+\ -}{\beta(i,\ P)}\ H = \underset{-\ +}{L(i,\ P)}$

Furthermore, since Y does not appear in any of the asset demand and supply functions, the asset markets are independent of any output effect, but asset price of the interest rate feeds into the generation of effective demand. Therefore, if we consider only the asset market, then the impact of a change in base money (H) can be captured by the following comparative static derivatives, *viz.*,

$$\text{(2.10a)} \qquad \left.\frac{di}{dH}\right|_{LL-LM} = \frac{1}{N}[-\alpha(H\beta_P - M_P) + \beta(H\alpha_P - L_P)]$$

$$\text{(2.10b)} \qquad \left.\frac{dY}{dH}\right|_{LL-LM} = \frac{1}{N}[-\beta(H\alpha_i - L_i) + \alpha(H\beta_i - M_i)]$$

where, $N = (H\alpha_i - L_i)(H\beta_P - M_P) - (H\beta_i - M_i)(H\alpha_P - L_P) < 0$

Interestingly, when we consider only the asset market, while di/dH is unambiguously negative, dP/dH can take any sign. Therefore, for a positive dP/dH we need the condition that the ratio of responsiveness of excess supply in the credit market to a monetary expansion induced reduction in i to responsiveness of excess supply in the money market to a monetary expansion induced reduction in i is less than the ratio between credit multiplier and money multiplier.[9]

Since asset markets do not have any direct output effect, it can be shown that,

9. Note that the condition is more restrictive than the Brunner and Meltzer (1993) condition that, "the responsiveness of the asset price level P to changes in monetary base ... is positive provided the interest elasticity of the credit market exceeds the corresponding elasticity of the money market" (p.87).

$$(2.11) \qquad \left.\frac{dY}{dH}\right|_{IS-LL-LM} = Y_i\left[\left.\frac{di}{dH}\right|_{LL-LM}\right] + Y_P\left[\left.\frac{dP}{dH}\right|_{LL-LM}\right]$$

Thus, as a result of an expansion in base money the initial expansionary impact on aggregate demand comes from a reduction in the rate of interest. However, this expansionary impact on output is likely to be reinforced by the rise in the nominal price of the real capital as long as the above condition for the relative responsiveness of excess-supply in the credit market *vis-à-vis* money market, is met.

How does the model differ from the standard IS-LM model? First, the notion of a liquidity trap gets diluted in this extended model with real capital and credit. After all convergence of excess supply of money to minus infinity would imply convergence of interest elasticity of excess supply of credit to plus infinity. Secondly, once the credit market is introduced, a change in reserve requirement will not only change the money multiplier but also the credit multiplier.

What role do banks play in the model? Note that, since there is no independent rate of interest for bank loans, credit market responses are made to be integral parts of asset market mechanism. Changes in high powered money, stock of government debt or the expected return to real capital are transmitted to the output market by changes in I and P that incorporate changes in the credit market. In particular, Brunner and Meltzer (1993) point out,

> There are no credit market effects independent of monetary effects. The issue of whether credit or money matters for output or asset prices has no meaning. This does not mean we cannot develop an analysis with separate shocks of money and credit. Such analysis would be useless for analysing financial systems like our own where money and credit are interrelated. (Brunner and Meltzer,1993: 90-91).

Thus, mere introduction of credit in an IS-LM framework does not establish an independent role of banks and the consequent credit channel. We need to assume something more, *viz.*, bank loans are special. It is this issue to which we now turn.

2.3.2 Banks in the Bernanke and Blinder (1988) Model

A slightly modified version of the Bernanke and Blinder (1988) model is presented below, where in an otherwise IS-LM model banks are specifically introduced in the operation of monetary policy. Let us assume an economy with three assets, *viz.*, money, bonds and bank loans. The major actors of the economy are households, firms and banks whose balance sheets, after clubbing firms and households under 'non-banks' are represented in Table 2.4.

Table 2.4

Hypothetical Balance Sheets of Non-Bank Public and Banks: Two Asset Model

Non-Bank Public				*Banks*			
Assets		*Liabilities*		*Assets*		*Liabilities*	
(1)		*(2)*		*(3)*		*(4)*	
Deposits	M	Bank Loans	L	Reserves (R)	μM	Deposits	M
Bonds	B_h	Bonds	B	Bank Loans	L		
Net Wealth	W			Bonds	B_b		

A few interesting points about this simplified economy are worth noting.

- First, currency is assumed away from the model, so that money and deposits (M) become synonymous.
- Secondly, there are two interest-yielding assets, *viz.*, bank loans and bonds, the returns from these assets are denoted by r and i respectively.[10] Hence, given the reserve ratio, μ the problem of the banking sector is to allocate the investible surplus, $(1-\mu)M$ among two opportunities, *viz.*, B_b, and L. This of course follows from the balance sheet identity for banks, whereby, $B_b+L= (1-\mu)M$. Furthermore, it is assumed that out of the investible surplus $(1-\mu)M$, the proportion of loan holding is λ, i.e., $\lambda = L/(B_b+L)$, where $\lambda = \lambda(i,r)$ and $\lambda < 1$.[11]
- Finally, once a second asset is introduced, the equality between money and credit is lost.

10. Technically, of course there is another interest rate in the model *viz.*, deposit rate (rD), which can be neglected either through the assumption that it is given or through the assumption of a constant spread (d), so that r=rD+d.

11. Unlike Bernanke and Blinder (1988), we have neglected excess reserves for the sake of simplicity.

Equations 2.12, 2.13 and 2.14 are basic behavioural equations in the model (Table 2.5). In order to make them comparable to the standard IS-LM model, i.e., to have them in (i, Y) plane, let us treat 2.13 separately, which clearly gives a positively sloped LM curve.

Table 2.5

Equilibrium Conditions in the Two Asset Model

Equation No.	*Items*	*Equation*
(1)	*(2)*	*(3)*
2.12	Equilibrium in the Commodity Market (IS)	$\underset{- \; -}{I(i, r)} = \underset{+}{S(Y)}$
2.13	Equilibrium in the Money Market (LM)	$\underset{- \; +}{M(i, Y)} = M$
2.14	Equilibrium in the Loan Market (LL)	$\underset{- \; + \; +}{L(r, i, Y)} = \underset{- \; +}{\mu (i, r)} (1-\mu)M$

Note: L(r, i, Y), and $\lambda(i,r)(1-\mu)M$ are demand for and supply of loans, respectively.

In order to reduce (2.12) and (2.14) in terms of a single equation, Bernanke-Blinder (1988) proceeded in the following manner. From the loan market equilibrium (2.14) the loan rate of interest r can be expressed as, $r=r(i,Y,M)$ with r_i, $r_y > 0$, and $r_M < 0$. This after substituting in the IS equation (2.12) yields a negatively sloped (i, Y) locus for all of which both the commodity and loan markets are in equilibrium. This curve is termed as CC curve, which is given by.

(2.15) $I(i,r(i,Y,M))=S(Y)$

Thus, equations (2.15) and (2.13) describe the reformed CC-LM model which takes into account the role of credit. Before we proceed further two special cases deserve mention.

- *Money only View*: The standard IS-LM model captures the money only view. In the CC-LM model this is captured by the following special cases whereby we are back to the original IS curve, *viz.*,
  - loans and bonds are perfect substitutes to borrowers, so that $L_r = -\infty$ and consequently di/dy (LL) $= \infty$;
  - loans and bonds are perfect substitutes to lenders so that $\lambda_r = \infty$, and consequently di/dy (LL) $= \infty$;

- Commodity demand is insensitive to loan rate so that $I_r = 0$.
- *Credit only View*: This is the case of liquidity trap where deposits and bonds are perfect substitutes, i.e., $M_i = -\infty$.

Monetary Transmission in Presence of Credit

While an expansionary monetary policy unambiguously lowers the interest rate in the standard IS-LM model, in the extended CC-LM model this is not necessarily so. After all, once bank credit is introduced, aggregate spending depends also on loan market conditions. Hence, any expansionary monetary policy will not only shift the LM curve but also the CC curve, so that while output will rise, interest rate may go either way or remain constant (Figure 2.1).[12] Any increase in M lowers i in the IS-LM case because of an additional demand for bonds. However, in the CC-LM case because of the existence of an additional asset, *viz.*, bank loans, the additional money may go into both of them, particularly under the assumption of imperfect substitutability between bank loans and bonds.

Algebraically, in the CC-LM model the impact of a change in money supply is given as follows,

$$\text{(2.16a)} \qquad \frac{dY}{dM} = \frac{I_r(r_M M_i + r_i) + I_i}{I_r(M_Y r_i - r_y M_i) + I_i M_y + S_y M_i}$$

$$\text{(2.16b)} \qquad \frac{di}{dM} = \frac{I_r(r_y + M_y r_M) - S_y}{I_r(M_y r_i - r_y M_i) + I_i M_y + S_y M_i}$$

Thus, given the signs of derivatives while dY/dM is unambiguously positive, di/dM > = < 0 according as $(r_y + M_Y r_M)$ < = > 0. But if i goes up then wherefrom does the expansion in effective demand come, so that Y goes up ultimately? Since there are two financial assets in the model, apart from money, *viz.*, bonds and bank loans, in the event of a rise in i the expansionary impact on investment comes from a fall in r. For positive di/dM, the only thing we need to ensure is that both di/dM and dr/dM are not positive simultaneously.

---

12. The new equilibrium could be at E1, E2, or E3 in the CC-LM model in Figure 2.1.

Figure 2.1

IS-LM and CC-LM Model

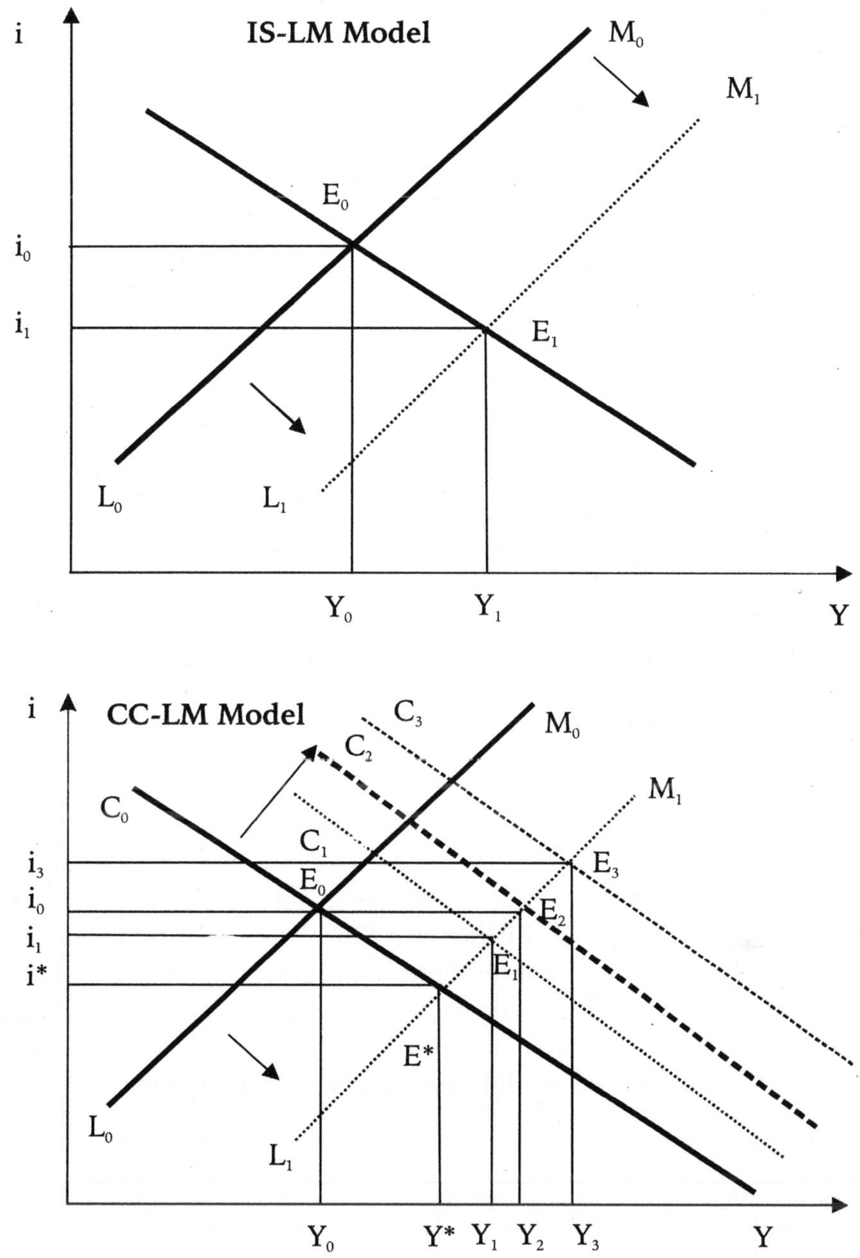

This is clearly brought out if we consider the comparative static derivatives with respect to the three equation structure, *viz.*, IS, LL and LM. The impact of a change in M on Y, i and r are given below.[13]

(2.17a) $$\frac{dY}{dM}=\frac{1}{J}\left[\left(\frac{\lambda_r}{\lambda}-\frac{L_r}{L}\right)\frac{I_i}{I_r}+\left(\frac{L_i}{L}-\frac{M_i}{M}\right)-\frac{\lambda_i}{\lambda}\right]$$

(2.17b) $$\frac{di}{dM}=\frac{1}{J}\left[\left(\frac{\lambda_r}{\lambda}-\frac{L_r}{L}\right)\frac{S_y}{I_r}-\left(\frac{L_y}{L}-\frac{M_y}{M}\right)\right]$$

(2.17c) $$\frac{dr}{dM}=\frac{1}{J}\left[\left(\frac{L_i}{l}-\frac{\lambda_i}{\lambda}-\frac{M_i}{M}\right)\frac{S_y}{I_r}+\frac{I_i}{I_r}\left(\frac{L_y}{L}-\frac{M_y}{M}\right)\right]$$

where, $$J=\left[\left(\frac{\lambda_i}{\lambda}-\frac{L_r}{L}\right)\left(\frac{M_i\,S_y+M_yI_i}{I_r}\right)+\left(\frac{L_iM_y-L_yM_i}{L}\right)-\frac{\lambda_i}{\lambda}M_y\right]>0$$

Note that while dY/dM is unambiguously positive, the signs of both dr/dM and di/dM may go either way. Though dY/dM is positive in both the IS-LM and IS-LL-LM models, it is interesting to compare them. Noting that $dY/dM|_{\text{IS-LM}} = I_i/(M_yS_y + M_yI_i)$, a consideration of the two comparative static derivatives yields the following condition for money to have a greater effect on output when the credit channel is operational, *viz.*, $(L_y/L) < (M_y/M)$.[14] Note that under this condition r goes down (see Case 2 below).

However, there are two special cases where we can have either di/dM or dr/dM to be negative.

Case 1: If $L_Y/L > M_y/M$ then di/dM <0;

Case 2: if $L_Y/L < M_y/M$ then dr/dM <0 (since, $I_i / I_r > 0$).

It needs to be noted that the above relationship is merely sufficient, and hence asymmetric in the sense that a reversal of the sign of inequality in the 'if' condition does not yield a positive di/dM or dr/dM. To comprehend the nature of transmission mechanism of

13. The particular form of derivatives follows Miron *et. al* (1994); instead of the original Bernanke and Blinder (1988) formulation of $\lambda = \lambda(i,r)$ they assumed that $\lambda = \lambda(\delta)$ (where δ is the spread between i and r), we have, however, worked out the derivatives in terms of the original model.

14. $(dY/dM)_{\text{IS-LL-LM}} - (dY/dM)_{\text{IS-LM}} = [J(M_iS_Y+M_YI_i]^{-1}\ [M_iS_Y(L_i/L-M_i/M-\lambda_i/\lambda) + I_iM_i\ (L_y/L-M_y/M)]$.

the loan rate and the bond rate of interest, it may be noted that the derivative concerning each rate has two terms; while the first term captures the cross-effect of the other rate, the second captures the output effect. As for example, in case of di/dM the term $(\lambda_r/\lambda - L_r/L)$ captures the effect from r, and the term $(L_Y/L - M_Y/M)$ measures the output effect. Intuitively, if the output elasticity of loan demand is more than output elasticity of money demand (i.e., Case 1) then out of a monetary expansion induced output increase, rise in loan demand will be higher than increase in money demand; consequently the bond rate of interest will go down. On the contrary, lower income elasticity of loan demand *vis-à-vis* money demand (i.e., Case 2) will yield a lower loan rate. It is interesting to note that dr/dM and di/dM cannot be positive simultaneously.[15] However, under the following condition, both i and r will go down simultaneously.

$$(2.18) \quad \left[\left(\frac{\lambda_y}{\lambda} - \frac{L_r}{L}\right)\frac{S_y}{I_r} < \left(\frac{L_y}{L} - \frac{M_y}{M}\right) < \left(\frac{\lambda_i}{\lambda} + \frac{M_i}{M} - \frac{L_i}{L}\right)\frac{S_y}{I_i}\right]$$

Thus, the usual channel of the expansionary impact on output from an expansionary monetary policy, through a reduction in rates of interest and resultant boosting of investment demand, remains unaltered in this model. Only when one of the rates of interest goes up, the burden of generating additional investment demand falls solely on the other. If both goes down then the expansionary impact of monetary policy gets reinforced through a credit channel. Note that in this model, the credit channel does not ever neutralise or reverse the expansionary effect of M on Y.

2.4 Loan and Deposits Substitutes for Banks and Corporates

The effect of a contractionary monetary policy on the economy would be primarily through a reduction in the effective demand. There

15. Note that di/dM > 0 => $(L_Y/L) < (M_Y/M)$ => dr/dM < 0, and dr/dM >0 => $(L_Y/L) > (M_Y/M)$ => di/dM < 0. This is, however, obvious in the model where excess reserves are assumed away. It may be noted that to avoid this problem of simultaneous increase in both the rates of increase (due to a monetary expansion) Bernanke and Blinder (1988) assumed that excess reserves are dependent on only the bond rate of interest (i).

are, however, two ways in which such contractionary monetary policy can be avoided, *viz.*, (a) when banks have deposit substitutes like certificates of deposit (CDs) and (b) when corporates have loan substitutes, like commercial papers (CPs).

2.4.1 Certificates of Deposit and Bank Behaviour

CDs and the Credit Channel: The Basic Model[16]

Certificates of deposit were perhaps the first major instrument of liability management brought about by banks.[17] A bank could issue CDs to fund loans; in many advanced countries these were in the nature of time deposits with maturity of three to four months. However, in a number of countries either CDs were free from reserve requirements or attracted, compared to deposits, a lower reserve ratio. In such cases where banks can raise funds from non-deposit resources, Romer and Romer (1990) have pointed out that the link between open market operations and the supply of credit to bank dependent borrowers is broken, particularly, if banks see deposits and CDs as perfect substitutes.

How can we incorporate CDs in the basic IS-LM model with credit? Instead of incorporating it as a separate item on the liability side, following Keeton (1992) and Miron *et al.* (1994), we assume that banks' holding of securities (B_b) is expressed in net terms so that it can be positive or negative. When B_b is negative, it simply means that banks have issued CDs, so that there will be an additional item in bank reserves, *viz.*, τB_b (where τ is the reserve requirement on CDs).[18] Thus, in the presence of CDs, the balance sheets of non-bank public and bank will have the following look (Table 2.6).

As earlier, λ is defined as the ratio of loans (L) to investible resources, i.e., B_b + L. Since B_b can be negative, λ can be greater than unity as well (when banks hold CDs); τ on the contrary is the reserve

16. This issue has been dealt with in Romer and Romer (1990, 1993), Keeton (1992), Kashyap and Stein (1994), Miron *et al.* (1994), and Hubbard (1994).

17. Walter B. Wriston of Citicorp is credited to have innovated CDs in the USA during the 1960s.

18. Note that such a treatment of CDs assumes away simultaneous holding of securities and CDs on the part of the banks.

Table 2.6

Balance Sheets of Non-Bank Public and Banks with CDs

Non-Bank				*Banks*			
Assets		*Liabilities*		*Assets*		*Liabilities*	
(1)		*(2)*		*(3)*		*(4)*	
Deposits	M	Bank Loans	L	Reserves (R)		Deposits	M
				on M	μM		
				On CDs	$-\tau B_b$		
		Bonds	B_p	Bank Loans	L		
Net Wealth	W			Bonds	B_b		

ratio on CDs. Thus, the loan supply function is derived from the bank's balance sheet as:

$$L^S = \frac{\lambda(i,r)(1-\mu)}{1+[\lambda(i,r)-1]\tau} M \tag{2.19}$$

However, the equilibrium conditions (12) and (13) of the original model remain unaltered; only the equilibrium condition in the loan market (14) is replaced by,

$$L(r,i,Y) = \frac{\lambda(i,r)(1-\mu)}{1+[\lambda(i,r)-1]\tau} M \tag{2.20}$$

where μ and τ are the reserve requirements on M and CDs, respectively.

How does the central bank influence commercial banks in the model with CDs? To comprehend this let us look at comparative statics results of a change in M on Y, i, and r in equations (12), (13), and (20). The relevant derivatives are as follows:[19]

$$\frac{dY}{dM} = \frac{1}{Q}\left[\left(k\frac{\lambda_r}{\lambda} - \frac{L_r}{L}\right)\frac{I_i}{I_r} + \left(\frac{L_i}{L} - \frac{M_i}{M}\right) - k\frac{\lambda_i}{\lambda}\right] \tag{2.21a}$$

$$\frac{di}{dM} = \frac{1}{Q}\left[\left(k\frac{\lambda_r}{\lambda} - \frac{L_r}{L}\right)\frac{S_y}{I_r} - \left(\frac{L_y}{L} - \frac{M_y}{M}\right)\right] \tag{2.21b}$$

19. Annex A-2.1 gives the details of algebra.

(2.21c) $$\frac{dr}{dM}=\frac{1}{Q}\left[\left(\frac{L_i}{L}-k\frac{\lambda_i}{\lambda}-\frac{M_i}{M}\right)\frac{S_y}{I_r}+\frac{I_i}{I_r}\left(\frac{L_y}{L}-\frac{M_y}{M}\right)\right]$$

where $$Q=\left[\left(k\frac{\lambda_r}{\lambda}-\frac{L_r}{L}\right)\left(\frac{M_i S_y+M_y I_i}{I_r}\right)+\left(\frac{L_i M_y-L_y M_i}{L}\right)-\frac{k\lambda_i M_y}{\lambda}\right]>0$$

and, $$k=\frac{1-\tau}{1+(\lambda-1)\tau}$$

Note that the expressions for comparative static derivatives in the CD-case have an additional multiplicative term k associated with λ_i and λ_r. We can term k as 'effective loan-deposit ratio' (in presence of CDs). If however, the reserve requirement on CDs is zero, (i.e., $\tau=0$), then the loan supply function is back to our original formulation $L^S = \lambda(.)(1-\mu)M$, and we get k=1. Consequently, with no reserve requirement on CDs, the transmission channel in the presence of CDs turns out to be no different from the situation where there are no CDs. It may be noted that banks innovated CDs precisely to evade the reserve requirement regulation. However, in many countries there are reserve requirements on CDs, and consequently we postulate the relationship $0 < \mu < \tau < 1$.

In the general case it is easy to check that as long as $0<\tau<1$ (k<1), the increase in output due to a monetary expansion in presence of CDs is less than in a situation were CDs are absent, i.e., $dY/dM|_{k<1} < dY/dM|_{k=1}$. This is due to the fact that in the presence of CDs, an expansion in money will not necessarily lead to a comparable reduction in loan and interest rates, as is observed in a situation without CDs.

Bank Behaviour in Presence of CDs

Following Kashyap and Stein (1994), the bank's optimal behaviour can be illustrated with the help of a simple partial equilibrium model. The representative bank can raise funds from deposits M and pay i_M as the interest cost, or can raise funds from CDs ($B_b < 0$) and pay i as the interest cost, which can only be invested in loans (L), the earning from which is r.[20] Assuming the bank is a price taker in the loan market, its profit (π) maximisation problem may be written as:

20. In Kashyap and Stein (1994)'s formulation, banks have been allowed to raise CDs and hold bonds.

(2.22) $$\underset{B_b, M}{Max}\ \pi(B_b, M) = rL + i(B_b)B_b - i_M(M)M$$

subject to,

(2.23a) $$R = \mu M - \tau B_b$$

(2.23b) $$R + L + B_b = M$$

Indicating the first order derivatives by prime (′), the first order conditions yield,

(2.24a) $$r(1-\tau) - i = B_b i'(B_b)$$

(2.24b) $$r(1-\mu) - i_M = M i'_M(M)$$

Note that two conditions are sufficient for arriving at the notion of perfect substitutability between loans and CDs, on the part of the banks, or to get $i=r$, *viz.*, (i) $\tau = 0$, and (ii) $i'(B_b)=0$. These are precisely the conditions under which Romer and Romer (1990) have argued that lending channel will not be operational. If banks face increasing marginal cost of issuing CDs then the situation is quite different.

However, even with $i'(B_b) = i'_M(M) = 0$, one gets the following relationship between the two rates of interest, i.e., i and i_M,

(2.25) $$\frac{i}{i_M} = \frac{1-\tau}{1-\mu}$$

It is, thus, clear that under the assumption of zero marginal cost of issuing CDs, and accepting deposits, the spread between the deposit rate and CD rate will solely be determined by the respective reserve requirement ratios.

2.4.2 *Existence of Bank-Dependent Borrowers and Commercial Paper*

For the central bank's policy actions to be successful in their demand management policies, a crucial precondition is the existence of bank-dependent borrowers. Instruments like commercial paper (CPs) really weaken this condition. CPs are a typical example of auction market credit, where a corporate can directly issue a paper to the bank, normally for a short term and receives the proceeds of the paper. CPs grew in the late nineteenth century in the US but disappeared during the depression years. Though it surfaced in the post-depression years, following the Penn Central failure in the 1970s it suffered a temporary halt. During the 1980s, particularly during the credit crunch period it continued to grow rapidly.[21] In this section, following Kashyap, Stein and Wilcox (1993), we present a model where the issue of commercial paper is considered explicitly. The model is essentially a variant of the Bernanke-Blinder (1988) model.

Let us retain our basic model and replace the notion of a bond by commercial paper, which are issued by the corporates and held by the banks, so that now i becomes the rate of interest of CPs. The financing decision of the firm is conceived as determining some proportion θ of total investment I to be raised as loans, so that $(1-\theta)$ comes from commercial paper. Speciality of bank loans in the model is formalised through a 'relationship advantage from bank borrowing' (A) such that,

(2.26) $$\frac{A}{I} = f(\theta), \text{with } f(.)' > 0, f(.)'' < 0$$

In such a framework the firm's optimal financing mix (θ_c) is given by,

(2.27) $$\theta_c = \theta_c(r-i), \text{with } \theta_c' < 0, \text{where}, \theta_c(.) = f'^{-1}(.)$$

Therefore, the net cost of capital (k) raised is not just the sum of the two interest costs but net of the per unit 'relationship advantage from bank borrowing' (A/I), so that,

(2.28) $$k = i + \theta_c(.)(r-i) - f(\theta_c)$$

Hence, the investment and the loan demand function in this model are given by,

(2.29) $$I = I(k, Y), \text{with } I_k < 0, I \; > 0$$

(2.30) $$L_d = \theta_c(.)I$$

Kashyap-Stein-Wilcox (1993) point to a number of implications of these functional forms insofar as the issue of substitutability between loans and CPs (and their empirical verification) is concerned.

First, consider the optimal financing mix θ_c and note that,

21. See Calomiris, Himmelberg and Wachtel (1995) for an extensive discussion on the CPs in the US.

(2.31) $$\frac{d\theta_c}{dM} = \theta'c\frac{d(r-i)}{dM}$$

Since perfect substitutability between loans and securities (in this case CPs) on the part of the corporates would imply r = i, therefore, the optimal financing mix will be independent of monetary policy under this assumption.

Secondly, note that the responsiveness of loan demand to monetary policy is given by,

(2.32) $$\frac{dL^d}{dM} = \theta_c\frac{dI}{dM} + I\theta'c\frac{d(r-i)}{dM}$$

Therefore, unlike θ_c, L^d will continue to be influenced by monetary policy even under perfect substitutability assumption. Consequently a high correlation between money and loans cannot necessarily be interpreted as lack of substitutability between loans and CPs.

Finally, the responsiveness of investment to monetary policy is given by,

(2.33) $$\frac{dI}{dM} = I_Y\frac{dY}{dM} + I_k\frac{di}{dM} + \frac{d(i-r)}{dM}$$

Thus, when loans and CPs are perfect substitutes then the third term becomes zero, so that investment will depend only on output and interest rates on CPs. However, the imperfect substitutability as represented by the spread (i.e., r-i) between loan and CP rate also affects investment.[22]

Let us turn to the other functions of the model. For simplicity, consumption is assumed away from the model so that commodity market equilibrium is described as,

(2.34) $$IS: Y = [I, K(i, \theta_c(r-i), Y] + G$$

The money market is described as a conventional LM curve of the form equation (2.13).

22. Dale and Haldane (1995) discuss about two cases regarding the spread between r and i, viz., overshooting and undershooting; they rationalised the co-existence of both a overshooting and undershooting for different kinds of borrowers. The issue is, however, primarily empirical.

The loan market equilibrium assumes a proportional relationship between loan supply and money supply, with $\gamma=\gamma(r-i)_{23}$, and $\gamma'>0$ as the proportionality coefficient, so that the LL curve is given by,[23]

(2.35) $$LL:\theta_c(r-i)I=\gamma(r-i)M$$

What is the transmission mechanism of the model? To comprehend this let us consider the comparative static derivatives of the IS-LM-LL system:

(2.36a) $$\frac{dY}{dM}=\frac{1}{S}[I_k(I\theta_c'-M\gamma')+\theta_c(\gamma-\theta_c)I_kM_i]$$

(2.36b) $$\frac{di}{dM}=\frac{1}{S}[(1-I_y)(I\theta_c'-M\gamma')-\theta_c(\gamma-\theta_c)I_kM_i]$$

(2.36c) $$\frac{dr}{dM}=\frac{1}{S}[(1-I_y)(I\theta_c'-M\gamma')+(1-\theta_c)(\gamma-\theta_c)I_kM_y+(y-\theta_c)(1-I_y)M_i]$$

where, $S=(I\theta_c'-M\gamma')[M_i(1-I_y)+M_yI_k]>0(\because I_y<1)$

Note that, so long as $\gamma>\theta_c$, dy/dM is positive, but dr/dM is negative. However, di/dM is negative exactly under a reverse inequality, *viz.*, $\gamma<\theta_c$. Thus as long as the 'proportion of investible surplus allocated to loans by the banks' (i.e., γ) exceeds the optimal proportion of investment finance raised through loans by firms (i.e. θ_c), an expansionary monetary policy reduces the loan rate, which in turn reduces the net capital cost of investment (k)—this leads to an expansion of output through the usual Keynesian multiplier channel. However, since in this situation there is every possibility of i going up, the burden of adjustment falls primarily on the loan rate, and in turn on loan supply.[24] Output suffers so long as there is paucity of loans to the firms. This is, however, a direct offshoot of the assumption capturing relationship advantage from bank borrowing (i.e., $\theta_c'<0$).

---

23. γ(r-i) can be conceived as λ(i,r) (1-μ) as per our original formulation of Bernanke and Blinder (1988) model, discussed earlier.

24. Note that the condition $\gamma<\theta_c$ is merely sufficient condition. Thus di/dM may still turn out to be negative even when $\gamma<\theta_c$.

Therefore, as long as we retain the assumption of imperfect substitutability between loans and securities, existence of non-intermediated forms of borrowing does not invalidate the credit view of monetary policy. Moreover, in practise, as CPs are successfully issued by firms with high credit rating, backed by bank guarantee, they are more in the nature of complementary rather than substitutes to bank loans.

2.5 Information Asymmetry and Bank Behaviour

2.5.1 Stein (1998)'s Model

Broadly speaking, the models discussed so far on the central bank's policy actions and commercial bank behaviour within the confines of the 'bank lending channel', assumed away any informational problem. What happens when the scenario is added with the complication of information asymmetry? Ever since Stiglitz and Weiss (1981) introduced the "asymmetry information-induced credit rationing", it is well known that asymmetry of information is capable of incorporating a number of worries in the macroeconomic equilibrium. It is in this context we turn to Stein (1998), which was an adverse-selection model of bank asset and liability management. Notwithstanding the microeconomic emphasis of the model, in view of the fact that it specifically tackled the problem of banks' asset-liability management in the event of a contractionary monetary policy, we discuss the model. The bank's balance sheet in Stein (1998) looks as follows (Table 2.7).

Table 2.7

Stylised Balance Sheet of a Typical Bank in Stein (1998) Model

Assets		*Liabilities*	
(1)		*(2)*	
Reserves	R	Insured Deposits	M
Old Assets	K	Non-deposit finance	P
New Loans	L	Incremental Non-deposit external finance	E

Assuming that old assets are completely supported by non-deposit financing like CDs, subordinated debt or preferred stock (so that

K=P), with τ as the reserve ratio, the balance sheet constraint of the bank is written as,

(2.37) $$L \leq (1-\tau)M + E$$

Since banks are assumed to be monopolist in the loan market, they face a loan demand schedule of the form:

(2.38) $$L^D = a - br$$

Stein (1998) postulated that there is an asymmetry of information about the level of the old asset K. In particular, for good banks (G) the value of K (K^G) is higher than that of the bad banks (K^B). Interestingly, bank managers know their type but outside investors do not. It has further been assumed that both K^G and K^B are sufficiently larger than L. In such a scenario, Stein (1998) asks the following question: if a bank is faced with an exogenous outflow of insured deposits, how will it react? That is to say, if M falls, whether L goes down or E goes up.[25]

In such a scenario, Stein (1998) had shown that there is a unique separating equilibrium, with the following properties:

- Bad banks will lend in an undistorted manner and raise $E^b = \max(o, a/2 - M(1-\tau))$
- Good banks, on the other hand, raise less external finance and, therefore, will lend less.

The divergence between the bahaviour of good and bad banks can be rationalised as follows. When M falls, bad banks will make up by E and leave their lending uninsured, but good banks will be reluctant to use uninsured sources of finance and hence their lending will go down. Thus, in any economy if a significant proportion of banks are good, a contractionary monetary policy will lead to a fall in bank lending.[26]

In a two-period setup the structure is slightly different. In the asset side, banks have an additional option in period 1, *viz.*, to hold securities (S). The difference between loans and securities in the model is as follows. While securities at time 1 may be costlessly

25. Note that by assuming P=K, we are not considering adjustment in terms of non-deposit resources like CDs.

26. This is, thus, contrary to Romer and Romer (1990), wherein CDs can substitute as non-deposit resources. The non-applicability of the Modigliani-Miller proposition for the banking firms is due to the presence of adverse selection.

liquidated in time 2, they can only liquidate an amount J (of the loans in period 1) in period 2, so that the balance sheet constraint at time 1 and 2 is written as,

(2.39a) $$L + S \leq M_1(1-\tau) + E_1 \qquad \text{(time 1)}$$

(2.39b) $$L - J \leq M_2(1-\tau) + E_1 + E_2 \qquad \text{(time 2)}$$

In such a set-up, if $E_1^B > 0$ good banks tend to react to a decrease in M by cutting lending. Since banks hold securities, in spite of their low yield, due to the cost of liquidation of the loans, bad banks in time 1 will hold so much securities that it may not have to worry for period 2. Good banks on the contrary, will not fully insulate themselves so that they will hold both of securities and loans. Thus, in the presence of asymmetry of information, even with securities, a fall in M would lead to a fall in L.

2.5.2 *Macro-Implications of Credit and Equity Rationing*

A major implication for information asymmetry is the existence of equilibrium of credit-rationing (Stiglitz and Weiss, 1981) and equity rationing (Greenwald and Stigliz, 1988, 1990), even without any government regulation about the downward movement of interest rate. While a discussion on micro-models is beyond the scope of the present book, following Greenwald and Stiglitz (1990), this section takes a look at the implications of these models for the macro behaviour of the economy.

The LL Curve from the Credit Rationing Model

Let the banks hold four kinds of assets, *viz.*, reserves (ìM), risky loans (L), safe Government bonds (G_b), and bank capital (K_b).[27] As before let λ be the proportion of banks' investible surplus devoted to loans, with the following functional from,

(2.40) $$\lambda = \lambda(\underset{-}{i}, \underset{+}{E_{f,-1}}, \underset{+}{E_{b,-1}})$$

27. We neglect Greenwald-Stiglitz (1990)'s distinction of real and nominal variable.

where, i is the interest rate on Government bonds, and $E_{f,-1}$ and $E_{b,-1}$ are one period earlier equity positions of the firms (f) and banks (b), respectively. Note that the lagged values of equity positions are taken on the premise that this was the value at which the firm (or bank) entered the current period. Thus the loan supply is given by,

(2.41) $$L_s = \lambda(i, E_{f,-1}, E_{b,-1})[(1-\mu)M + K_{b,-1}]$$

The loan demand, on the other hand, is specified in terms of contractual rate of interest in the credit rationed equilibrium (r) and is given by,

(2.42) $$r = r(i, E_{f,-1})$$

While $r_i \geq 0$, we cannot say for certain about the sign of $\delta r / \delta E_{f,-1}$. Since higher level of firms' equity lowers the default rate, which is expected to lower r, and on the contrary higher levels of equity may raise loans, and in turn loan rate, the net effect may go either way.

The LM Curve

There are four financial markets in the model, *viz.*, money (comprising demand deposits), government bond, loans, and equity of firms. Of the four, the stock market is ignored through the assumption of absence of equity sales. On the other hand, the government bond market and money market can be solved simultaneously so as to yield a traditional LM curve of the form:

(2.43a) $$i = i(\underset{+}{Y}, \underset{+}{G}, \underset{-}{M})$$

Where, G is the outstanding amount of government debt. However, treating G as a parameter will continue to describe the LM curve of the more standard form, *viz.*,

(2.43b) $$LM: M = M(\underset{-}{i}, \underset{+}{Y})$$

The IS Curve

The commodity market equilibrium can be written as,

(2.44) $$IS: I(\underset{+}{L}, \underset{-}{r}) = S(\underset{+}{Y}, \underset{+}{i})$$

Note that apart from the presence of both i and r (as in Bernanke-Blinder, 1988), because of credit rationing L appears as argument in the IS equation. The presence of both r and L may be reflective of both price and quantity rationing in the loan market that the firm face.

The CC Curve

Greenwald and Stiglitz (1990) proceed in the similar manner as in Bernanke-Blinder (1988). Note that, L_s and r determine L and r as functions of i and M, given δ, $E_{f,-1}$, $E_{b,-1}$, $K_{b,,-1}$. Thus, if we substitute them in the IS equation we arrive at the usual CC Curve given by,

$$(2.45) \qquad I[\underset{+\ ?}{r(i,M)}, \underset{+\ -\ +}{L(i,M)}] = \underset{+\ +}{S(Y,i)}$$

Greenwald and Stiglitz (1990) call the CC curve as "credit rationing modified IS curve."[28] Thus equations (2.45) and (2.43) describe the CC-LM model in Greenwald and Stiglitz (1988).

Transmission Mechanism in Greenwald-Stiglitz (G-S) Model

Note that, as in Bernanke-Blinder (B-B), in this case too a change in money will shift both the CC and LM curve, and a situation may arise where a monetary expansion can lead both to higher output and higher interest rate (e.g., point E3 in Figure 2.1).

This is also clear from the comparative static derivatives given as follows,

$$(2.46a) \qquad \frac{dY}{dM} = \frac{1}{R}[(I_r R_M + I_L L_M)M_i + (I_r r_i + I_L L - S_i)]$$

$$(2.46b) \qquad \frac{di}{dM} = \frac{1}{R}[S_y - M_y(I_r r_M + I_L L_M)]$$

where, $R = S_y M_i + M_y(I_r r_i + I_L L_i - S_i) < 0$

So long as $r_M \le 0$ ($r = 0$, under credit rationing), we have dY/dM > 0; if $r_M > 0$, then the sign of dY/dM turns out to be indeterminate, and it may even turn out to be negative.[29] Moreover, the sign of di/dM is also indeterminate, and in fact,

---

28. Note that, $(di/dY)_{cc} = [S_Y/(I_r r_i + I_L L_i)] < 0$

29. The necessary condition for dY/dM to be negative is: $r_M > [\{S_i - I_r r_i - I_L(L_i + L_M M_i)\}/I_r M_i] > 0$. That is to say, under a severe credit rationing, the impact of an expansionary monetary policy on output may turn out to be adverse.

$$\frac{di}{dM} >=< 0 \text{ according as } S_y <=> M_y(I_L L_M + I_r r_M)$$

How does the Greenwald-Stiglitz (G-S) story differ from monetary transmission in the Bernanke-Blinder (B-B)? A look at the functional forms enables us to discern two minor points of difference.

First, in G-S the loan market is not sensitive to output ($r_y=0$).

Secondly, in our simplified version of the B-B model interest sensitivity of saving is assumed away ($S_i=0$).

Under these two assumptions, let us consider dY/dM in both the cases. From (2.16a) and (2.46a) we get,

$$\frac{dY}{dM}(B-B; r_y = 0) = \frac{I_r(R_M M_i + r_i) + I_i}{I_r M_y r_i + S_y M_i + M_y I_i}$$

$$\frac{dY}{dM}(G-S; S_i = 0) = \frac{I_r(R_M M_i + r_i) + I_L(:_M M_i + L_i)}{I_r M_y r_i + S_y M_i + M_y I_L L_i}$$

Thus, the basic difference between the two models is the treatment of i in the investment function. In B-B, i enters either directly or through r, while in G-S it either through L or through r. This clearly explains the difference in the comparative static derivatives.[30]

2.6 Concluding Observations

The present chapter takes a broad overview of the central bank's policy actions and commercial bank behaviour. In this context, we have noted that the role of commercial banks in transmitting monetary policy actions has in particular been pursued in the literature of credit channel of monetary transmission, which, however, is not a substitute to the usual rate of interest channel. In the Keynesian transmission mechanism, it adds another independent channel through which monetary policy actions get transmitted, *viz.*, loan rate or loan amount or both (depending on which version of the model one is adopting). What follows below are the major issues that emerge from the present chapter.

---

30. Note that, $dI/di\,(G-S) = I_r r_i + L_i I_L$, while $dI/di\,(B-B) = I_r r_i + I_i$.

First, mere incorporation of bank loans in the banks' and firms' balance sheet does not add an independent role of commercial banks in transmitting monetary policy actions. After all, money is fungible and hence so long as there is no segmentation between loans and securities market, there is no force that inhibits the equalisation of loan rate of interest and bond rate of interest.

Second, the market segmentation between loans and securities is often ensured from information asymmetry based explanations of speciality of banks and bank loans, and existence of bank-dependent borrowers.

Third, a detailed examination of the Bernanke-Blinder (1988) model and Greenwald-Stiglitz (1990) model establishes the fact that given the assumption of speciality of bank loans it is possible to reconstruct a standard IS-LM model, with bank loans (as another asset for banks and as another source of financing for corporates) in which there is an independent credit channel and a consequent role of commercial banks in transmission of monetary policy actions.

Fourth, the newer financial instruments like CPs or CDs, as prime examples of non-intermediated borrowing, may weaken the speciality of bank credit, but so long as some degree of speciality of bank loan exist, the independent role of banks in transmitting monetary policy actions is not nullified.

Annex A-2.1

Comparative Static Analysis in the Two Asset Model

Following, Miron, Romer and Weil (1994), consider a simplified balance sheet of the non-bank public and banks in the presence of CDs.

Balance Sheets of Non-Bank Public and Banks with CDs

Non-Banks				*Banks*			
Assets		*Liabilities*		*Assets*		*Liabilities*	
(1)		*(2)*		*(3)*		*(4)*	
Deposits	M	Bank Loans	L	Reserves (R)		Deposits	M
				On M	μM		
				On CDs	$-\tau B^b$		
		Bonds	B^p	Bank Loans	L		
Net Wealth	W			Bonds	B^b		

In such a set up, the basic IS-LM-LL equations are given as follows:

(A2.1.1) $IS: S(Y) = I(i, r)$

(A2.1.2) $LM: M(i, Y) = \bar{M}$

(A2.1.3) $$LL: L(r, i, Y) = \frac{\lambda(i, r)(1-\mu)}{1+(\lambda(i, r)-1)\tau}M$$
$$\Rightarrow L(r, i, Y)[1+(\lambda(i, r)-1)\tau] = \lambda(i, r)(1-\mu)M$$

While IS and LM equations are fairly standard ones, the LL equations needs some clarification. First, note that, μ and τ are the reserve requirements on Deposits (M) or CDs (B^b), respectively. Second, note that, λ is defined as the ratio of loans (L) to investible resources, i.e., B^b + L. Since B^b can be negative, λ can be greater than unity as well (when banks hold CDs).

Differentiating (A2.1.1) - (A2.1.3), with respect to M, we get the following system of linear equations

(A2.1.5) $$\begin{bmatrix} -S_y & I_i & I_r \\ M_y & M_i & 0 \\ A_1 & A_2 & A_3 \end{bmatrix} \begin{bmatrix} dT/dM \\ di/dM \\ dr/dM \end{bmatrix} = \begin{bmatrix} 0 \\ 1 \\ 0 \end{bmatrix}$$

where, $A_1 = (1+(\lambda-1)\tau)Ly - \lambda(1-\mu)M_Y$

$A_2 = L\,\tau\lambda_i + (1+(\lambda-1)\tau)L_i - (1-\mu)M\,\lambda_i - \lambda(1-\mu)M_i$

$A_3 = L\,\tau\lambda_r + (1+(\lambda-1)\tau)L_r - (1-\mu)M\lambda_r$

Simplifying,

$$\text{(A2.1.6)} \qquad \frac{dY}{dM} = \frac{A_2 I_r - A_3 I_i}{I_r(A_2 M_Y - A_1 M_i) - A_3(S_Y M_i + M_Y I_i)}$$

Substituting the values of A_i's we get,

$$\text{(A2.1.7a)} \qquad \frac{dY}{dM} = \frac{1}{Q}\left[(k\frac{\lambda_r}{\lambda} - \frac{L_r}{L})\frac{I_i}{I_r} + (\frac{L_i}{L} - \frac{M_i}{M}) - k\frac{\lambda_i}{\lambda}\right]$$

$$\text{where } Q = \left[(k\frac{\lambda_r}{\lambda} - \frac{L_r}{L})(\frac{M_i S_y + M_y I_i}{I_r}) + (\frac{L_i M_y - L_y M_i}{L}) - \frac{k\lambda_i M_y}{\lambda}\right] > 0$$

and, $k = \dfrac{1-\tau}{1+(\lambda-1)\tau}$

This is the result reported in equation (2.21a).

Note that, in the Bernanke and Blinder (1988) model, CDs are absent so that, $\tau = 0$, and $k = 1$. Hence (A2.1.7a) gets reduced to,

$$\text{(A2.1.7b)} \qquad \left(\frac{dY}{dM}\right)_{k=1} = \frac{1}{J}\left[\left(\frac{\lambda_r}{\lambda} - \frac{L_r}{L}\right)\frac{I_i}{I_r} + \left(\frac{L_i}{L} - \frac{M_i}{M}\right) - \frac{\lambda_i}{\lambda}\right]$$

$$\text{where, } J = \left[\left(\frac{\lambda_r}{\lambda} - \frac{L_r}{L}\right)\left(\frac{M_i S_y + M_y I_i}{I_r}\right) + \left(\frac{L_i M_y - L_y M_i}{L}\right) - \frac{\lambda_i}{\lambda}M_y\right]$$

3

Monetary Policy and Bank Behaviour in India

Some Stylised Facts

3.1 Introduction

Having delineated the theoretical issues on monetary policy action and commercial bank behaviour, the present chapter provides a selective account of the experience of the Indian economy. The chronicle starts at the early 1990s, *i.e.*, since the initiation of the reform programme. The stylised facts that are going to emanate from this account are expected to provide a perspective to the empirical questions that are going to be pursued in the rest of the book.

It would perhaps be proper to go a little back in time. Following the pattern of planned economic development, the primary focus of Indian financial policies was on channelising resources from the savers to the investors in accordance with planned priorities. Accordingly, efforts were on to build a banking system, with a widespread network, not only in terms of geographical spread but also in terms of socio-economic reach (Ajit and Banger, 1997). This was reinforced by gradual extension of 'social control' over banking—by the nationalisation of private commercial banks in 1969 and 1980.[1]

The objective of creating a large bank network was satisfied by the 1980s with the number of bank branches increasing from 8,262 in 1969 to around 60,000 in the early 1990s and finally to more than 68,000 in 2004. The absolute number of branches might not indicate the extent of financial progress. In terms of per capita deposits and credit too, there was tremendous progress. During a large part of the 20-year period 1970-1990, the primary emphasis of the banking policy was on branch expansion and ensuring financial deepening of the

1. See Burgess and Pande (2005) for a discussion on impact of Indian social banking.

economy. At the same time, with the ever-increasing support of the central bank through the monetisation of Government deficit necessitating large pre-emption of lendable resources, the emphasis of the monetary policy was to control credit extended by commercial banks. Thus, during the two decades of the 1970s and 1980s, a large chunk of the policy actions of the central bank permeated to the commercial banks *via* administrative fiats in terms of pre-assigned proportions of credit going to the desired sectors of the economy. Apart from the stipulations on priority sector lending, there were also commodity specific norms for working capital requirement.[2]

The initiation of the financial sector reform programme apropos the recommendations of the Committee on the Financial System (Chairman: M. Narasimham) in 1992, changed the scenario a great deal.[3] Apart from the gradual lowering of the statutory pre-emptions, commercial banks were given a substantial degree of operational autonomy with the deregulation of credit prescriptions and interest rate, both, on deposit and lending side. Along with open market operations through auctions of Government securities, repos and reverse repos, income recognition and asset classification norms as well as capital adequacy measures *a la* Basel I were introduced in order to ensure safe and sound banking.

In the backdrop of Indian macroeconomic trends during the sample period of the present book, namely, 1990-91 through 2003-04, this chapter gives a synoptic account of two specific issues, *viz.*, (a) what were the forms of central bank's policy actions?, and (b) what do various parameters of commercial bank behaviour indicate?

The rest of the chapter is organised as follows. A quick rundown of the broad contours of the Indian macroeconomic trends during the sample period of 1991-92 through 2003-04 is provided in Section 3.2.[4] Section 3.3 gives a synoptic account of the central bank's policy actions. The behaviour of various parameters of commercial banks is summarised in Section 3.4. Concluding observations are presented in Section 3.5.

---

2. These were specified in various reports, such as, Tandon and Chore Committee; see Chakravarty Committee Report for details (RBI, 1985).
3. Hereafter referred to as Narasimham Committee I (RBI, 1992).
4. While for all practical purpose the sample period is 1992-93 through 2003-04, reference is made to 1991-92 (and occasionally 1990-91) for placing the issues in perspectives.

3.2 Macroeconomic and Monetary Trends

The 1990s began with a severe balance of payments crisis and a high rate of inflation, reflecting the growing pressure on internal balances of the 1980s (Figure 3.1 and Table 3.1). The rapidly deteriorating balance of payments situation in the wake of the Gulf war of August 1990 required stiff monetary and credit measures aimed at demand containment and import compression. The Reserve Bank continued to attempt to curtail monetary expansion to combat growing inflation, which crossed double digits for the first time since 1980-81. Non-food credit expansion was also lower at 12.4 per cent in 1990-91 from 18.5 per cent in 1989-90. Notwithstanding the deterioration in the balance of payments, output growth was satisfactory in 1990-91 at 5.6 per cent.

Table 3.1

Growth and Inflation

(Per Cent)

Year	*Growth of Real GDP*	*Growth of IIP*	*Inflation*
(1)	*(2)*	*(3)*	*(4)*
1991-92	1.3	0.6	13.7
1992-93	5.1	2.3	10.1
1993-94	5.9	6.0	8.4
1994-95	7.3	9.4	12.6
1995-96	7.3	13.0	8.0
1996 97	7.8	6.1	4.6
1997-98	4.8	6.7	4.4
1998-99	6.5	4.1	5.9
1999-00	6.1	6.7	3.3
2000-01	4.4	5.0	7.2
2001-02	5.8	2.7	3.6
2002-03	4.0	5.7	3.4
2003-04	8.5	7.0	5.5

Notes: 1. GDP growth rates up to 2002-03 are from old series (base 1993-94) and data from 2003-04 onwards are from new series (base 1999-2000).
2. While growth rates of IIP up to 1994-95 are from the old series (base 1980-81), data from 1995-96 onwards are from the new series (base 1993-94).
3. Inflation rates are based on average of weeks for the wholesale price index number. While upto 1993-94, these are from the 1981-82 base, data from 1994-95 onwards are from the 1993-94 base.

Source: RBI. *Handbook of Statistics on the Indian Economy*, various issues.

Figure 3.1

Growth and Inflation in India

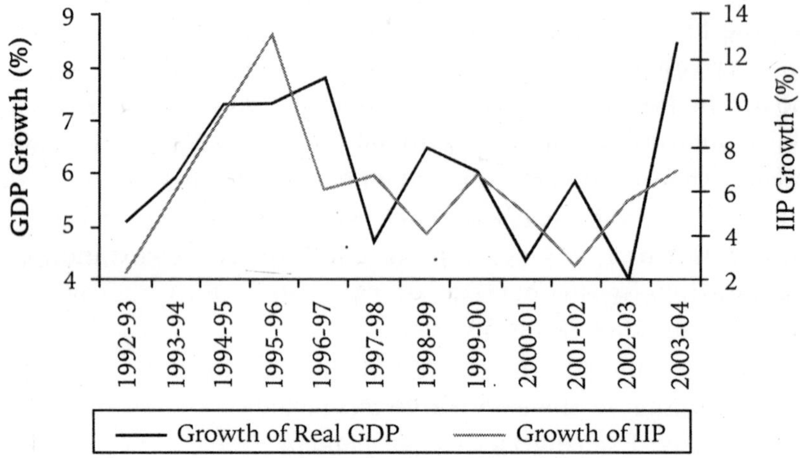

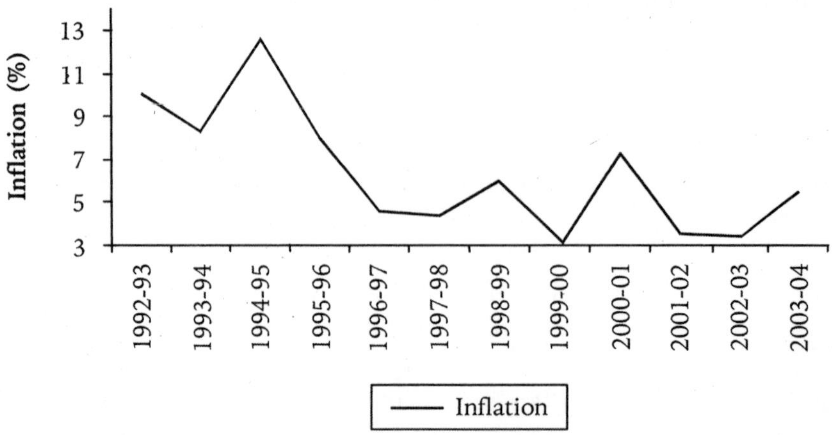

The payments situation deteriorated further in 1991-92 till the foreign exchange reserves contracted to a low of US $ 975 million as on July 12, 1991, sparked off by a sudden withdrawal of Foreign Currency Non-Residents (Accounts) [FCNR(A)] deposits of nearly US $ 1 billion in the first quarter ended June 1991. In response, the Reserve Bank of India (RBI) continued to tighten monetary conditions to contain domestic demand and compress imports. Faced with the adverse shock, the GDP growth rate decelerated to 1.3 per cent in 1991-92. At the same time, inflation increased to 13.7 per cent in 1991-92, as monetary expansion worked out to 19.3 per cent, far above the 13 per cent projection of the April 1991 monetary and credit policy, driven by the overriding need to re-attract non-resident deposits in the latter half of the year. In tandem, bank deposit mobilisation was substantial. Non-food credit recorded a lower growth of 8.2 per cent in line with the measures of credit restriction, pushing the surplus liquidity in government paper.

Fiscal 1992-93 saw a revival in economic activity, with the real GDP growth rate climbing to 5.1 per cent. As a result, the Indian economy, like most other emerging market economies, attracted large-scale capital flows following the success of the initial stabilisation efforts and liberalisation of the external sector, including the introduction of the Liberalised Exchange Rate Management System in March 1992. The Reserve Bank absorbed surplus capital flows in its balance sheet in order to maintain the export competitiveness of the economy and at the same time, attempted to sterilise the monetary impact as inflation persisted in double digits for the third successive year. The RBI introduced open market operations to offload government paper to neutralise the bank liquidity fostered by capital flows. Aggregate deposits slowed down to 16.4 per cent but the accretion to time deposits was stronger at 19.6 per cent, perhaps reflecting the 'flight to safety' in the wake of uncertainties arising out of irregularities in securities transactions.[5] Non-food credit revived at 20.1 per cent, two-and-half times the increase of the previous year, reflecting the easing of monetary conditions, including reductions in statutory pre-emptions and easing of lending norms.

The macroeconomic performance began to strengthen, with the real GDP growth rate climbing further to 5.9 per cent in 1993-94. Inflation decelerated to single digit levels. Capital flows continued unabated—

5. It may be recalled that during April 1991 to May 1992, there was a diversion of funds to the tune of over Rs. 3500 crore from the banking system to various stockbrokers in a series of transactions (primarily in Government securities). Reforms in the stock market were accelerated following the stock market scam that revealed serious weaknesses in the regulatory mechanism; see Ahluwalia (2002).

combined with a buoyant capital market and a revival of economic activity. The RBI attempted to reduce the cost of funds by cutting cash reserve requirements by 50 basis points each in April and May 1993. At the same time, it continued to absorb the excess foreign exchange in its balance sheet by conducting open market operations in order to nullify the resultant monetary (and inflationary) impact of capital flows. Monetary expansion, nevertheless, climbed to 18.4 per cent, driven by a sharp increase in cash demand, with the revival of economic activity (Table 3.2). In conjunction, demand deposits also recorded a sharp growth of 21.8 per cent, reflecting the buoyancy in the capital market. Non-food credit, on the other hand, slowed down to 5.7 per cent as corporates began to access the capital market. The resultant surplus bank liquidity was parked in government paper, driving the banks' investment in government securities to grow at 33.3 per cent, up from 21.1 per cent in the previous year.

Table 3.2

Growth in Select Monetary Aggregates

(Per cent)

Year	*Reserve Money*	M_3	*Other Banks credit to Government*	*Other Banks credit to Commercial Sector*	*Net Forex Assets of Banking Sector*
(1)	(2)	(3)	(4)	(5)	(6)
1991-92	13.4	19.3	25.1	9.3	100.6
1992-93	11.3	14.8	21.1	18.4	15.2
1993-94	25.2	18.4	34.5	8.1	123.4
1994-95	22.1	22.4	15.6	23.7	44.7
1995-96	14.9	13.6	12.8	18.1	3.9
1996-97	2.8	16.2	20.5	9.6	28.4
1997-98	13.2	18.0	18.9	14.9	30.9
1998-99	14.5	19.4	19.8	13.8	28.8
1999-00	8.2	14.6	25.2	18.1	15.6
2000-01	8.1	16.8	22.2	16.6	21.5
2001-02	11.4	14.1	22.1	13.2	24.6
2002-03	9.2	14.7	27.1	18.9	26.6
2003-04	18.3	16.6	25.6	13.2	33.7

Source: RBI. *Handbook of Statistics on the Indian Economy*, various issues.

The economy continued to record strong growth during 1994-95, with the real GDP growth rate at 7.3 per cent. At the same time, inflation tended to remain high, returning to double-digit levels, reflecting the excessive monetary expansion fostered by continuing capital inflows. The data on monetary and credit growth during 1994-1995 are, however, amplified by the fact that the last reporting Friday coincided with the balance sheet date of March 31, so that the full impact of year-end interest application and 'window dressing' is reflected in the annual numbers. The RBI had raised reserve requirements by one percentage point in June, July and August. After two years of steady capital inflows, the domestic currency came under slight pressures during November 1994 and in mid-March 1995, but stability was quickly restored.

Fiscal 1995-96 saw continued high growth, with the real GDP growth rate continuing at 7.3 per cent, driven by an IIP growth of 13.0 per cent. With the tightening of monetary policy, inflation began to abate to 8.1 per cent during the year, notwithstanding a drop in crop production. There was a return of tight liquidity conditions on account of strong demand for credit and the decline in capital inflows.[6] The RBI used the opportunity to reduce reserve requirements by 50 basis points in the latter half of the year and push liberalisation measures, such as, the increase in the ceiling interest rate for 2-year deposits and deregulation for larger tenors. The year saw the first of the sudden switches in capital flows which would characterise the Indian economy in the latter half of the 1990s. The first serious pressure in the foreign exchange markets began in late August 1995, with increased import demand, slowdown in capital inflows and strengthening of the US dollar against other major world currencies. The RBI intervened by selling US dollars, especially in the forward market, in an attempt to bring forward premia in alignment with the interest differentials. This was supplemented by a withdrawal of money market support, which pushed up call rates towards end-October and early November (touching the peak of 85.0 per cent on November 3, 1995) to choke off the possibility of speculative pressures on the exchange rate. With the return of stability in the spot foreign exchange market, the RBI

6. At the same time, the deceleration in the monetary and credit aggregates is overemphasised by the base effect of the spurt on March 31, 1995.

re-injected liquidity through repos with two primary dealers, *viz.*, Discount and Finance House of India (DFHI) and Securities Trading Corporation of India (STCI), enhanced banks' refinance facilities against Government securities and cut the CRR to stabilise the inter-bank market. The forex market once more became volatile in February 1996, pushing up call rates but stability returned soon with the revival of capital flows coupled with measures to accelerate repatriation of export proceeds and prevent acceleration of import payments.

Real GDP growth accelerated to 7.8 per cent during 1996-97, although industrial production began to decelerate to 6.1 per cent. There was a sharp drop in the inflation rate to 4.6 per cent reflecting a revival of agriculture. Bank liquidity improved with the accretion of US $ 5,323 million to the Reserve Bank's foreign currency assets in 1996-97 on account of a contraction in the current account deficit on the one hand and an increase in capital inflows on the other. With the return of exchange rate stability, the Reserve Bank was able to ease liquidity conditions further by cutting the CRR by as much as 4.0 percentage points (thereby releasing Rs.17,850 crore of lendable resources to banks during April 1996-January 1997) with a view to moderating interest rates and facilitating credit off-take. In response, there was a significant softening of interest rates across the spectrum.

As the reasonable growth in industry could not compensate for a dip in agricultural production, the year 1997-98 saw real GDP growth falling to 4.8 per cent. As inflation ruled at sub-5 per cent levels, the conduct of monetary policy had to shift gears to create enabling conditions for revival of economic activity, especially as industry was beginning to show a downward trend. This was facilitated by easy liquidity conditions in the first half of 1997-98, driven by sustained capital inflows that resulted in substantial accretion of the Reserve Bank's net foreign exchange assets (NFA) by Rs.11,546 crore (adjusted for revaluation). The stability in the foreign exchange market enabled the Reserve Bank to announce further reductions in reserve requirements by 2.0 percentage points in October 1997. The situation changed dramatically in the second half of the year as the contagion from the South-Asian financial crisis began affecting the Indian financial markets, pushing the exchange rate beyond Rs.40 per US dollar in mid-January 1998. The Reserve Bank responded with a two-pronged strategy of mitigating excess demand conditions in the foreign exchange market, and tightening monetary conditions, on the other, to reduce the scope for arbitrage between the easy money market and the volatile foreign exchange market.

Fiscal 1998-99 saw a revival of growth beyond 6 per cent, driven by agricultural recovery. The sharp drop in industrial growth to 4.1 per cent, however, posed a challenge to the monetary policy. Inflation remained relatively benign, barring a sudden mid-year spurt in agricultural prices. The monetary strategy of easing liquidity conditions was contained by a return of volatility in the foreign exchange market in mid-May 1998, in reaction to the impending sanctions by the US to register protests against India's nuclear experimentation. As a result, the Rupee-US$ exchange rate weakened to Rs. 42.38 by June 11, 1998 from Rs. 39.73 per US dollar at the beginning of May. The Reserve Bank once again had to tighten monetary conditions to stabilise the foreign exchange market, although a carefully crafted strategy of managing liquidity conditions by combining monetisation of the fiscal deficit and open market sales was able to contain the resultant impact on the interest cost of public debt and to some extent, longer-term interest rates. The mobilisation of US $ 4.2 billion through Resurgent India Bonds (RIBs) in August 1998 helped to stabilise expectations and the result was an accretion of US $ 3.7 billion to the foreign exchange reserves. This helped in the Reserve Bank easing liquidity conditions in the latter half of the year. The M_3 expansion, net of RIBs, decelerated marginally in 1998 containing demand side pressures on prices. Bank credit also decelerated in response to the weakening of credit demand as a result of the slowdown in industrial activity.

Real GDP growth continued to rule at 6.0 per cent plus, driven by a modicum of industrial recovery during 1999-2000. The inflation rate slipped to about 3.0 per cent partly reflecting the base effects of the supply shocks of the previous year. The Reserve Bank continued to ease liquidity conditions. Although the foreign exchange market witnessed a degree of volatility during end-May 1999 and August 1999, the central bank was quickly able to restore stability. The return of stability in the foreign exchange market allowed the Reserve Bank to further ease monetary conditions by releasing lendable resources of about Rs.10,000 crore through a one percentage point cut in the cash reserve ratio (as well as phasing out of incremental CRR on FCNR(B) deposits) during November and December of 1999. Commercial bank non-food credit accelerated to 16.6 per cent from 13.0 per cent in the previous year in response to industrial recovery.

The macroeconomic performance deteriorated in 2000-01 with the real GDP slowing down to sub-5.0 per cent levels. Industrial growth continued to be subdued (5.0 per cent). In addition, there was a decline in agricultural production for the second consecutive year. The inflation rate climbed beyond 7.0 per cent, driven by a spurt in oil prices, following tensions in the Middle East. The concerns over the rising import bill spilled over into the foreign exchange markets. The Reserve Bank had to once again tighten monetary conditions to restore stability. Aggressive repo operations under the Liquidity Adjustment Facility, a new monetary instrument introduced in June 2000, stabilised markets in the face of sudden capital outflows. Foreign exchange inflows through India Millennium Deposits (IMD) stabilised markets in November 2000, allowing the Reserve Bank to ease monetary conditions in January-March 2001. Reflective of the weak credit demand, bank credit decelerated to 14.9 per cent. The surplus liquidity generated by capital flows began to pour into the gilt market, inducing a rally in the government security prices.

Fiscal 2001-02 proved to be another challenging year for the Indian economy. Although real GDP growth revived to 5.8 per cent, driven by a recovery in agricultural production, industrial growth slipped to 2.7 per cent, with manufacturing growth falling to 2.9 per cent from 5.3 per cent in the previous year. Inflation fell for a second time below 4.0 per cent. Although the Reserve Bank continued to ease monetary conditions, weak credit demand further pulled non-food credit off-take to 13.6 per cent. With bank deposits growing somewhat strongly at 14.6 per cent (net of IMDs), reflecting strong capital flows and a flight to safety, and the downturn in the capital market, surplus bank liquidity began to fund a rally in the government securities markets.

There was a drought-like situation in 2002-03 with absolute declines in agricultural activity dragging the real GDP growth to 4 per cent. Inflation was, however, under control at 3.4 per cent and broad money (M_3) slowed down. There was a policy bias towards soft interest rates and a flexible interest rate structure. Accordingly, the CRR was reduced from 5.5 per cent to 5.0 per cent in June 2002, to 4.75 per cent in November 2002 and further to 4.5 per cent in June 2003, augmenting the lendable resources of banks by about Rs.13,500 crore. Further, the Bank Rate and the LAF reverse repo rate were reduced by 25 basis points each in October 2002 followed by a 50 basis point cut in the LAF repo rate on March 3, 2003. Comfortable liquidity conditions engendered by large capital inflows enabled a general reduction in market interest rates with varying sensitivity to policy signals across the maturity spectrum. Lending rates of banks exhibited somewhat sluggish downward movements. The softening of interest rates was enabled by a benign inflation environment.

There was a sharp turnaround in agriculture in 2003-04, aided by a normal monsoon. Industrial and services sector activities strengthened significantly and India's real GDP grew at an impressive 8.2 per cent during 2003-04.[7] The year was marked by a generally stable inflation situation. With orderly and easy conditions in the financial markets engendered by domestic and international sources of liquidity, interest rates continued to be low. Monetary policy supported this with a 25 basis point cut in the Bank Rate in end-April 2003 and in the CRR in mid-June, followed by a 50 basis point reduction in the LAF reverse repo rate towards the end of August. Banks took advantage of easy liquidity conditions to reduce deposit rates and lending rates. Responding to the Reserve Bank's initiative, banks switched over from tenor-linked prime lending rates (PLRs) to benchmark PLRs (BPLRs). As at end-March 2004, BPLRs were lower by 25-20 basis points than the PLRs which prevailed a year ago. Beginning the second quarter, massive sterilisation operations were conducted through open market sales of Government securities and LAF reverse repos. The large scale sterilisation necessitated by the relentless expansion in the net foreign assets of the Reserve Bank resulted in reverse repos outstanding under the LAF soaring to over

7. In the post-Independence pre-1990s history, India's real GDP grew by over 8.0 per cent only on three occasions [*viz.*, 1967-68 (8.1 per cent), 1975-76 (9.0 per cent) and 1988-89 (10.5 per cent)]. In these three occasions, however, the share of agriculture in GDP was much higher than in 2003-04.

Rs. 50,000 crore by March 2004 and large scale open market sales from the stock of Government securities in the Reserve Bank's portfolio. To further strengthen the Reserve Bank's ability to conduct monetary and exchange rate management, a Market Stabilisation Scheme (MSS) was introduced in April 2004.[8]

3.3 Monetary Policy Action[9]

Notwithstanding the spread of banking institutions, the Indian banking system as it emerged in the early 1990s suffered from three major structural bottlenecks:

a) There were multiple restrictions on bank portfolios which segmented financial markets.

b) A regime of administered interest rates blunted the process of price discovery.

c) Bank profitability was affected by the need to compensate the depositor for the rising inflation, partly driven by the monetary expansion emanating from deficit financing and partly by the imperative to provide soft loans to spur industrial development.[10]

As pointed out earlier, India embarked upon a massive programme of stabilisation and structural adjustment in the midst of the unprecedented balance of payment and fiscal crisis in mid-1991.[11] A basic component of the new economic policy since 1992-93 was reforms in the financial sector, aiming at providing a diversified, efficient and competitive operating environment with the ultimate objective of improving the allocative efficiency of available resources.

Narasimham Committee I, which laid down the blue print of financial sector reforms, recognised that a vibrant and competitive

---

8. See Mohan (2006b) for a discussion on MSS.
9. See Joshi and Little (1994, 1996), Jadhav (1994) Rangarajan (1998), Reddy (1999, 2005), and Mohan (2005) for a discussion of Indian monetary policy.
10. Joshi and Little (1996), in this context, noted, "By 1991, the country had erected an unprofitable, inefficient, and financially unsound banking sector" (p.111).
11. The Reserve Bank began to liberalise the Indian banking industry in fact in the 1980s, following the recommendations of the Chakravarty Committee (RBI, 1985); e.g., the Credit Authorisation Scheme was withdrawn in 1988.

financial system was central to the wide-ranging structural reforms. In order to ensure that the financial system operates on the basis of operational flexibility and functional autonomy with a view to enhancing efficiency, productivity and profitability, the Committee recommended a series of measures aimed at changes according greater flexibility to bank operations, especially by phasing out statutory per-emptions and directed credit programmes, improving asset quality, institution of prudential norms, greater disclosures and better house-keeping, in terms of accounting practices. In this backdrop the next section turns to the broad contours of the central bank's policy actions.

3.3.1 Direct Measures for Controlling Banks' Balance Sheets

The 1990s saw a significant change in terms of the macro-economic role of financial systems—from channelising financial resources from the saver to the investor in line with social commitments of the planning process to a gradual transformation of allocating resources in response to market signals. While these are not 'either-or' processes, there was a distinct shift towards market orientation as far as monetary policy and banking operations were concerned. The issue of greater autonomy of bank operations was, however, linked to the management of Government finances. At the heart of the banking reforms, at the macro-level, thus, was the need to contain the ability of the fisc to obtain resources from the banking system by an administrative 'fiat.' What were the major instruments with the central bank? What follows is a quick rundown of the major instruments of monetary policy during this period.

Statutory Liquidity Ratio (SLR)

The SLR, originally a stipulation for ensuring bank solvency, was progressively hiked to 38.5 per cent of net demand and time liabilities in September 1990 to provide a captive market for government paper. While there could be doubt as to whether one can consider SLR to be a monetary policy instrument in the Indian context, this was one of the instruments which inhibited the normal activities of loan disbursement of commercial banks all through the 1980s. After almost reaching the statutory maximum, the monetary authorities started reducing the SLR since January 1993 and it came back to its statutory minimum of 25.0 per cent of net demand and time liabilities (NDTL) by October 1997 (Figure 3.2). This clearly increased the lendable resources of the banking sector, and accordingly had implications for the composition of portfolio of the commercial banks.

Figure 3.2

Movement of CRR and SLR (As per cent of Net Demand and Time Liabilities)

A. Changes in Cash Reserve Ratio (CRR): 1991-2004

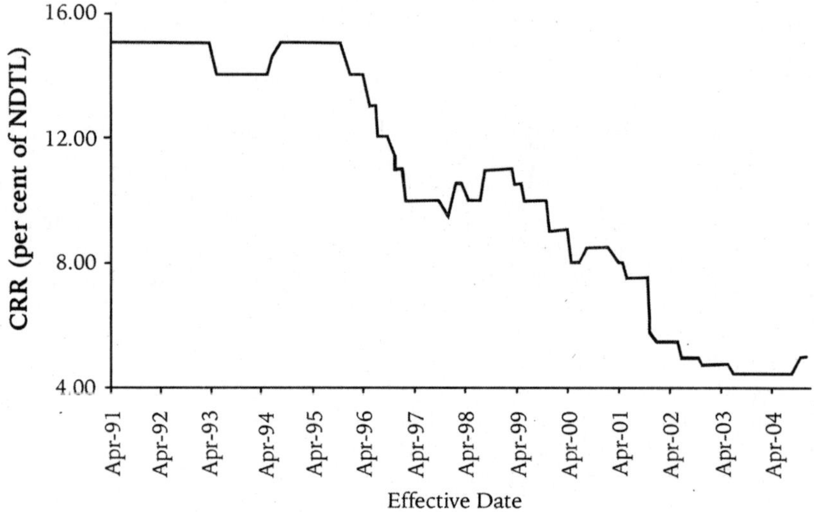

B. Changes in Statutory Liquidity Ratio (SLR): 1991-2004

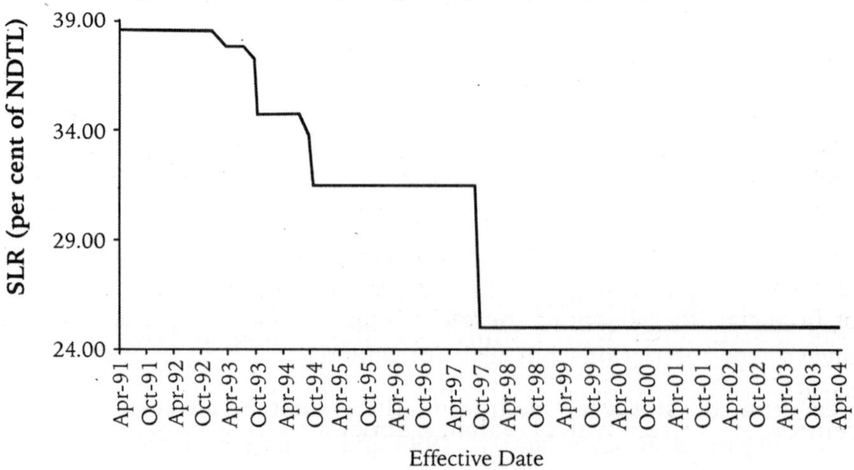

Cash Reserve Ratio (CRR)

The Reserve Bank had progressively raised the CRR throughout the 1970s and 1980s in order to neutralise the monetary impact of the monetisation of the fiscal deficit. The CRR, thus, stood at 15 per cent during July 1989 to October 1992. The CRR was reduced to 4.5 per cent of net demand and time liabilities (NDTL) by June 2003, in pursuance of the medium-term goal of finally bringing it down to the statutory minimum of 3.0 per cent. The reduction in CRR was, in particular, facilitated by phasing out of the automatic monetisation of the Government deficit with the abolition of the earlier practise of issuance of *ad hoc* Treasury bills, which allowed the Reserve Bank to regain control over its balance sheet.

The reduction in statutory pre-emptions from over 60 per cent of deposit mobilisation to less than 30 per cent of deposit mobilisation, thus, accorded the banks the freedom to determine their own portfolio. To be sure, banks' investments in government securities continued to remain well above the statutory minimum but this was market driven rather than by administrative 'fiat.' Besides the reductions in pre-emption of resources of commercial banks, there were two other developments relating to policy. First, in terms of price, the RBI asked the banks to mark government paper to the market, and second, the practice of placing the Government borrowing programme to the market began since 1992-93. This process of according greater autonomy to bank portfolios was reinforced by phasing out of directed credit programmes, on the one hand, and deregulation of the regime of administered interest rates, on the other.

3.3.2 Development of Market-related Instruments

The process of banking reforms was backed by the evolution of financial markets which were capable of re-igniting the process of price discovery. There were critical problems. Indian financial markets were segmented. Institutions were restricted to certain segments of operations and there were no markets of various tenors. The process of financial liberalisation, therefore, entailed not only relaxations in investment restrictions but also introduction of new instruments of varying risks and tenors. The process of developing markets was reinforced by removal of balance sheet restrictions which earlier confined financial intermediaries to their primary segments of the financial markets. Banks were gradually allowed to operate in equity markets and foreign exchange markets as investors, although there remained prudential caps on the position they could take.

The process of price discovery, especially at the shorter end, was limited by missing markets. The old Scottish practice of offering lines of cash credit had placed the onus of cash management to the lender. The Reserve Bank, used to offer 91-day 4.6 per cent Treasury bills on tap, with a discounting facility, and thereby effectively took the entire fluctuation in liquidity onto its own balance sheet. The need to develop short-term money markets was emphasised by the Chakravarty Committee as early as in the mid-1980s. Following the recommendations of the Working Group on the Money Market (Chairman: N. Vaghul) in 1987, the Reserve Bank introduced a number of money market instruments in the late 1980s together with deregulation of interest rates on existing money market instruments (RBI, 1987). At the same time, banks were instructed to convert a large part of their loan portfolio into term loans, so that day-to-day cash management reverted to the borrower. More significantly, the Reserve Bank phased out the 91-day tap Treasury bills. This paved the way for a vibrant money market in the Indian economy. Further, the Reserve Bank put in place a Liquidity Adjustment Facility (LAF) since July 2000. Through repo (selling securities) and reverse repo (buying securities) auctions of daily and longer-term tenor RBI started to manage market liquidity. This instrument at the same time provides the RBI with an operating tool to transmit interest rate signals through changes in the repo/reverse repo rates. The three-pronged strategy of: i) phasing out of non-banks from the call money market, ii) placing restrictions on banks' call money transactions and iii) development of a non-bank repo market, now insulates the central bank balance sheet from day-to-day cash management of the economy.

Another major development was the nurturing of a market for government paper which allowed banks to increasingly determine their gilt-edged investments according to commercial judgment. The Reserve Bank has introduced, as the manager of public debt, a number of new instruments, such as, 364-day treasury bills, zero coupon bonds, floating rate bonds, partly paid stock. These options met different objectives of—managing the maturity profile of the gilts, meeting the requirements of different investor groups (*e.g.*, insurance companies with a demand for long-term paper whereas mutual funds looked for shorter maturity paper) and creating liquidity in scrips through reissuance while at the same time avoiding bunching of repayments for the issuer. A system of Delivery *versus* Payment was introduced to facilitate synchronised transfer of securities synchronises and the cash payment. This improved payment and settlement system in Government securities transactions, reducing the settlement risk. This was further reinforced by the institution of a Negotiated Dealing System (NDS), providing on-line dealing and reporting of transactions in money market instruments and government paper and setting up of the Clearing Corporation of India Ltd (CCIL), an industry service organisation for clearing and settlement of trades in foreign exchange, government securities and other debt instruments.

3.3.3 Deregulation of Interest Rates

The Reserve Bank began to deregulate the deposit and lending rates in the early 1990s. At present, commercial banks have full freedom to set domestic term deposit rates of seven days and above on a uniform basis for all clients. The RBI, however, continued to fix interest rates on savings accounts (at 3.0 per cent per annum at present) and issued guidelines on non-resident deposits from time to time depending on the evolving macro-economic situation. Banks were also free to fix their lending rates for all classes of loans, with only small loans below Rs. 2 lakh and export credit for which the ceiling rates are prescribed to be linked to the prime lending rate (PLR) being exceptions. In order to instil transparency, banks were required to announce their benchmark prime lending rates (BPLR), reflecting some kind of actual average costs and also their range of effective lending rates.

In tandem with easy liquidity conditions and reflective of the Reserve Bank's policy preference for a softer interest rate regime, there was a gradual softening of interest rates across the board in the 1990s (Table 3.3). Concomitantly there were reductions in the redemption yields on the GoI securities as well (Table 3.4). Bank lending rates have, however, been relatively rigid in recent years. The rigidities in lending rates reflected the impact of a number of factors, such as, high reserve requirements, stickiness in small saving interest rates, large government borrowing, overhang of non-performing assets (NPAs) and finally, high operating expenses of banks.

Table 3.3

Interest Rates

(Per cent)

Year	*Call Rate*	*Deposit Rates*			*SBI Advance Rate*
		1 to 3 yrs.	*Over 3 yrs. and up to 5 yrs.*	*1 to 3 yrs.*	
(1)	*(2)*	*(3)*	*(4)*	*(5)*	*(6)*
1991-92	19.57	12.00	13.00	13.00	16.50
1992-93	14.42	11.00	11.00	11.00	19.00
1993-94	6.99	10.00	10.00	10.00	19.00
1994-95	9.40	11.00	11.00	11.00	15.00
1995-96	17.73	12.00	13.00	13.00	16.50
1996-97	7.84	11.00-12.00	12.00-13.00	12.50-13.00	14.50
1997-98	8.69	10.50-11.00	11.50-12.00	11.50-12.00	14.00
1998-99	7.83	9.00-11.00	10.50-11.50	10.50-11.50	12.00-14.00
1999-00	8.87	8.50-9.50	10.00-10.50	10.00-10.50	12.00
2000-01	9.15	8.50-9.00	9.50–10.00	9.50-10.00	11.50
2001-02	7.16	7.50-8.50	8.00–8.50	8.00-8.50	11.50
2002-03	5.89	4.25-6.00	5.50–6.25	5.50-6.25	10.75
2003-04	4.62	4.00-5.25	5.25-5.50	5.25-5.50	10.25

Note: Deposits Rates refer to that of 5 major public sector banks as at end-March.
Source: RBI. *Handbook of Statistics on the Indian Economy*, various issues.

The greater policy concern is that the real interest rates for borrowers have actually been increasing. In fact, they have risen much more than the increase in interest rates for depositors. Mohan (2002) has shown that if real interest rates are calculated as the weighted average lending rate of scheduled commercial banks 'less' manufacturing inflation for borrowers and average cost of time

Table 3.4

Annual (Gross) Redemption Yield of Government of India Securities

(Per cent)

Year	Short-term (1-5 yrs.)	Medium-term (5-15 yrs.)	Long-term (15 yrs. and above)
(1)	(2)	(3)	(4)
1991-92	8.37-26.26	9.50-13.42	9.91-12.38
1992-93	9.08-23.77	9.50-14.78	8.82-12.47
1993-94	11.86-12.86	12.70-13.30	12.85-13.43
1994-95	9.75-11.76	11.30-13.86	11.77-13.47
1995-96	6.00-14.28	5.75-14.07	11.84-13.02
1996-97	5.21-16.21	5.75-14.44	9.00-14.20
1997-98	5.50-17.69	5.20-14.00	9.00-13.17
1998-99	4.45-17.73	5.75-13.74	10.00-13.46
1999-00	3.18-14.30	6.50-13.84	9.79-13.11
2000-01	4.94-16.66	9.37-12.50	10.58-11.89
2001-02	5.32-10.96	5.14-13.85	7.41-10.86
2002-03	5.12-10.98	5.60-9.27	6.10-8.76
2003-04	3.93-7.16	4.41-6.78	5.44-7.72

Note: These are based on redemption yield which is computed from 2000-01 as the mean of the daily weighted average yield of the transactions in each traded security. The weight is calculated as the share of the transaction in a given security in the aggregated value of transactions in the said security. Prior to 2000-2001, the redemption yield was not weighted and was computed as an average of daily prices of each security.

Source: RBI. *Handbook of Statistics on the Indian Economy*, various issues.

deposits 'less' inflation for depositors (based on the consumer price index for industrial workers), then there has been a marked rise in the real lending rates (Table 3.5).[12] This has effectively meant that banks have not fully passed on the benefits of the reduction in deposit rates to borrowers.

12. Mohan (2002) calculated the real interest rate for borrowers and lenders separately for two separate periods, *viz.*, period I: 1990-91 through 1995-96, and period II: 1996-1997 to 2001-02. He found that while the real interest rate has increased for depositors from (-) 0.3 per cent in period I to 1.9 per cent in period II, the same has gone up much sharply for borrowers from 6.5 per cent in period I to 12.5 per cent in period II.

Table 3.5

Nominal and Real Interest Rates

(Per cent)

Year	Nominal Interest Rate			Real Interest Rate		
	Deposit Rate (PSBs) (1 year and above)	Average/ Median Lending Rate of SCBs	Weighted average interest rate of Central Govt. Securities	Deposits	Borrower	Govt.
(1)	(2)	(3)	(4)	(5)	(6)	(7)
1995-96	12.00-13.00	17.10	13.75	3.90-4.90	9.00	5.65
1996-97	11.00-13.00	16.94	13.69	6.40-8.40	12.34	9.09
1997-98	10.50-12.00	16.32	12.01	6.10-7.60	11.92	7.61
1998-99	9.00-11.50	15.51	11.86	3.06-5.56	9.57	5.92
1999-00	8.50-10.50	14.95	11.77	5.21-7.21	11.66	8.48
2000-01	8.00-10.50	14.29	10.95	0.85-3.35	7.14	3.80
2001-02	7.25-8.75	13.92	9.44	3.61-5.11	10.28	5.80
2002-03	5.25-7.00	13.50	7.34	1.84-3.59	10.09	3.93
2003-04	5.00-6.00	11.00-14.00	5.71	0.36-1.36	6.36-9.36	1.07

Source: RBI. Calculated from the data from *Handbook of Statistics on the Indian Economy*, various issues.

3.3.4 Deregulation of Bank Operations

The Reserve Bank began to rationalise the sector-specific directed lending programme in the early 1990s. This has taken three inter-related forms. First, most credit controls have been gradually phased out in the early 1990s. Second, the list of borrowers eligible for loans under the priority sector has been expanded. In case banks were not able to meet priority sector lending targets, they could place the money under the Rural Infrastructure Development Fund (RIDF) or the Small Industrial Development Bank of India (SIDBI), depending on whether the shortfall in priority sector is in agriculture or in small-scale industry target, respectively. Finally, interest rates on priority sector lending had been rationalised and were linked to prime lending rates.

The Reserve Bank also attempted to introduce competitive forces in the Indian banking system. For well over two decades after the two-stage nationalisation of banks in 1969 and 1980, no banks had been allowed to be set up in the private sector. After a long gap, in 1993 the Reserve Bank allowed new banks in the private sector. So far 11 private sector banks became operational. Considering that the objective of providing adequate banking infrastructure throughout the country, particularly in rural areas, had been broadly achieved, the Reserve Bank further liberalised the branch licensing policy. Banks are now permitted to rationalise their existing branches, spin-off of business at other centres, open specialised branches, and even convert the existing non-viable rural branches into satellite offices. Banks have also been permitted to close down their branches subject to certain conditions other than in rural areas.

3.3.5 Prudential Regulation

The increasing market orientation of the banking system is perhaps a double-edged sword. While it is true that ensuring a process of price discovery facilitates a better allocation of lendable resources, the process of financial deregulation also implies that financial markets are more susceptible to fluctuation. More importantly, these fluctuations transmit across the segments of the markets much more swiftly. This, in turn, implies that bank balance sheets get linked to the fluctuations in financial markets. The challenge before the regulator, therefore, is to harness the benefits of competition, while at the same time, limit the threat to financial stability. Most economies presently follow a standard package of prudential norms and disclosure standards in order to strengthen financial stability—and India is no exception.

The cornerstone of the strategy of strengthening financial stability was the institution of prudential norms relating to income recognition, asset classification and provisioning requirements and incentive-based regulation through the prescription of capital to risk-weighted assets ratio. This had been supplemented by the institution of asset-liability management and risk management systems. Over the period, the guidelines had only been tightened to bring them in line with the best international practices.

Capital Adequacy

At the core of prudential norms is the issue of adequacy of capital in relation to the risks of banking. The RBI had prescribed banks capital to risk-weighted assets ratio (CRAR) in 1992-93 (Table 3.6). The CRAR stipulations had been gradually increased, especially in the case of domestic banks, from 4 per cent during 1992-93 to 9 per cent in 1999-2000. The notion of risk-weighted assets had been gradually expanded from credit risk also to encompass market and operational risks. In order to ensure a smooth transition, the Government has recapitalised a number of nationalised banks and allowed foreign banks to bring capital from their parent bank abroad.

Table 3.6

Changes in Prescribed CRAR and Mark-to-Market on Investment Portfolio

Year	*CRAR (Per cent to Risk Weighted Assets)*			*Mark-to-Market on Investment Portfolio (%)*
	Domestic Banks (with international Business)	*Other Domestic Banks*	*Foreign Banks*	
(1)	*(2)*	*(3)*	*(4)*	*(5)*
1992-93	4	4	8	30
1993-94	8	4	8	30
1994-95	8	4	8	30
1995-96	8	8	8	40
1996-97	8	8	8	50
1997-98	8	8	8	60
1998-99	8	8	8	70
1999-00	9	9	9	75
2000-01	9	9	9	*
2001-02	9	9	9	*
2002-03	9	9	9	*
2003-04	9	9	9	*

Note: *: According to the revised classification norms for investment portfolio (including: SLR and non-SLR securities) effective half-year ended September 30, 2000, banks should classify the same into three categories, *viz.*, Held to Maturity (HTM), Available for Sale (AFS) and Held for Trading (HFT) categories. The investments under HTM should not exceed 25 per cent of banks' total investments.

Source: RBI. *Report on Trend and Progress of Banking in India*, various issues.

Non-Performing Assets (NPA)

An equally important issue of the Indian banking sector is the asset quality. Banks were earlier instructed to rate their loan portfolio on a health code matrix introduced in 1985. Following the recommendations of the Narasimham Committee I, the RBI required banks to classify their loan portfolio into 'standard assets' (if the accounts are satisfactory) and into 'non-performing assets', if principal/instalment of interest are due after a stipulated time period (Table 3.7). Depending on the time period for which such payments are not received by the bank, 'non-performing assets' are further divided into 'sub-standard assets', 'doubtful assets' and 'loss assets'. While incomes are typically recognised on an accrual basis, no income should be recognised in case of these non-performing assets.

Table 3.7

Changes in NPA and Provisioning Requirements

Year	*NPA@ (Periods in Quarters)*			*Provisioning Requirements (Per cent to Corresponding Assets)*		
	Sub-standard Assets	*Doubtful Assets (exceeding the period)*	*Standard Assets**	*Sub-standard Assets***	*Doubtful Assets: Secured Assets #*	*Doubtful Assets: Unsecured Assets*
1	*2*	*3*	*4*	*5*	*6*	*7*
1992-93	4-8	8	–	10	20-50	100
1993-94	3-8	8	–	10	20-50	100
1994-95	2-8	8	–	10	20-50	100
1995-96	2-8	8	–	10	20-50	100
1996-97	2-8	8	–	10	20-50	100
1997-98	2-8	8	–	10	20-50	100
1998-99	2-8	8	–	10	20-50	100
1999-00	2-8	8	0.25	10	20-50	100
2000-01	2-6	6	0.25	10	20-50	100
2001-02	2-6	6	0.25	10	20-50	100
2002-03	2-6	6	0.25	10-20	20-50	100
2003-04	1-6	6	0.25	10-20	20-50	100

Note: – : Not prescribed.

@ : Banks are required to classify non-performing assets in to three categories: sub-standard assets, doubtful assets and loss assets. A loss asset is one where loss has been identified by the bank or internal or external auditors or the RBI inspection but the amount has not been written off wholly. If loss assets are permitted to remain in the books for any reason, 100 percent of the outstanding should be provided for.

* : General provisioning of standard assets on global portfolio basis started from March 31, 2000.

** : Effective March 31, 2003, banks were advised to make additional provision of 10 per cent for the unsecured portion of sub-standard assets in addition to the existing 10 per cent.

: 20 per cent if an asset is doubtful for 1 year; 30 per cent for 1-3 years; 50 per cent for more than 3 years.

Source: RBI. *Report on Trend and Progress of Banking in India,* various Issues.

The international experience suggests that the identification of the non-performing assets could be objective—with the supervisor setting the criteria, as in the Indian case—or subjective—with bank managements using their discretion. While the objective methodology has the merit of uniformity, the subjective case often has the benefit of man-on-the-spot judgment. In case of a large and diversified system, such as India's, objective prescriptions enjoy the benefit of rules over discretion. The Reserve Bank later advised banks to monitor "special mention accounts", *i.e.*, accounts which the banks perceive could potentially turn into non-performing assets.

The overhang of non-performing loans posed a challenge to the banking system. This implied two clear constraints for monetary policy. First, a large stock of NPAs placed a floor to interest rate spreads and, thus, constrained the effectiveness of the interest rate channel of monetary transmission. Second, large NPAs posed a threat to financial stability especially as banks now operate across all markets. From a policy perspective, it became imperative that a reduction in NPAs would require both a 'stock' (a one-time cleansing of balance sheet) and a 'flow' (preventing substantial accretion) solution. Several measures have been taken to address the 'flow' problem (*viz.*, *Lok Adalats* and settlement advisory committees), whereas the Securitisation and Reconstruction of Financial Assets and Enforcement of Security Interest Act, 2002 was set to address the problem of the stock, by empowering secured creditors to enforce any security interest credited in their favour without any intervention of court or tribunal. As part of the process, two asset management companies, with statutory mandate for their business of asset reconstruction, have been put into operation. A Corporate Debt Recovery (CDR) mechanism has also been instituted to explore the bad assets of large borrowers (corporates) and suggest remedial measures.

Provisioning Norms

Strict provisioning norms had been specified in case of the various categories of NPAs, *viz.*, sub-standard assets (10 per cent), doubtful assets (100 per cent of unsecured portion and 20-50 per cent of the balance depending on the time profile) and loss assets (100 per cent).

In addition, a nominal 0.25 per cent had to be provided for standard assets (since increased to 0.40 per cent in the October 2005 Monetary Policy). Further, a conservative policy was put in place in respect of loans which have been either rescheduled or renegotiated.

Valuation Norms

While market determined prices are necessary for economic efficiency, they also tended to expose bank balance sheets to volatility in the financial markets. This, in turn, implied that bank balance sheets have to be assessed at their true values as market prices keep changing over time. The Reserve Bank has also repeatedly stressed the need for marking assets to the market in order to capture true current values. Banks were initially required to mark to market 30 per cent of their investment portfolio in 1992-93—the proportion was gradually raised to 75 per cent in 1999-2000. Subsequently, the investment portfolio is required to be classified into 'held to maturity' (HTM), 'available for sale' (AFS) (at least annual revaluation) and 'held for trading' (HFT) (at least monthly revaluation) in accordance with Generally Accepted Accounting Principles (GAAP). While the 'held to maturity' component could be held at historical cost, subject to a cap of 25 per cent of the investment portfolio, the balance has to be 'marked to market' at prescribed frequencies.

Since 2002-03, there has been a sustained decline in interest rates driven by a combination of strong capital flows on the supply side and weak credit-offtake on the demand side. The combination of falling interest rates and a widening government securities market provided banks an avenue for treasury operations. The importance of valuation norms and necessary provisions escalated because the rise in bank profitability emerging from easy liquidity conditions has led to an interest in bank stocks. This, in its wake, forged a new link between the debt and equity markets. While treasury income emerged as a key driver of bank profitability, it was necessary to guard against the possibility of a reversal in interest rates. Banks were advised, in March 2002, to build up, by March 2007, an investment fluctuation reserve (of up to 5.0 per cent of the investments held in HFT and AFS categories in five years) as a cushion against diminution in investment portfolios owing to interest rate changes. Subsequently in 2003-04, in recognition of the interest rate risks in a rising interest rate scenario the target date of building the IFR was advanced to March 2006 and banks were advised to build up the minimum levels of the Investment Fluctuation Reserve (IFR) (5 per cent of investments in 'Held for Trading' (HFT) and 'Available for Sale' (AFS) categories) by March 2006 instead of the target date of March 2007 set earlier.

Disclosure Norms

It needs to be recognised that the asymmetry of information between banks and their clientele often distorts credit markets. A major step in this regard was the implementation of the transparency and disclosure standards recommended in the International Accounting Standards in a phased manner for the Indian banking system. Illustratively, the formats of commercial banks' balance sheet and profit and loss Account Statements were revised in 1992 in order to bring about greater transparency. Disclosure requirements were gradually broad-based and banks were advised to disclose the key business ratios in the 'Notes to Accounts' from the year ended March 31, 1996. These disclosures have gradually been expanded.

Risk Management

It is necessary to note that the range of risks had widened from the risks associated with the quality of loans to interest rate risks embedded in the investment portfolio as well as the exchange rate risk involved in the management of foreign assets and liabilities. Banks were required to follow prudential norms of not booking unrealised gains but booking unrealised losses. The Reserve Bank had been taking several initiatives to move towards better risk management. Pursuant to the RBI guidelines of February 1999 (and December 1999 for FIs), banks and FIs had already put in place asset-liability management systems, typically supervised by an Asset Liability Committee. The RBI had also issued guidelines on risk management systems in October 1999, supplemented by guidance notes on credit risk and market risk management in October 2002, intended to serve as a benchmark to the banks, which were yet to establish integrated risk management systems. Besides, the Reserve Bank had also directed banks to constitute committees looking after audit and risk management. Furthermore, a credit information bureau called the Credit Information Bureau (India) Limited (CIBIL) had been set up in August 2001 with a view to improving dissemination of data relating to defaulters-borrowers.

3.3.6 Changing Fiscal Scenario

Another important element of the Indian macro scenario had been the easing fiscal situation. In fact, it was largely perceived that one of the major reasons of the 1991 crisis was fiscal profligacy. The reforms programme initiated in 1991, thus, had a significant fiscal content. Elimination of the system of automatic monetisation of budget deficit, clearer delineation of roles of the RBI and the Government in financing of development and reduction in fiscal dominance are some of the major highlights of the reforms programme (Reddy, 2003). These measurers yielded some positive results. The financing of the fiscal deficit is almost entirely domestic and the measures have been

Table 3.8

Select Fiscal Indicators of the Central Government

(As percentage to GDP)

Year	*Gross Fiscal Deficit*	*Revenue Deficit*	*Direct Taxes*	*Indirect Taxes*	*Gross Tax*	*Interest payments*	*Subsidies*
(1)	(2)	(3)	(4)	(5)	(6)	(7)	(8)
1991-92	5.6	2.5	2.3	8.0	10.3	4.1	1.9
1992-93	5.4	2.5	2.4	7.5	10.0	4.2	1.4
1993-94	7.0	3.8	2.4	6.5	8.8	4.3	1.4
1994-95	5.7	3.1	2.7	6.5	9.1	4.4	1.2
1995-96	5.1	2.5	2.8	6.5	9.4	4.2	1.1
1996-97	4.9	2.4	2.8	6.6	9.4	4.3	1.1
1997-98	5.8	3.1	3.2	6.0	9.1	4.3	1.2
1998-99	6.5	3.8	2.7	5.6	8.3	4.5	1.4
1999-00	5.3	3.5	3.0	5.8	8.8	4.6	1.3
2000-01	5.6	4.0	3.2	5.7	8.9	4.7	1.3
2001-02	6.2	4.4	3.0	5.2	8.2	4.7	1.4
2002-03	5.9	4.4	3.4	5.4	8.8	4.8	1.8
2003-04	4.5	3.6	3.8	5.4	9.2	4.5	1.6

Source: Mohan (2006c).

quite successful in meeting these objectives. Illustratively, the gross fiscal deficit has come down from 7 per cent in 1993-94 to 4.5 per cent in 2004-05. Tax Revenue has recovered to 10 per cent of GDP (Table 3.8). On the expenditure management side, however, the fiscal policy initiatives have been relatively less successful. The reduction of fiscal dominance has added to the operational autonomy of commercial banks during the 1990s.

3.4 Commercial Bank Behaviour

3.4.1 Aggregative Parameters

The Indian economy continued to remain a bank-based system with banks accounting for the bulk of the financial activity. The size of the banking sector in the economy tended to increase in the initial phase of development, with the increase in monetisation of the economy and thereafter declined once financial deepening sparked off a process of financial disintermediation. In the Indian case, the banking system expanded rapidly in the 1970s and 1980s after the spread of the banking network in rural areas following the bank nationalisation of 1969. During the 1990s, the proportion of deposit growth in GDP began to plateau out as the push effect of wider banking began to be countered by the pull effect of financial innovations such as anytime banking, which allowed a greater churning of the same stock of deposit money to fund a larger number of transactions (Sarkar, 2004; Bhaumik and Mukherjee, 2003). The ratio of credit to output, an indicator of financial development, continued to climb suggesting that banks remained 'special' as sources of finance in the Indian economy. Since the early 1990s, the Indian commercial banking sector experienced healthy growth in deposits; the growth experience of bank advances was, however, not too spectacular, with at least three years, *viz.*, 1991-92, 1993-94 and 1996-97 experiencing single digit credit growth (Table 3.9).

3.4.2 Portfolio Composition of Commercial Banks

Apart from the bank-specific factors, the changes in the composition of the bank balance sheet in a sense are outcomes of the changes in the macroeconomic environment brought forward by

Table 3.9

Growth in Select Aggregates of Scheduled Commercial Banks

(*Per cent*)

Year	*Demand Deposits*	*Time Deposits*	*Aggregate Deposits*	*Bank Credit*	*Non-food Credit*	*Balances with RBI*	*Investment in Government Securities*	*Total Invest-ment*
(1)	(2)	(3)	(4)	(5)	(6)	(7)	(8)	(9)
1991-92	35.8	16.5	19.8	8.0	8.2	43.2	25.5	20.2
1992-93	3.0	19.6	16.4	21.0	20.1	-16.5	21.1	17.1
1993-94	21.8	16.4	17.3	8.2	5.7	67.4	33.3	25.4
1994-95	35.9	19.9	22.8	28.7	29.8	25.7	16.3	12.6
1995-96	4.8	14.0	12.1	20.1	22.5	-15.6	12.4	10.4
1996-97	12.4	17.5	16.5	9.6	10.9	-1.6	20.2	15.6
1997-98	13.1	21.2	19.8	16.4	15.1	15.7	17.7	14.8
1998-99	14.5	20.3	19.3	13.8	13.0	10.1	19.4	16.4
1999-00	8.5	15.0	13.9	18.2	16.6	-9.6	24.7	21.3
2000-01	11.9	19.5	18.4	17.3	14.9	3.7	22.1	19.8
2001-02	7.4	15.9	14.6	15.3	13.6	4.8	20.9	18.4
2002-03	11.3	16.9 (13.7)	16.1 (13.4)	23.7	26.9	-6.5	27.3	24.9
2003-04	32.1	15.2	17.5	15.3	18.4	18.3	25.1	23.8

Note: Figures in parentheses exclude the impact of mergers on May 3, 2002 and the impact of conversion of a non-banking entity into a banking entity on October 11, 2004.

Source: RBI. *Handbook of Statistics on the Indian Economy*, various issues.

financial sector reforms. What have been the main distinguishing features of the changes in the composition of bank balance sheets?

First, there was a gradual decline in the share of balances held with the Reserve Bank from 10.2 per cent of aggregate assets as at end-March 1993 to 5.7 per cent as at end-March 2004, reflecting a sharp reduction in reserve requirements (Table 3.10). Banks had to earlier set aside as much as 15 per cent of their deposit mobilisation for CRR and could earn an effective return of 3-4 per cent on these balances by way of interest on CRR. The reduction in CRR not only enabled them to deploy assets more efficiently but also pare interest charged on non-priority loans.

Second, banks were allowed to increasingly take exposures in foreign currencies as part of the liberalisation of the external account in the 1990s. As a result, there was a doubling of banks' foreign assets during the period under consideration. This reflected the impact of the large capital inflows following the opening up of the economy coupled with relaxations in the norms governing investments in foreign assets. Besides, banks were now allowed to advance foreign currency loans to residents out of their dollar liabilities. This required banks to manage their foreign currency risk better, especially as the central bank stopped providing exchange rate guarantees to non-resident deposits by the mid-1990s.

Third, while it is true that the share of bank credit had not appreciably increased despite the reduction in statutory pre-emptions, this was in the backdrop of the weakening of credit demand in the latter half of the 1990s. The situation changed in the 1990s when banks were accorded the freedom to align their credit allocation in consonance with their portfolio decisions. Besides, there was a growing indirect securitisation of bank credit, as banks were now permitted to invest in money and equity markets. Besides conventional credit in the form of loans and advances and bills purchased and discounted, banks invested heavily in non-SLR investments with the relaxation of investment norms and their share in deposits climbing to more than 7 per cent by end-March 2004.

Finally, the share of government paper in the bank portfolio, climbed to 41 per cent of assets as at end-March 2004 from 26 per cent as at end-March 1993. There was, however, a major shift in the rationale of such investment. Unlike till the mid-1990s, when gilt investment was largely on account of high SLR requirements prescribed by the central bank, during the latter half of the 1990s, the persistent preference for government paper reflected lack of alternative avenues of investments with the weakening of domestic credit demand (Sarkar, 1999; 2004). The decision of the banking system to park funds in government paper allowed them to earn attractive returns in a scenario of falling interest rates during the downturn in economic activity in the latter half of the 1990s. Besides, investments in government paper allowed banks to avoid the problems of adverse selection, which are usual, in economic slowdowns. This was reflected

Table 3.10

Composition of Portfolio of Scheduled Commercial Banks

(As per cent of total assets/liabilities)

Year	Capital	Reserves and Surplus	Deposits	Borrowings	Other Liabilities	Cash and Balance with RBI	Balances with Banks and Call Money	Investments	Advances	Other Assets*
(1)	(2)	(3)	(4)	(5)	(6)	(7)	(8)	(9)	(10)	(11)
1992-93	1.3	1.7	78.4	7.7	11	10.2	3.8	30.5	45.0	10.5
1993-94	2.4	2.6	80.3	3.4	11.2	11.9	2.9	35.4	38.7	11.1
1994-95	3.1	3.0	78.9	4.9	10.0	12.2	3.4	33.6	40.5	10.3
1995-96	2.7	3.4	76.4	7.1	10.4	11.7	5.1	31.0	42.1	10.1
1996-97	2.5	4.0	79.9	3.5	10.1	9.1	7.0	33.3	41.0	9.7
1997-98	2.4	4.3	81.0	3.2	9.1	9.0	7.6	34.2	40.8	8.5
1998-99	1.9	3.9	81.1	4.2	8.9	8.6	9.3	35.7	38.8	7.5
1999-00	1.7	3.9	81.1	4.1	9.2	7.7	7.3	37.3	40.2	7.5
2000-01	1.5	3.8	81.5	4.3	9.0	6.5	8.2	38.0	40.6	6.8
2001-02	1.4	4.1	78.5	6.7	9.4	5.6	7.7	38.2	42.0	6.4
2002-03	1.3	4.5	79.8	5.1	9.3	5.1	4.4	40.8	43.6	6.1
2003-04	1.1	4.8	79.8	4.9	9.5	5.7	4.2	40.6	43.8	5.7

Note: * Including Fixed Assets

Source: RBI. *Handbook of Statistics on the Indian Economy*, various years, and *Report on Trend and Progress of Banking in India, 2003-04*.

in the fact that the fresh accretion to NPAs has been marginal in recent years notwithstanding the economic slowdown.

The deregulation of bank portfolios during the 1990s created a set of large and strong balance sheets which were able to invest across a number of markets deepening interlinkages between them. As a result, banks now respond to market signals in allocating their funds across their CRR balances with the RBI, the inter-bank market and government paper depending on relative returns. There was a switch towards gilts during the late 1990s away from credit with an industrial slowdown. Similarly, there was evidence that banks have switched resources between foreign investments and foreign currency loans to residents on the one hand and foreign currency and Rupee assets on the other in recent years.

Certificates of Deposit (CDs)

As already pointed out in Chapter 2, Certificates of Deposits (CDs) are debt instruments issued by banks to investors. Following the recommendations of the 1987 Working Group on the Money Market (Chairman: N. Vaghul), certificates of deposit (CDs) were introduced in India in June 1989. Transaction cost of CDs was often lower as compared to that of retail deposits. It may be noted that when there is a pick-up in credit, banks try to meet their liquidity gap by issuing CDs, often at a premium. As banks offered higher interest rates on CDs, subscribers found it profitable to hold CDs till maturity. As a result, the secondary market for CDs was slow to develop (RBI, 2001). The Reserve Bank initially limited the issuance of CDs at a certain percentage of the fortnightly average of the outstanding aggregate deposits of 1989-1990. Over-time, bank-wise limits were raised and finally abolished from October 16, 1993. This enabled CDs to emerge as a market related instrument. Interestingly, the outstanding CDs as a proportion of aggregate deposits was rather small in the Indian context (Table 3.11), indicating that CDs failed to merge as a major source of non-deposit resources for Indian banks.

3.4.3 Profitability Indicators

What has been the impact of all these to banks' bottomlines? There is very little doubt that the profitability of the banking system

Table 3.11

Issue of CDs by Scheduled Commercial Banks

(Rupees crore)

Year	*Outstanding CDs (Rs. Crore)*	*Outstanding CDs as per cent of Aggregate Deposits*	*Rate of Interest(per cent)@*		
			Low		*High*
(1)	(2)	(3)	(4)		
1992-93	9803	3.7	12.50	-	16.50
1993-94	5571	1.8	7.00	-	12.20
1994-95	8017	2.1	10.00	-	15.00
1995-96	16316	3.8	12.00	-	22.25
1996-97	12134	2.4	7.00	-	14.25
1997-98	14296	2.4	7.20	-	26.00
1998-99	3717	0.5	8.00	-	12.50
1999-00	1227	0.2	7.50	-	12.00
2000-01	771	0.1	5.50	-	11.00
2001-02	1576	0.1	5.00	-	10.03
2002-03	908	0.1	5.00	-	7.10
2003-04	4461	0.3	3.87	-	5.16

Note: @ Effective Discount Rate per annum

Source: RBI. *Handbook of Statistics on the Indian Economy*, 2003-04.

improved during the 1990s (Table 3.12). Net profits of the scheduled commercial banks climbed steadily from 0.2 per cent of total assets as at end-March 1996 to 1.1 per cent as at end-March 2004, notwithstanding a narrowing of spreads and higher provisions for non-performing loans (Koeva, 2003). Besides, there had been distinctive productivity improvements in Indian banking (Mohan, 2006a). Illustratively, at 1993-94 prices, profits per employee improved to 0.15 million in 2004 from Rs. 0.02 million in 1992 (Table 3.13).

How was this increase in profitability possible? While *a priori* competitive forces during a period of financial sector reforms could drive the profits down, they could also result in making a bank more cost-conscious. In fact, in the Indian case, the improvement in profitability was primarily due to a combined effect of larger trading incomes and a curtailment in operating expenses, including the wage bill.

Table 3.12

Key Performance Ratios for Scheduled Commercial Banks

(As % of Total Assets)

Item	*1991-92*	*1992-93*	*1993-94*	*1994-95*	*1995-96*	*1996-97*	*1997-98*	*1998-99*	*1999-00*	*2000-01*	*2001-02*	*2002-03*	*2003-04*
(1)	*(2)*	*(3)*	*(4)*	*(5)*	*(6)*	*(7)*	*(8)*	*(9)*	*(10)*	*(11)*	*(12)*	*(13)*	*(14)*
1. Income	11.6	10.9	10.1	10.0	10.9	11.3	10.8	10.5	10.4	10.2	9.8	10.1	9.3
a) Interest Income	10.3	9.7	8.7	8.6	9.4	9.9	9.3	9.2	9.0	8.9	8.3	8.3	7.3
b) Other Income	1.4	1.2	1.4	1.4	1.5	1.5	1.5	1.3	1.4	1.3	1.6	1.9	2.0
2. Expenditure	11.3	12.0	10.9	9.6	10.7	10.7	10.0	10.0	9.7	9.7	9.1	9.1	8.2
a) Interest Expenses	7.0	7.2	6.2	5.6	6.2	6.7	6.3	6.4	6.3	6.0	5.7	5.5	4.4
b) Operating Expenses	2.6	2.6	2.6	2.8	2.9	2.9	2.6	2.7	2.5	2.6	2.2	2.2	2.2
o/w Wage Bill	1.7	1.8	1.7	1.9	2.1	1.9	1.8	1.8	1.7	1.8	1.4	1.4	1.3
c) Provisions and Contingencies	1.7	2.1	2.1	1.2	1.5	1.2	1.0	1.0	1.0	1.0	1.2	1.4	1.5
3. Net Profit/Loss	0.4	-1.1	-0.9	0.4	0.2	0.7	0.8	0.5	0.7	0.5	0.8	1.0	1.1
4. Spread	3.3	2.5	2.5	3.0	3.1	3.2	3.0	2.8	2.7	2.9	2.6	2.6	2.9
5. NPA (Gross)	n.a	n.a	n.a	n.a	n.a	n.a (15.7)	6.4 (14.4)	6.2 (14.7)	5.5 (12.7)	4.9 (11.4)	4.6 (10.4)	4.0 (8.8)	3.3 (7.2)

Note: Figures within brackets are percentages to total advances.

Source: RBI. *Report on Trend and Progress of Banking in India*, various issues.

Table 3.13

Select Productivity Indicators of Scheduled Commercial Banks

(Rs. million at 1993-94 prices)

Year	*Business per Employee*	*Profit per Employee*	*Business per Branch*
(1)	(2)	(3)	(4)
1992	5.4	0.02	109.9
1993	5.4	-0.05	110.4
1994	5.4	-0.04	109.2
1995	5.6	0.02	113.0
1996	6.0	0.01	119.6
1997	6.6	0.04	129.0
1998	7.5	0.05	144.9
1999	8.4	0.03	158.7
2000	9.7	0.05	179.4
2001	11.5	0.05	196.2
2002	13.7	0.09	214.9
2003	15.0	0.12	234.8
2004	16.3	0.15	254.5

Source: Mohan (2006a).

The macroeconomic environment in which banks operate changed dramatically in the 1990s. This largely explained the changes in the performance of the banking system. There were three clear sources of change emanating from the shift in the monetary policy framework. First, banks were able to deploy a much larger proportion of their resources in accordance with their portfolio decisions with the reduction in reserve requirements, earn a higher rate of return on the erstwhile impounded resources and thus reduced their spreads. Secondly, the evolution of a reasonably deep government securities market had opened a new opportunity for generating substantial treasury incomes in the recent years. Finally, the deregulation of interest rates had gradually reduced the cross-subsidies inherent in the 'priority sector' loans.

How far are these results sensitive to ownership question? There is a large literature on Indian banking that examines whether the public sector banks are less efficient than their private sector counterparts.[13] Existing empirical evidence indicates that the ownership effect in Indian banking is rather weak. In fact, it is found that the improvement in profitability has been fairly broad-based cutting across bank groups. If we define 'Government-owned PSBs'[14] as the set of select PSBs which were divested at end-March 2002, and 'Divested PSBs' as the set of select PSBs, which had accessed capital market and consequently, had a lowered Government holding[15], then an important highlight of the entire process has been the sharp improvement in the performance of divested public sector banks as well (RBI, 2003a). This suggests that the issue of ownership is not as strong a factor in bank performance as is often made out to be.

The improvement in the profitability of the banking system has been reinforced by an improvement in its health. The CRAR of the banking system, as at end-March 2004, worked out to 12.9 per cent of assets, far above the stipulated 9 per cent. The ratio of net non-performing assets to net advances declined to 2.9 per cent as at end-March 2004 from 8.1 per cent as at end-March 1997. It may be appreciated that the improvement in CRAR partly reflects the recapitalisation of banks by the Government. At the same time, it is also true that a number of banks had been accessing the capital market for funds since the early-1990s.

3.5 Concluding Observations

What are the important take-aways from the Indian experience insofar as the relationship between the central bank's policy actions and commercial bank behaviour is concerned? While presenting the broad generalisation, let us note that to brand the whole experience of the 1990s as one of unbridled financial de-control would perhaps be erroneous. After all, the measures towards deregulation of interest

---

13. See Kumbhakar and Sarkar (2003) and Sarkar *et al.* (1998) on the ownership question of Indian banking.

14. These included: Bank of Maharashtra, Central Bank of India, Punjab and Sind Bank, UCO Bank and United Bank of India.

15. These included: State Bank of India (December 1993 and October 1996), Oriental Bank of Commerce (October 1994), Bank of Baroda (December 1996), Bank of India (February 1997) and State Bank of Bikaner and Jaipur (November 1997), with the date of going public in brackets.

rates and reducing the extent of statutory pre-emption were accompanied by a simultaneous imposition of capital adequacy and provisioning norms. Illustratively, when a contractionary monetary policy (say, as captured by an increase in CRR) is accompanied by a reduction in loan extended by commercial banks, some part of the reduction could be due to a simultaneous imposition of capital adequacy on the commercial banks. Take the recent behaviour of commercial banks, when it is widely known that commercial banks hold large volumes of government securities far in excess of the required SLR. While one may argue that this could be due to a depressed investment climate that there is no pick-up in the credit demand, there are allegations of 'lazy banking' as well—whereby banks prefer to hold government securities instead of extending loans to the clientele. The norms related to non-performing assets are widely believed to be a responsible factor in this regard. Considering the fact that interest rates are already at very low levels, it is also alleged that the banks have merely substituted interest rate risk for credit risk.

Thus, given the sample period of 1992-93 through 2003-04, two broad stylised facts come out. First, in general, barring a few occasions, the stance of monetary policy was non-contractionary. Second, as far as the balance sheet of the commercial banks were concerned, there were two opposing forces—(a) reductions in statutory requirement made banks' investible and lendable resources higher, and (b) imposition of prudential norms could have made the granting of loans somewhat difficult. In this backdrop, the next three chapters would empirically address the question of relationship of monetary policy and select variables of commercial banks' behaviour.

4

Impact of Monetary Policy on Banks' Balance Sheet

The Macro Behaviour

4.1 Introduction

The channels through which the central bank's policy actions get transmitted to the rest of the economy operate through the behaviour of the commercial banks. Illustratively, when the central bank increases cash reserve ratio (CRR) the value of money multiplier gets depressed through which the economy attains a lower money supply. But what happens to the commercial banks' balance sheets? How do the deposits get affected? Is it credit or the investment that bear the bulk of the adjustment of a change in the monetary policy stance? Some of these questions are addressed in the present chapter.

Major attempts to look empirically into the impact of central bank's policy actions on commercial bank behaviour (as captured by various balance sheet variables) have largely emanated from the genre of studies delving into monetary transmission channel. This is, of course, over and above the large macro-econometric models in which normally there is a block for the banking/monetary sector. While traditionally the monetary transmission channel looks into the impact of the central bank's policy variables on the various macro variables like price and output, the intermediate impact of monetary policy actions on commercial banks' balance sheet is often relegated into the background. This is one of the reasons that make the monetary transmission channel a 'black box.'

In the present chapter, the primary focus is on this question of impact of central bank's policy actions on commercial bank behaviour as captured by their major balance sheet variables. How do we measure the impact of monetary policy on the portfolios of commercial banks? At the risk of being naive, one may note that apart from the single equation models, methodologically two distinct approaches have emerged. First, ever since Sims (1980), a number of studies looked into the impact of monetary policy actions on macro variables within the broad structure of vector autoregression (VAR) models. VAR models are typically dynamic systems of equations aiming to examine the inter-relationships between economic variables, using minimal assumptions about the underlying structure of the economy and aim to provide good statistical representations of the past interactions between variables. Second, following Romer and Romer (1990), a number of studies have used what is called 'narrative evidence' of monetary policy. The present chapter is confined to the first kind of evidence that can generically be located within the 'VAR studies of monetary policy' (Söderlind, 1999).

The rest of this chapter is organised as follows. Section 4.2 gives a synoptic account of the received empirical literature on monetary policy and bank portfolios. Section 4.3 is devoted to the specification of the VAR models, choice of variables, time span and other related issues. Results from the base-line model are discussed in Section 4.4. Section 4.5 is devoted to some robustness exercise, including, time series properties of the variables and unrestricted difference VARs, as well as, the sensitiveness of the impulse responses with respect to ordering of variables. Conclusions are presented in Section 4.6.

4.2 Monetary Policy and Bank Portfolio: A Select Review

4.2.1 Methodology of Measuring the Impact

Since the econometric foundation of this chapter and the next is couched in terms of the vector autoregression (VAR) model, a brief review of the VAR models is perhaps appropriate. VAR models are simply vector extensions of an autoregressive process whereby a variable is explained by its own lagged terms. Thus, a VAR is an "n-equation, n-variable linear model in which the current value of a variable is explained by its own lagged values, plus current and past values of the remaining n-1 variables" (Stock and Watson, 2001; p.101). Ever since Sims (1980) published his influential article, VAR models have been applied in a number of empirical investigations on dealing with the nature of monetary transmission channel. While Annex A-4.1 offers a brief review of the methodological development on and issues relating to VAR, in order to appreciate the results presented later in this chapter the following features of VAR models may be noted here.[1] First, typically in the VAR models a small number of variables are considered without any distinction between exogenous and endogenous variables. Second, following Stock and Watson (2001), taxonomically the VAR models can be divided into three groups, *viz.*, (a) reduced form VAR, (b) recursive VAR, and (c) structural VAR. The conclusions could differ substantially depending on which type of VAR model the researcher uses.

4.2.2 Monetary VAR Models: A Review

Since VAR models have been extensively used in analysis of monetary policy, within which a number of empirical models to gauge the impact of monetary policy on commercial banks can be located, this section presents a select review of monetary VAR models.

In his seminal paper, Sims (1980) using monthly US data for 1947-1978, estimated a level VAR with the following variables, (in that order) *viz.*, interest rate (4 to 6 months commercial paper rate), narrow money, prices, and output. Using a recursive structure, Sims found that proportion of output explained by money seemed to have gone down once interest rate is added to the model. Since then there have been various attempts to explain Sims' finding.

Litterman and Weiss (1985) in an influential paper found that while an unexpected increase in nominal interest rates, implied major revisions in output forecasts, an unexpected increase in real rate signalled 'no' change in output prospects. Two explanations had been offered in this context. First, while nominal interest rate had information on output, a distinction between real interest rate and expected inflation might have masked this. Secondly, it had also been pointed out that expected inflation innovations were crucial components of nominal rate changes.

---

1. See Nachane (2006) and Bank of England (2000) for a discussion of VAR models, and Christiano, Eichenbaum and Evans (1999) for a discussion of various kinds of VAR models for capturing monetary shocks.

Eichenbaum and Singleton (1986) find that the statistical association between money and output gets substantially weakened when the model is taken in differences rather than levels (with a time trend). To probe into the robustness of Sims' results, Todd (1990) made a number of small modifications. Although he found that in several respects Sims' results appeared to be non-robust, none of the critiques' alternative results seemed to have contradicted Sims' basic result that in presence of interest rate, money seemed to have little influence on output.

In an influential paper, Sims (1992) included two more variables, namely, exchange rate and world export commodity price index to his earlier 1980 model, and looked into the impact of monetary policy on real variables for five OECD countries. The following major findings of the paper deserve special mention. First, output impulse to money typically tended to follow a hump-shaped pattern. Second, responses of output to money innovations are either small or predominantly negative in all countries excepting Germany.[2] Third, once interest rate is introduced, explanatory power of monetary aggregate goes down. Fourth, though the impact of interest rate innovations turned out to be far from uniform across countries, yet they represented indicators of monetary policy disturbances. Fifth, prices initially rise and then fall eventually due to an interest rate shock.[3]

Latter application of VAR models to monetary policy continued its search for an appropriate indicator of monetary policy. Illustratively, while Bernanke and Blinder (1992) took the federal funds rate as the appropriate indicator of monetary policy, Christiano and Eichenbaum (1992) preferred innovations to non-borrowed reserves as reflective of exogenous shocks to policy.

Strongin (1995) started with the following problem: when monetary aggregates are used to measure exogenous policy disturbances, three problems of consistency arise: (a) innovations in standard monetary aggregates are associated with 'rising' rather than falling interest rates, (b) monetary aggregates do not Granger-cause

2. This has been interpreted as indicative of the fact that money stock innovations are poor indicators of monetary policy shocks.

3. This phenomenon is referred to as "price puzzle".

output when interest rates are included, (c) innovations in money explain a small proportion of output variance in VARs relative to interest rate innovations. As a solution to these problems, Strongin proposed that a significant proportion of the variance in reserves is due to accommodation of demand innovations rather than policy-induced supply innovations.[4] He found the following: (a) interest rates fall in response to expansionary monetary policy disturbances; (b) monetary policy disturbances account for a higher percentage of the variance of interest rates and output; (c) the marginal explanatory power of interest rates relative to the new measure is negligible in Granger-causality tests; (d) accommodative policy leads to permanent and significant increases in prices; and (e) output responses to policy innovations are insensitive to different VAR orderings.

Bernanke and Mihov (1998) generalised the approach of Bernanke and Blinder (1992) and Christiano and Eichenbaum (1992) by considering a vector of policy variables, instead of just one policy variable. In the first stage, the estimation of an unrestricted VAR generated two subvectors of innovations, one related to non-policy variables and the other to policy variables. In the estimation of the orthogonalised economically meaningful (structural) innovations in the second stage, a recursive causal block-order is assumed from the set of non-policy variables to the set of policy variables. Moreover, the recursive causal order is established for the non-policy variables. In terms of relationship between fundamental innovations and structural innovations, which are mutually and serially uncorrelated, they find that innovations to the federal funds rate (Bernanke and Blinder, 1992) are a good measure of policy innovations during the periods 1965-1979 and 1988-1994. For the period 1979-1994, innovations to the component of non-borrowed reserves that is orthogonal to total reserves seemed to be the best choice. They developed a new measure of policy stance that conformed well to qualitative indicators of policy, such as, the Boschen-Mills (1995) index. Innovations to their measure led to reasonable and precisely estimated dynamic responses by variables such as real GDP and the GDP deflator.

---

4. He considered two VAR models, *viz.*, (a) a 3-variable VAR with total reserves, non-borrowed reserves and federal funds rates, and (b) a 5-variable VAR with industrial production, prices, total reserves, non-borrowed reserves and federal funds rates.

VAR models had been applied in the European context as well. Mojon and Peersman (2003) analysed the transmission mechanism of monetary policy in ten countries (Austria, Belgium, Finland, France, Germany, Greece, Ireland, Italy, the Netherlands and Spain). While imposing the same identification of monetary policy shocks across countries, they noted that there were differences in the monetary policy regime of each country within the European Monetary System (EMS). For instance, Germany could follow an independent monetary policy as the *de facto* anchor of the EMS while the interest rate in a country like Austria was tied by fixed exchange rate with the Deutsche Mark during most of the past 20 years. They stressed that, given that the confidence bands around the responses were generally large, one could not use VAR models to conclude that some countries were characterised by larger effects of monetary policy than others.

4.2.3 Monetary Policy and Bank Portfolios[5]

Broadly speaking the recent work on monetary policy and bank portfolios can be located in the credit channel literature. The aggregative models on monetary policy and bank portfolios often had root in VAR models.

An early influential work is Bernanke and Blinder (1992), who took the federal funds rate as the appropriate indicator of monetary policy and estimated a VAR model for the US over the period 1959:8 to 1979:9, comprising the following variables, *viz.*, federal funds rate, unemployment rate, consumer price index and bank balance sheet variables (deposits, securities, and loans, all deflated by the CPI). Their calculated impulse response functions to an innovation to the funds rate indicated that contraction of bank loans seemed to follow an unanticipated hike of the funds rate.

Following Bernanke and Blinder (1992), McMillin (1996) estimated a model using monthly data for the period 1973:1-1994:11 for the U.S economy. The basic Bernanke and Blinder model was extended to include commercial paper issued by non-financial firms and the spread

5. This section selectively reviews aggregative evidence on the relationship between monetary policy and bank portfolio. Evidence arrived at for a more disaggregative level is surveyed in the next two chapters.

between the loan rate and the commercial paper rate. He found that when commercial paper and the spread were added to the basic Bernanke-Blinder model, the results for the unemployment rate, loans, deposits, and securities following a contractionary monetary policy shock were very similar in pattern to those of Bernanke and Blinder. The movements in commercial paper and the spread were consistent with the operation of a bank lending channel for monetary policy and suggest that the behaviour of loans did not stem from feedback from economic activity. There was little evidence of systematic movement in bank loans in the direction predicted by the bank lending channel, although the basic pattern of movement in the other variables was very similar to the full sample. His results indicated the importance of accounting for changes in the behaviour of the monetary authority.

Ehrmann *et al.* (2003) analysed the role of banks in monetary policy transmission in the euro area. It was shown that bank lending contracts significantly after a monetary tightening both in the euro area aggregate as well as at the country level. One of their major findings was that the way banks tended to respond to monetary policy could be explained by the structure of the banking system. This finding emerged when comparing the banking systems between Europe and the US, and matching the empirical findings with differences in the banking structures, as well as in the same comparison across euro area countries.

Some Indian Evidence

At an academic plane, the impact of monetary policy in commercial banks has been a somewhat neglected question in India. There are some notable exceptions, however. Illustratively, Khusro (1996) built up an econometric model for commercial bank behaviour in India. This negligence is quite understandable. After all, in a predominant regime of 'financial repression' with more than 90 per cent of banking assets being held by public sector banks, the issue loses much of its intellectual appeal.

Nevertheless, the issue of impact of monetary policy on banks' portfolios has attracted attention in the Indian context in recent years at a policy level. The motivation for such an interest came from some perceived notion of a "credit crunch", reported to be faced by the corporate sector during 1995-96 (Desai, 2001).[6] The sudden loss of industrial momentum, which occurred in late-1996 has attracted lots of attention in terms of tracing out the sources and origin of the industrial deceleration. The issue had also found place in Finance Minister P. Chidambaram's budget speech for 1997-98: "...in 1995-96, the growth in money supply was reduced sharply to 13.2 per cent. Although this helped to contain inflation, it also led to high real interest rates, a widespread perception of a liquidity crunch and a slackening of investment proposals. Since June 1996, corrective action has been taken which has eased the availability of money and brought down the interest rates." It is worthwhile to turn to this debate in the present context.

Sarkar (1999) noted that post-reform trends in credit and investment allocations of Indian banks were somewhat consistent with the credit crunch hypothesis. Reforms characterised by relatively large increases in riskless assets were more likely to see a substitution away from riskier loans—a flight to government paper, for instance, caused a 'credit crunch.' Such flight could be reinforced by prudential norms that require provisioning for risky assets, such as, loans in contrast to zero provisioning for riskless assets such as government securities. Returns on government securities have risen sharply to move closer to the PLRs of banks. During 1996-97, while the yields in primary auctions of dated securities ranged between 13.40 and 13.85 per cent for stocks of two- to 10-year maturity, the loan rate (as captured by the prime lending rate) ranged between 14.5 and 16.5 per cent. Provisioning norms have also been tightened in the recent years. Besides maintaining a capital adequacy ratio of eight per cent for risk-weighted assets, banks, during the period under review were required to classify all loans and advances into four categories and make appropriate provisions for NPAs. As mentioned earlier, such provisioning requirements have increased. In contrast, government securities have always been classified as risk-free and hence have been

---

6. In fact, Desai (2001) noted that, "The 1996 squeeze bit so deep because it was largely a squeeze on the quantity of credit. Industrial producers had ordered machinery from abroad; just as it started arriving, they were told there was no credit to finance them. Producers had begun to ship production to the market; just then there was no money to finance the pipeline inventories".

exempted from any provisioning requirements. Investments in government securities were also exempted in calculating the capital adequacy requirement whereas regular bank advances have been attached a weightage of 100 per cent. Sarkar (1999), thus, noted that all these could have led to a scenario of credit crunch.

Notwithstanding the fact that there is legitimate ground in subscribing to the credit crunch hypothesis, several competing hypotheses had been put forward to explain the decline in credit growth during the 1990s. One of these was the apparent stickiness of government securities investment and the inability of banks to adjust their investment portfolio to changes in regulatory and market conditions due to the absence of an active secondary market for such securities. The other was a demand side explanation that relates the slowdown of credit growth to the slowdown in economic conditions. Illustratively, a recent analysis (Bhaumik and Mukherjee, 2003) concluded that a significant part of the first half of 1996-97 witnessed a lack of adequate demand for credit, as opposed to credit rationing by banks. The Reserve Bank also noted that the introduction of capital adequacy requirements was not the prime reason for higher investments in government securities as non-food credit expanded by more than 20 per cent in the years 1994-95 and 1995-96 when pressure was great to maintain a capital adequacy requirement. The share of gross non-food credit going to industry between 1992 and 1996 also improved marginally. Moreover, while there has been some shift in the asset portfolio mix of banks towards investments, the commercial sector has not been starved of genuine credit needs.

However, Acharya (2002) felt that the unexpected and temporary tightening of liquidity in money markets, resulting from large dollar sales by the RBI in late 1995 in support of a suddenly unstable rupee-dollar exchange rate was mistaken as an expression of deflationary monetary policy. Indeed, between October 1995 and June 1996, the total 'net' liquidity impact of foreign exchange transactions and CRR reductions by the Reserve Bank was an injection of primary liquidity of over Rs.14,000 crore. The CRR reduction which had begun in November 1995 continued throughout 1996-97. Between April 1996 and January 1997, the CRR was reduced by 4 percentage points from 14 to 10 per cent. Since non-food bank credit grew by 22.5 per cent in 1995-96, Acharya felt that it would be hard to reconcile this with any 'credit squeeze' view.

Apart from such narrative studies of credit crunch, there have been some recent studies in the VAR tradition on this issue. RBI (2003a) has examined the transmission mechanism in India using monthly data for the period spanning April 1994 to December 2002 *vis-à-vis* the 1980s (April 1981 to June 1990) using a VAR framework with five endogenous variables in the following order: index of industrial production, wholesale price index, non-food credit, broad money, and call money rate. The results indicated that while a positive shock to broad money over time had led to higher output, a positive shock to the call money rate produced the reverse effect. Furthermore, shocks to the call money rate in recent years were found to take almost a year to have the expected negative effect on output, reflecting the monetary policy lags. A positive shock to non-food credit has the expected positive effect on output and the response during the post-1994 period was quicker, supportive of the existence of a narrow credit channel in the Indian context.

In a more recent paper, Pandit *et al.* (2006) built up a structural VAR framework to examine the monetary policy transmission mechanism with the following variables: index of industrial production, wholesale price index, commercial paper rate and broad money apart from the policy instruments (*viz.*, CRR or Bank Rate). Their results demonstrated that cash reserve ratio seemed to have greater potency as an instrument of monetary policy, as compared to the Bank Rate. Their results were supportive of the existence of a bank lending channel in the Indian context, suggesting that the central bank, while operationalising monetary policy, is likely to encounter independent shifts in the loan supply. These changes in bank loan supply would also induce changes in bank portfolios.

4.3 Specification of the VAR and the Variables

4.3.1 VAR Specification

To gauge the impact of monetary policy on balance sheet variable, in line with RBI (2003a), we run a VAR of the following form:

$$(4.1) \qquad X_t = G_0 + \sum_{i=1}^{N} g_i X_{t-i} + \sum_{i=1}^{11} c_i D_i$$

with $X_t = \{MP_t, B_t, Y_t, P_t\}$; where MP_t is a measure of monetary policy stance, B_t is a balance sheet variable, Y_t, and P_t are real activity and prices, respectively, and D_i's are the 11 monthly dummies so as to take care of seasonality pattern of the data. Note that, three balance sheet variables were considered: aggregate deposits (AD), aggregate bank credit (BC) and aggregate investment (INVA)

Specification of Monetary Stance: A Digression

There was a dilemma while choosing a variable capturing monetary stance. In India, prior to reforms initiated in the financial sector since 1992 and for a greater part of the decade of the 1990s, greater reliance was placed on the use of direct instruments, mainly CRR, in the conduct of monetary policy. The choice of instrument was partly circumscribed by the extent of development of financial markets. In the erstwhile monetary targeting framework, reserve money, more specifically, bank reserves were the operating target, which was influenced by frequent changes in CRR. Moreover, the financing of large fiscal deficits by the central bank resulted in greater monetisation, the liquidity impact of which was absorbed through increases in CRR. However, with the financial sector reforms gaining momentum, the emphasis shifted to the development and deepening of money, government securities and forex markets. This facilitated moving away from the use of direct instruments of monetary control to indirect measures, such as, open market operations and interest rate signals (Jadhav *et al.*, 2005).

Traditionally, there are several arguments in favour of CRR. First, they improve the precision in the conduct of monetary policy. Second, variations in CRR can themselves be used for implementing policy changes. Third, reserves ensure that banks hold enough deposits with the clearing institution to facilitate the payment and settlement process. However, it is expensive to administer frequent changes in reserve requirements and increases in reserve requirements put a strain on banks with low excess reserves, which has to be cushioned by liquidity injection from the central bank. In addition, fluctuating reserve requirements create more uncertainty and render the task of liquidity management more difficult for banks.

In the Indian context, during the 1980s and particularly in the 1990s, CRR, with its quick and predictable impact was most effective, both as an instrument of monetary control and as an anti-inflationary tool. During the period 1990-1999, changes in CRR were frequent, as many as 29 times. Besides, there were incremental CRR prescriptions on liabilities over some base period, specific category of liabilities like non-resident deposits. In 1992, over and above the CRR requirement of 15 per cent, there was an additional requirement of 10 per cent over the liability of some base period such that the resources impounded by CRR were as high as 25 per cent and effective CRR was 16.5 per cent. Moreover, specific contingencies during the decade that could have posed problems for monetary stability and liquidity management were also met by changes in CRR. For example, CRR was increased in January 1998 to tighten liquidity conditions and prevent speculative attack on the rupee arising out of the East Asian crisis. Similarly, the liquidity impact of inflows from Resurgent India Bonds (RIB) was contained by raising CRR in August 1998.

The reactivation of the Bank Rate and the signing of the Supplemental Agreement between the Government of India and the Reserve Bank on Ways and Means Advances in April 1997 provided additional instruments of monetary regulation to the RBI. While refinance facilities were linked to the Bank Rate, the conversion of *ad hoc* Treasury bills into special securities increased the stock of securities at the disposal of the RBI for conducting open market operations. While quantity adjustments were made by varying the refinance entitlements of banks and through OMO, the Bank Rate acted as a policy signal of the stance of monetary policy. Towards the end of the 1990s, successive reduction in CRR helped in augmenting systemic liquidity reflecting a policy bias towards soft interest rates.

In recent years, the CRR prescription was greatly simplified and the level was sharply brought down. CRR has been gradually lowered from 15 per cent in the early 1990s to five per cent by 2004, notwithstanding minor upward adjustments to deal with the evolving liquidity situation in the economy (Table 4.1), while the medium term objective of monetary policy is to reduce the CRR to the statutory minimum level of 3 per cent.[7]

Table 4.1

Changes in CRR

Effective Date	*Rate*
(1)	(2)
08-10-1992	15.00 @
17-04-1993	14.50
15-05-1993	14.00
11-06-1994	14.50
09-07-1994	14.75
06-08-1994	15.00
11-11-1995	14.50
09-12-1995	14.00
27-04-1996	13.50
11-05-1996	13.00
06-07-1996	12.00
26-10-1996	11.50
09-11-1996	11.00
04-01-1997	10.50
18-01-1997	10.00
25-10-1997	9.75
22-11-1997	9.50
06-12-1997	10.00
17-01-1998	10.50
28-03-1998	10.25
11-04-1998	10.00
29-08-1998	11.00
13-03-1999	10.50
08-05-1999	10.00
06-11-1999	9.50
20-11-1999	9.00
08-04-2000	8.50

contd...

7. At the minimum level, CRR would cease to be an instrument of monetary control and would act as more of a prudential measure facilitating the payment and settlement system.

...contd...

Effective Date	Rate
(1)	(2)
22-04-2000	8.00
29-07-2000	8.25
12-08-2000	8.50
24-02-2001	8.25
10-03-2001	8.00
19-05-2001	7.50
03-11-2001	5.75
29-12-2001	5.50
01-06-2002	5.00
16-11-2002	4.75
14-06-2003	4.50

Note: @ Excluding additional reserve requirements or release/exemption of CRR on incremental NDTL.

Source: RBI. *Handbook of Statistics on the Indian Economy*.

Thus, notwithstanding various reform measures and a professed consistent policy to reduce the CRR to its statutory minimum, CRR continued to be an effective tool of monetary management.[8] The adoption of reverse repo and repo operations and the use of the relevant rates as an effective signalling device emerged later during the period under study and hence it would be difficult to use the rates associated with repo/reverse repo without loosing sufficient number of observations.

During the period under review the CRR has been raised on the following occasions:

- *June 1994-August 1994*: During the financial year 1994-95, the CRR was progressively raised from 14.0 to 15.0 per cent in three phases during the period June-August, 1994 in order to

8. It is instructive to turn to Reddy (1999), who while speaking at a Seminar at the Bank organised by the Bank of International Settlement (BIS) in Switzerland, as a Deputy Governor commented that,

> The reform of the monetary and financial sector has enabled the Reserve Bank to expand the array of instruments at its command. The operational target of monetary policy continued to be banks' reserves which are controlled by changes in reserve requirement effected *mainly through the cash reserve ratio* (CRR) (p.104; emphasis added).

sterilise the expansionary impact of the increase in net foreign exchange assets.

- *December 1997-January 1998*: In order to insulate the domestic financial markets from the contagious disruption arising out of the East Asian crisis, the CRR was raised from 9.5 per cent to 10.5 per cent in two steps during December-January 1997-98.
- *August 1998*: In order to tackle inflows from Resurgent India Bonds (RIB), the CRR was raised from 10 per cent to 11 per cent in August 1998.
- *July-August 2000*: Finally, in view of the depreciation in the Indian Rupee, CRR was increased by 0.5 percentage point from 8 per cent to 8.5 per cent in two stages by 0.25 percentage point each effective from fortnights beginning July 29, 2000 and August 12, 2000, respectively.

VAR Specification

In general terms, the VAR models are framed in terms of the following variables: (a) a balance sheet variable, such as, deposits, credits and investment, (b) policy variables, such as, CRR, (c) output and (d) prices. Thus, in some way, the question is posed: how did banks' balance sheet variable respond to monetary policy after the influence of growth and inflation are taken into consideration. It is clear that such a simplistic story neglects the operation of various other factors that might impinge upon the relationship between commercial banks and monetary policy. Nevertheless, given that a small number of tractable variables are typically used in a VAR model to discern the nature of impulses as against the exact parameter estimates, such a characterisation seems to be plausible.

Thus, to begin with we estimate the following three VAR models, *viz.*,

VAR 1: $X_t = \{CRR_t, AD_t, Y_t, P_t\}$

VAR 2: $X_t = \{CRR_t, BC_t, Y_t, P_t\}$

VAR 3: $X_t = \{CRR_t, INVA_t, Y_t, P_t\}$

where, AD, BC and INVA refer to aggregate deposits, credit and investment of scheduled commercial banks, and Y and P refer to output and prices respectively.

The VAR models are identified using a recursive Cholesky factorisation. As far as the ordering of the variables is concerned, we place the policy variable first, followed by the balance sheet variables, and finally by the real activity and prices. We have placed the CRR in the first place so as to capture the policy stance of the Reserve Bank in India; the banking variable is placed next in order to capture the policy-induced behaviour of the commercial banks. The placement of Y and P in the end is to account for the concerns of the policy makers and commercial banks to the state of activity and inflation in the economy. The impact of monetary policy on the balance sheet variable (B_t) has been sought to be described in terms of the impulse response of CRR on B_t. As the impulses under Cholesky factorisation are sensitive to ordering, various robustness exercises are performed to probe into the role of ordering in the conclusion.

4.3.2 Choice of Variables and Time Span

As a prelude to the exercise of estimating the VAR models let us first turn to the set of variables and time span. Based on monthly data, the data base is built up over the 14-year period 1990-91 through 2003-04. The year 1990-91 is taken to be the starting point so as to coincide with the post-reform period and to avoid any problem of structural breaks. Since we need to estimate different VARs with varying lags, for the purpose of uniformity all the VARs have been estimated using monthly data for the 12-year period 1992-93 through 2003-04, (i.e., spanning over April 1992 through March 2004). Besides, much of the 1990-91 and 1991-92 was really part of the crisis period, and hence 'abnormal.'[9]

Broadly we take four kinds of variables in our empirical investigation, *viz.*, output, prices, policy actions and balance sheet variables. Let us discuss them separately.

Output Indicators: The standard output indicator, namely GDP is available only at a yearly interval in India. Thus, to avoid problems associated with paucity of data points, we for most of the period under study choose to work with monthly data. Accordingly, we had

9. Neglecting the initial years of reform has been a standard practice among the researchers. As for example, Singh and Kalirajan (2003), started the period from January 1993, so as to avoid 'the initial teething problem period.'

chosen the monthly Index of Industrial Production (IIP). Since the share of the industrial sector in GDP hovered around 25 per cent of GDP during the period under consideration, our choice of IIP as an activity variable is deficient. Nevertheless, when it comes to the purview of monetary policy actions in India, one would reasonably expect that the representativeness of IIP as an activity variable would be much more than the share of the industrial sector in GDP.[10] However, as part of the robustness checks, we have used quarterly GDP for a more limited period as an activity variable.

Price Indicators: Since in the Indian context there is no grand consumer price index covering all sections of population, we had to use the wholesale price index (WPI) for this purpose.[11] Nevertheless, for all practical purposes, prices for a number of commodities covered under the WPI do not include traders' margins, and hence, conceptually in Indian case, WPI stands somewhat midway between an index for producers' price and the same for wholesale price.

Policy Variables: As already indicated, we have taken cash reserve ratio as the policy variable.

Banking Variables: As far as banking variables are concerned we have concentrated on the data from the fortnightly returns of scheduled commercial banks submitted to the Reserve Bank of India under section 42(2) of the Reserve Bank of India Act, 1934. The last reporting fortnight values have been taken to be the representative of the monthly values. We have concentrated on three banking variables, *viz.*, aggregate deposits, bank credit and aggregate investment.

While the output, price and policy variables are collected from the *Handbook of Statistics on the Indian Economy*, Reserve Bank of India, various issues, the banking variables are collected from *Selected Banking Indicators*, 1980-2002, Reserve Bank of India and updated from the data available on the RBI website.

---

10. IIP underwent a change of base during the period under consideration. While data for the period April 1991 through March 1993 are available with the base 1980, data from April 1993 onwards are available with the base 1993-94. In order to construct the whole series into the new base of 1993-94, we spliced the series with respect to the common period, viz., April 1993 through March 1994 for the base with 1993-94.

11. WPI too has undergone a revision of base. For the sake of uniformity, we have spliced the entire series with respect to 1993-94 base, using the common values.

4.3.3 Treatment of Seasonality

In the context of the VAR model with quarterly or monthly data treatment of seasonality is extremely important. There had been some debate whether to take the data in the deseasonalised form or not. On one extreme, we find Sims (1974) who has showed seasonally unadjusted data over-emphasises the fit of seasonal frequencies or Wallis (1974) who has showed that in case of dynamic models such as autoregressive distributed lag models seasonal adjustment may result in an estimation bias; on the other, there is an equally strong argument against using deseasonalised data.[12]

Furthermore, Ericsson, Hendry and Tran (1994) have shown that seasonally adjusted data can affect the exogeneity properties of the VAR process. This apart, Ghysels, Granger and Siklos (1995) demonstrated that X-11 method of deseasonalisation might result in a seasonally adjusted series which have non-linear properties, even when the original series was linear.

Thus, in the present chapter instead of making the data deseasonalised through some standard but arbitrary filters like X-11, we choose to take the data in non-deseasonalised form; however, to take care of seasonality, we introduced monthly dummy variables in each VAR. This is primarily to avoid any bias that may arise out of the particular deseasonalisation method employed.[13] On the contrary, while estimating the VAR in difference form, we have also taken the annualised differences, i.e., $x_t - x_{t-12}$ as the basic variables. This is also expected to take care of the seasonality problems associated with monthly data.

Excepting CRR, for modelling purpose, all variables are taken in logarithms denoted by prefix L, so that Lx = log(x).

---

12. The argument has been succinctly summarised in Ghysels (1993): "The basic argument against the use of seasonal adjustment filters used to be that modern economic theory rarely, if ever, justifies the traditional practice of decomposing economic time series into orthogonal secular, cyclical, and seasonal components. Hence, as one important branch of empirical macroeconomics seeks to interpret aggregate time series data in terms of the parameters which describe the preferences, technology, and information set of market participants, it was always believed to be inappropriate to filter the data with any seasonal adjustment filter whatsoever" (p. 2).

13. Note that inclusion of monthly dummies failed to have taken care of any stochastic seasonality. This has been further tested in terms of presence of seasonal unit roots in Annex A-4.5.

4.4 Results from the Basic Model

4.4.1 Selection of Lag Length

VAR results are sensitive to selection of lag length, or the order of the VAR. Furthermore, as Canova (1995) has pointed out, in choosing the lag length of a finite order unrestricted VAR, the researcher faces a tradeoff between two opposite considerations, the "curse of dimensionality" and the correct specification of the model. Even then there is no unanimity as to what is the best selection criterion for selecting the order of a VAR model. It has been shown that under some regularity conditions, Schwartz Bayesian Information Criterion (SBIC) and Hannan-Quinn Criterion (HQC) are asymptotically superior (or consistent) to Akaike Information Criteria (AIC).[14] However, as both SBIC and HQ often lead to selection of a lower order of VAR as compared with AIC, and over-parameterised VAR is preferable to under-parameterised VAR, we have selected the order of the above three VARs on the basis of the Akaike Information Criteria (AIC).[15] The lag-lengths for the three VARs are uniformly found to be two (Annex 4.2).[16]

4.4.2 Impulse Responses

Having estimated the VARs, in order to understand the impact of monetary policy on the balance sheet variables, let us now turn to various impulse responses. Each impulse response represents a moving average coefficient normalised by its standard error. Such normalisation is necessary to compare the impulse responses across variables that have different variations. Symbolically, let $\mathbf{X}_t = \mathbf{A}_1\mathbf{X}_{t-1} + \mathbf{u}_t$ represent a VAR having a vector moving average representation. This can be

14. See Lutkepohl (1991) for a formal proof of this proposition, as well as for a discussion of the different selection criteria for selecting the order of a VAR.

15. Computation of the AIC values is done through the software MICROFIT (version 4.0). For a VAR with an intercept and N lags, Microfit defines, AIC(N) from a VAR of order N as, $AIC = -(nN/2)(1+\log 2\pi) - (T/2)\log|\Sigma_N| - n(nN+1)$, where, T is the total number of observations, n is the number of variables, and $|\Sigma_N|$ is the value of the determinant of the variance-covariance matrix of the error process of the VAR(N). Hence, we have selected that value of N for which the calculated AIC is maximum. This is contrary to the usual procedure of selecting N for which AIC is minimum corresponding to the usual formula of AIC, whereby, $AIC = T\log|\Sigma_N| + 2n(nN+1)$. However, the two different formula would yield same choice of N; see Pesaran and Pesaran (1997, p. 353).

16. The results were reconfirmed by selection of the order of the VAR through LR and modified LR test.

orthogonalised so that the error terms are not correlated: $X_t = \sum_{i=0}^{\infty} \varphi_i e_{t-i}$, where the residuals e_{t-i}'s are orthogonal. The matrices's are the impulse response functions (IRFs) since they represent the behaviour of the modelled series in response to the shocks (innovations). The vector e_t is the vector of innovations: the vector of impacts induced for particular variables when such impacts are independent of each other.

As Runkle (1987) has shown, since the IRFs could have wide variations in the reporting of impulse responses, due care needs to be taken in deriving the impulse responses. Furthermore, as the IRFs are related to the VAR coefficients in a non-linear form, the derivation and computation of standard errors in analytical form is difficult. In order to overcome such difficulties, we have adopted the Monte Carlo simulation procedure to compute the standard errors of the IRFs as follows.[17] At each repetition, a random sample from the asymptotic distribution of the VAR coefficients is drawn. Subsequently, the IRFs are computed from the asymptotic distribution of the VAR coefficients.[18] After repeating this process a number of times, the 95 per cent confidence interval by the percentile method is constructed. Figures 4.1, 4.2 and 4.3 report the impulse responses in the three VAR models, over a five year-horizon (60 months), with the standard deviations of the simulated impulse responses across 10,000 replications as the dotted lines. In general, the patterns of standard errors indicate reliability of the estimates of impulses.

Concentrating primarily on the impulses of a unit standard deviation shock in CRR on three balance sheet variables on the three VARs, a look at these Figures allows us to discern the following stylised facts. First, as a result of a shock in CRR, there is a mild rise in the aggregate deposits of the commercial banks in the first month, which tapers off from the second month, before finally getting flattened after two years. Second, a mild downward trend is noticeable in the behaviour of aggregate investment. Third, aggregate bank credit follows a sharp upward path as a result of the CRR shock in the first month.

How do we interpret the above stylised facts? To appreciate the results let us consider a thought experiment. What happens when the

---

17. Analytical formulas for calculating standard error bands of the IRF have also been developed; see Lutkepohl (1991).

18. See Hamilton (1992).

Figure 4.1

Impulse Response in VAR Model with Deposits

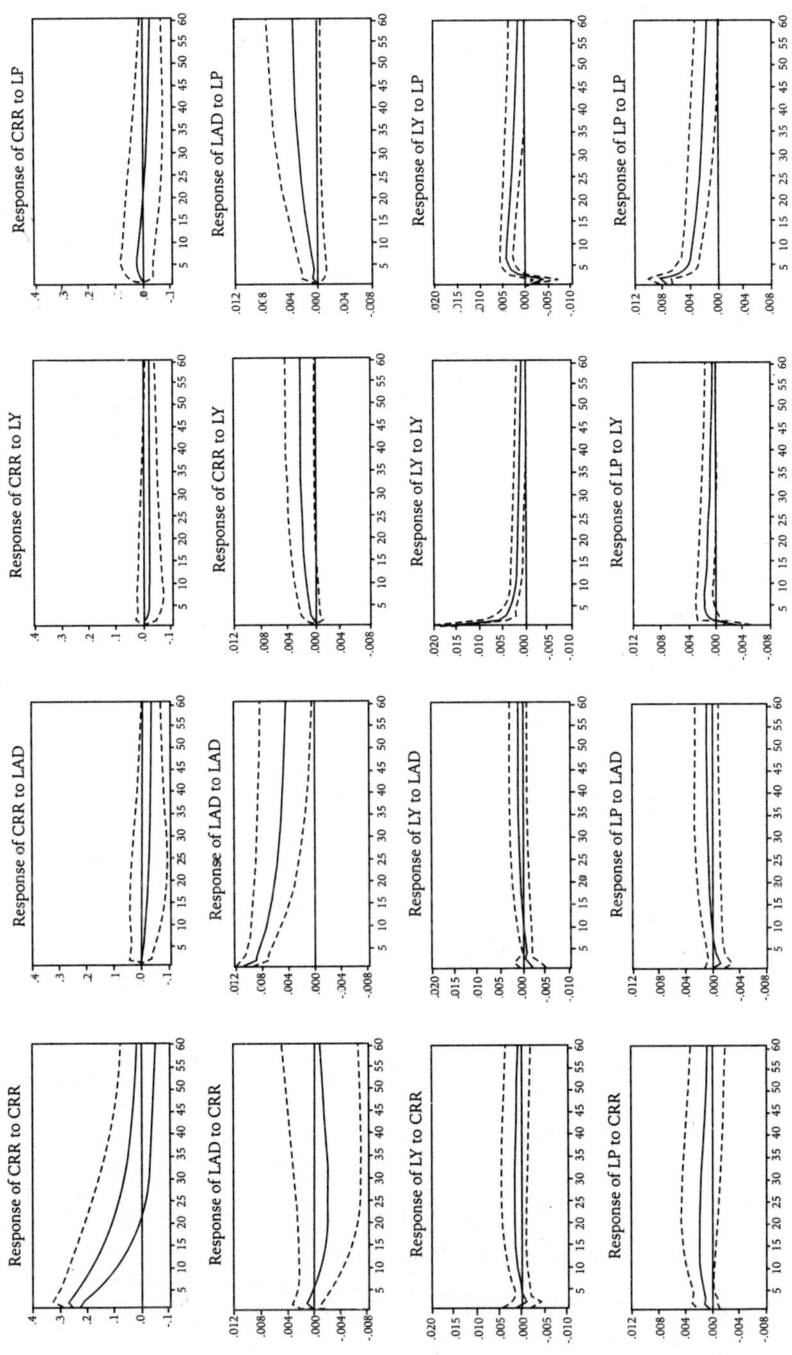

Figure 4.2

Impulse Response in VAR Model with Credit

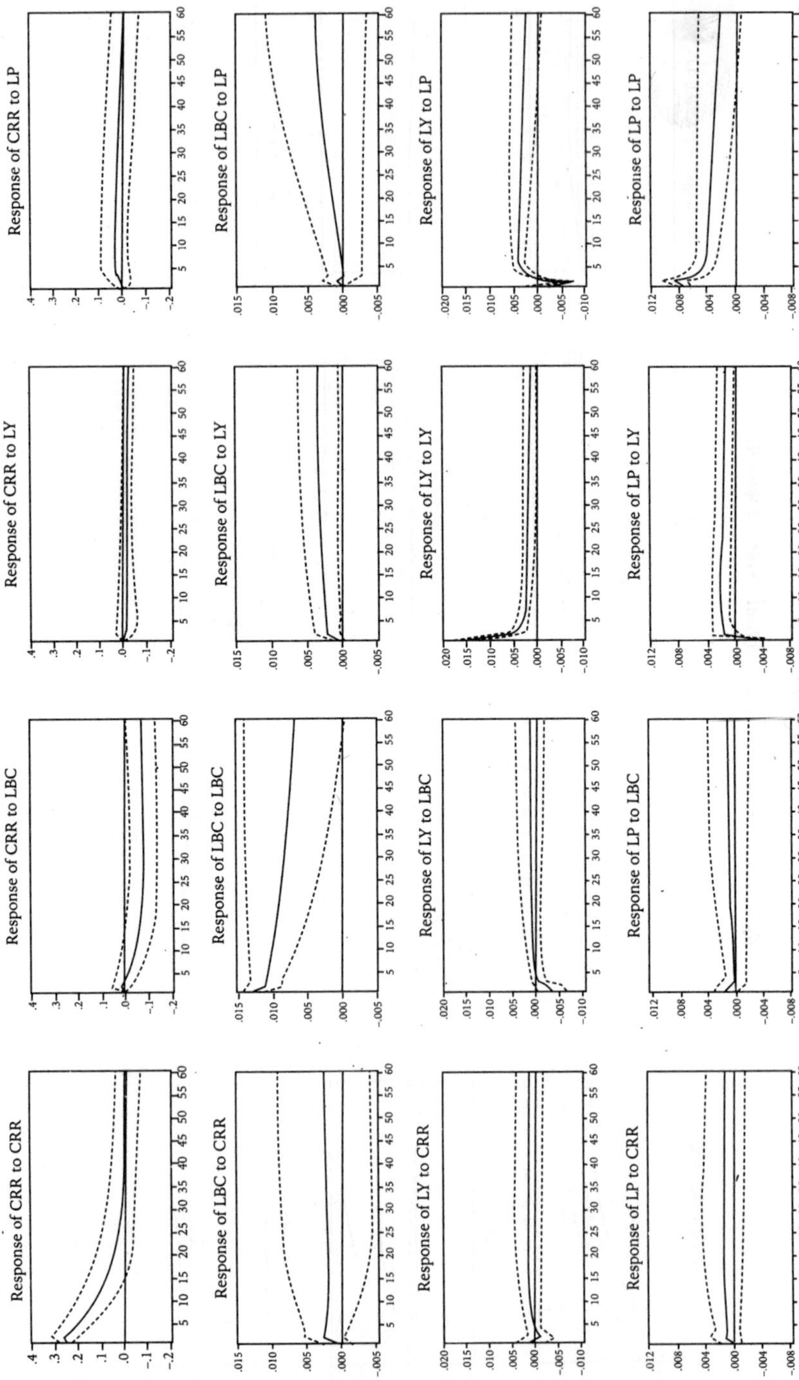

Figure 4.3

Impulse Response in VAR Model with Investment

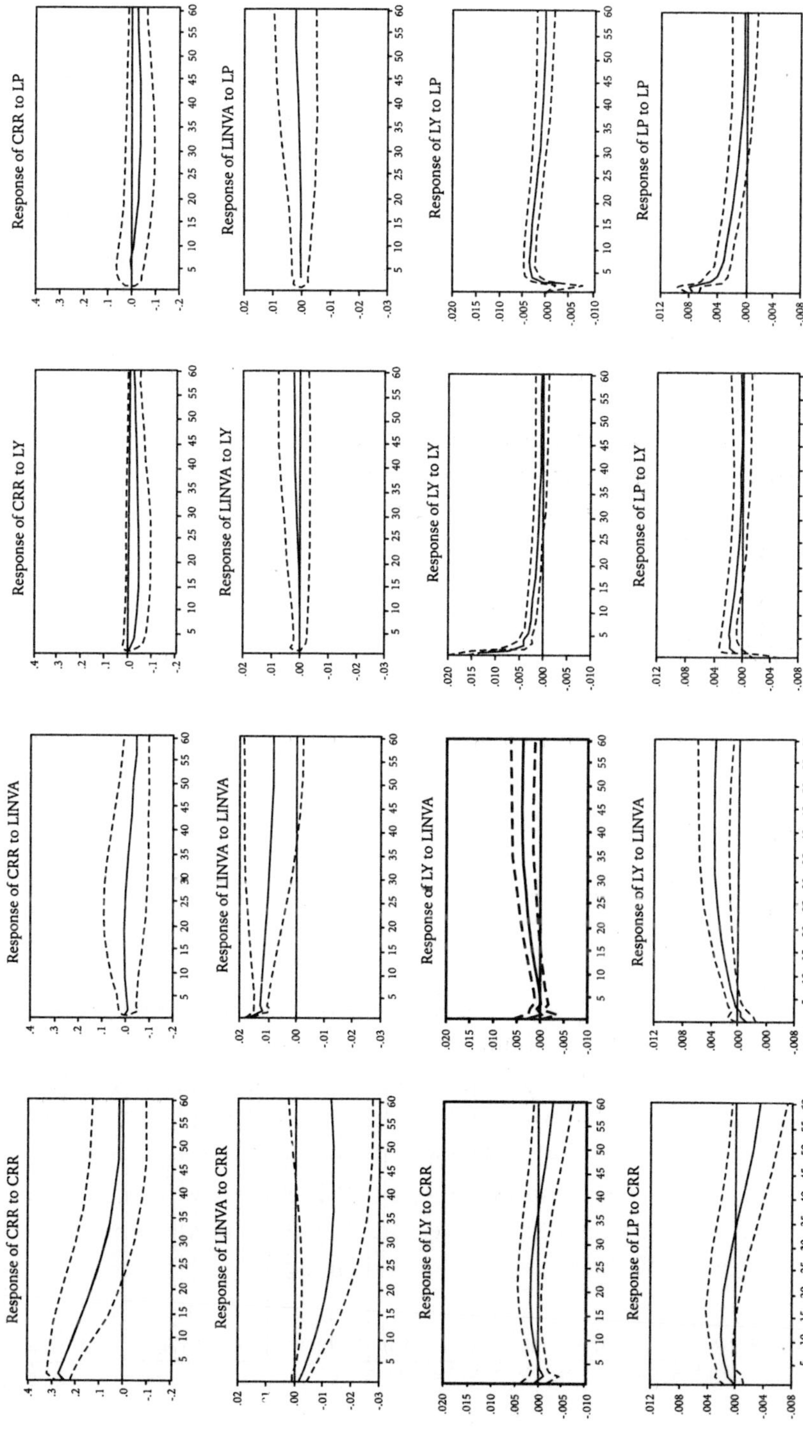

CRR goes up? Assume for the sake of argument that the current level of CRR is 10 per cent of NDTL and banks are accordingly managing their asset portfolio. Once CRR is raised to, say 20 per cent, banks will find themselves with insufficient reserves (assuming of course they do not have access to non-deposit resources on which CRR is not imposed). Therefore, they will sell some bonds and/or call in some loans. The buyers of bonds and/or the borrowers will draw down their deposits. As a result, deposits as a whole will come down and banks will be left with a lower amount of resources for the purpose of lending or investment. If the bank manages to maintain higher reserves by shifting funds from cash in hand and is not required to sell off bonds or call in loans, then it will again be left with lower liquid resources, which can be deployed as loan or investment. Thus, in either case, increase in CRR reduces the credit creation ability of banks. The process of reduction in loans/investment and/or deposits continues in sequel to the hike in CRR until and unless the reserves maintenance is equivalent to the enhanced requisite percentage of the NDTL. Thus, increase in CRR reduces the tempo of credit and deposit growth as also that of the money supply growth.

Thus, an increase in CRR would call an adjustment in the asset side of the balance sheet—the two major items being advances and investment. The results indicate that as a result of contractionary monetary policy there is actually an increase in bank credit initially. In other words, while commercial banks are able to insulate their loan portfolio from the impact of a contractionary monetary policy, it is their investment portfolio that bears the brunt.

Does it mean that it is not credit but the investment that bears the brunt of a contractionary monetary policy contrary to the existing economic reality? Two issues can be raised as counterfactual. First, the sample period has been marked by a downward trend in CRR. Second, in the recent period, commercial banks have been allegedly skirting away from their responsibility of disbursing credit and instead have been more interested in investing in Government securities.[19] Let us take each of these arguments separately.

---

19. Note that as the sample period ends at 2004, the more recent credit boom (during 2005 and 2006) is out of our purview.

As regards the first aspect, it may be noted that while the period 1992-2004 was indeed marked by a decreasing trend in CRR, there are four instances when the RBI has used CRR as a device for monetary contraction. In fact, while the simple correlations between CRR and bank credit, and CRR and bank investment are negative for the period, April 1992 through March 2004, the same during these episodes are positive, indicating that despite the rise in CRR, bank credit did not experience a fall.[20] Impulse responses from the VAR model could have picked up this underlying empirical regularity.

More fundamentally, this result is contrary to the view that credit disbursements on the part of the banks have taken a back seat in the recent years. Illustratively Banerjee, Cole and Duflo (2004) have argued that banks were under-lending because of the incentive structure of the employees of the public sector banks; after all employees of the public sector banks were under the potential threat of an indictment by the Central Vigilance Commission for the bad loans. As an alternative there could be preference on the part of the bank managers for the Government securities which are of zero risks. While this phenomenon could be true for select banks/branches, which constitute the sample in Banerjee, Cole and Duflo (2004), there is a possibility that this may not be true for the macro trends of credit disbursements.

Let us, at this juncture, recall the pattern of investment and credit behaviour of scheduled commercial banks (SCBs). Figure 4.4 below depicts the credit-deposit (C-D) ratio and investment-deposit (I-D) ratio of SCBs. While C-D ratio is seen to have a mild downward trend and I-D ratio is seen to have mild upward trend in the entire sample period, there are sub-periods when C-D ratio too exhibits upward trend.

More interestingly, if we take the credit and investment with respect to some other normalising variables, like aggregate assets of all SCBs or GDP at current market prices, much of the downward trends is not in evidence (Figure 4.5).

---

20. Illustratively, while the correlation coefficient between CRR and bank credit is -0.96 for the period April 1992 to March 2004, the same for the periods, (a) May 1994 to October 1995, (b) January 1998 to February 1999, and (c) August 2000 to January 2001, are 0.55, 0.75, and 0.57, respectively.

Figure 4.4

Credit-Deposit and Investment-Deposit Ratio

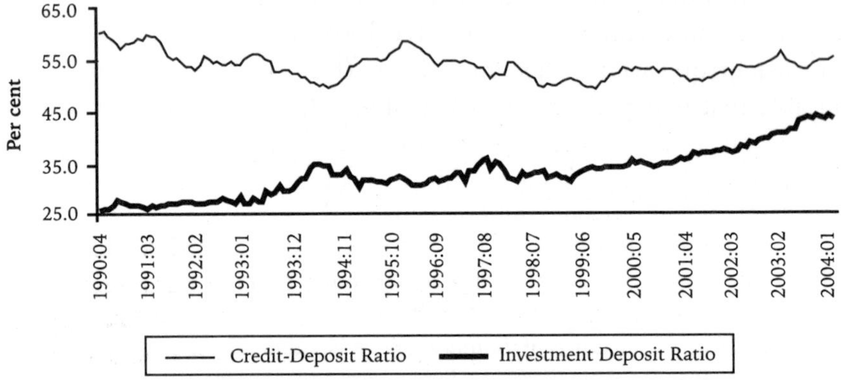

Figure 4.5

Credit and Investment Behaviour of Commercial Banks

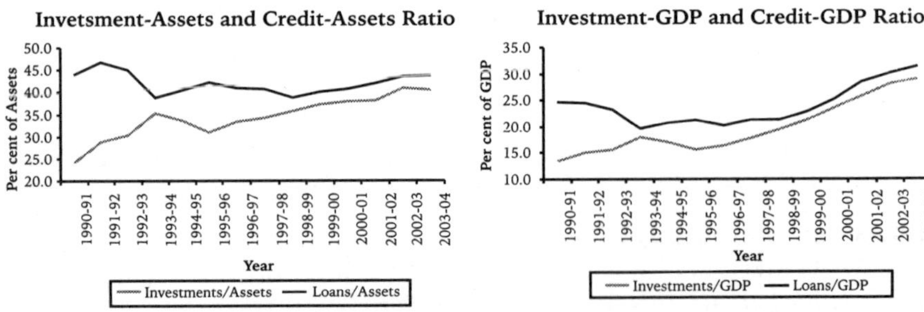

Thus, it seems that at the aggregative level, excepting the initial period up to 1993-94, credit too seemed to have followed an upward trend.[21]

Before we go on to check the robustness of the trends in impulse response functions, let us turn to the forecast error variance decomposition of the VAR models.

---

21. This is, however, the aggregative pattern and it may be quite true that some particular type of banks is under-lending. This will be examined in the next chapter.

4.4.3 Variance Decomposition

How far is the monetary policy important for the commercial banks? In order to decide about the effectiveness of monetary policy for the commercial banks, we have looked into the proportion of forecast error variance decomposition (FEVD) of the balance sheet variable that is explained by CRR (Table 4.2). Interestingly, it is found that as far as aggregate deposit is concerned, CRR does not matter much; though it explains a significant proportion of credit variance, it is indeed the investment where it matters.

Table 4.2

Proportion of Variance of Balance Sheet Variable Explained by CRR: Results from Forecast Error Variance Decomposition

Steps (Months)	*VAR 1 with Deposits*	*VAR 2 with Credit*	*VAR 3 with Investment*
(1)	(2)	(3)	(4)
1	0.07	0.18	1.13
12	1.03	3.60	15.91
24	3.62	3.92	32.79
36	4.90	4.41	44.19
48	4.95	4.99	50.61
60	4.52	5.59	53.78

4.5 Some Robustness Tests

4.5.1 How Far are the Above Results Sensitive to Ordering?

We have already noted that Choleski decomposition is sensitive to ordering of the variables. As the first check on robustness of the results, we look into this aspect of impulse responses.

Correlation Matrix

The sensitiveness of impulse responses is distinctly more when the residuals from the VAR model are correlated. To this end, Table 4.3 presents the correlation matrix of the VAR residuals. One may note that for the period of estimation, being April 1992 through March 2004 (i.e., 132 observations) any correlation coefficient exceeding 0.2

is significantly different from zero.[22] By that standard, correlation coefficients between residuals of CRR and balance sheet variables in all the VARs are quite low and insignificant. It is only that correlation between price and output that turns out to be significant. However, this could influence any conclusion regarding the impulses about a price or output shock. This is indicative of the robustness of the conclusions about the monetary policy shocks presented above.

Results from Generalised Impulse Function and FEVD

There is still another way to circumvent the problem of dependence of the orthogonalised impulse responses on the ordering of VAR. The method of generalised impulse responses, introduced in Koop *et al.* (1996), in the context of non-linear multivariate models, has been applied in case of linear VAR model by Pesaran and Shin (1998). Figure 4.6 reports select orthogonalized impulse responses *vis-à-vis* generalised impulse responses of a CRR shock on the balance sheet variables in the three VAR models.[23] The absence of any major difference between the two types of impulse responses is indicative of the robustness of the conclusions.

Similarly, Table 4.4 reports the FEVD of various balance sheet variables consequent upon the monetary policy shock. A comparison of the results of Tables 4.4 and 4.5 establishes the robustness of the conclusion regarding primacy of the monetary policy shock on investment decisions of banks.

4.5.2 Unrestricted Difference VAR

We have already mentioned that, following Hamilton (1992), we would follow an eclectic approach to modeling whereby we run VAR in both level as well as first difference (if variables under consideration are I(1)). In order to check the robustness of the conclusions, we need to turn to estimation of a VAR in differences. But before we do so, we consider the time series properties of the variables.

22. By testing the hypothesis on correlation coefficient (r), H_0: $r = 0$ against H_1: $r \neq 0$, by $r\sqrt{[\{1/(1-r^2)\}\{1/(n-2)\}]} \sim t_{n-2}$, we get the critical value of r to be 0.2 (where n is number of observations).

23. Annex A-4.3 delves into the methodological details of the Pesaran and Shin (1998)—type generalised impulse response analysis.

Table 4.3

Correlation Matrix of the VAR Residuals

VAR	*Variables*	*CRR*	*Balance sheet Variable*	*Output*	*Prices*
(1)	(2)	(3)	(4)	(5)	(6)
VAR 1	CRR	1.00			
	Deposits	0.03	1.00		
	Output	0.05	-0.13	1.00	
	Prices	0.04	0.00	-0.48*	1.00
VAR 2	CRR	1.00			
	Advances	0.04	1.00		
	Output	0.06	-0.18	1.00	
	Prices	0.03	0.17	-0.48*	1.00
VAR 3	CRR	1.00			
	Investment	-0.11	1.00		
	Output	0.03	0.16	1.00	
	Prices	0.02	-0.18	-0.50*	1.00

*Note:** significant at 1 per cent.

Time Series Properties of Variables

Presence of Unit Root in the Data

What are the time series properties of the different variables? In order to test for the presence of unit root in the data, the Dickey-Fuller and the augmented Dickey-Fuller tests are used. The results for the level variables indicate that we are unable to reject the null hypothesis that series are I(1). We, thus, concentrate on the differences. Instead of taking the usual first differences in the data, we took the annualised first difference, i.e., $\Delta_{12}x_t = x_t - x_{t-12}$, so as to get around the problem of seasonality. The variables in annualised first differences indicate that all the series are I(1).[24] The results are reported in Annex A-4.4.

Presence of Seasonal Unit Roots in the Data

In dealing with the monthly data like ours, there could be two sources of seasonality, *viz.*, deterministic and stochastic. While the former has

24. We have also run the Dickey-Fuller regressions for the first differenced data—the results indicated that the series are I(1).

Figure 4.6

Select Orthogonalised vis-à-vis Generalised Impulse Responses of a Unit Standard Deviation Shock in CRR on the Balance Sheet Variables

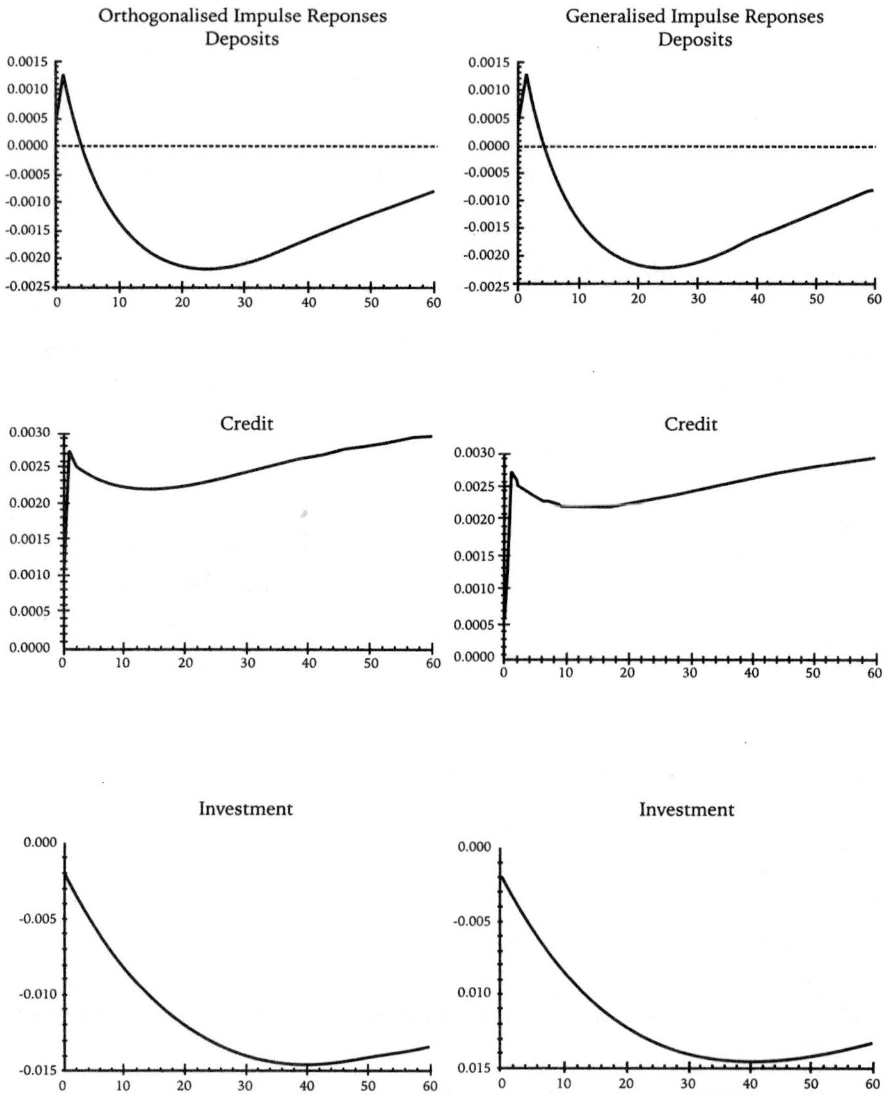

Table 4.4

Proportion of Variance of Balance Sheet Variable Explained by CRR: Results from Generalised Forecast Error Variance Decomposition

Steps (Months)	*VAR 1 with Deposits*	*VAR 2 with Credit*	*VAR 3 with Investment*
(1)	(2)	(3)	(4)
1	0.07	0.18	1.13
12	1.03	3.60	15.92
24	3.60	3.93	32.80
36	4.88	4.42	44.20
48	4.93	5.01	50.62
60	4.49	5.61	53.79

been tackled by incorporating monthly dummies in various VARs, the latter has remained unattended. One of the major forms in which the latter source of seasonality can occur is non-stationary stochastic seasonality due to seasonal unit roots. This issue is of considerable importance as the distinction needs to be drawn between unit roots at the zero frequency, and unit roots at some or all of the seasonal frequencies in the case of non-annual data. Hence we checked for presence of seasonal unit roots in the data through the Beaulieu and Miron (1993) seasonal unit root test. The methodology is reported in Annex A-4.5. In fact, based on the results on the whole we reject the presence of seasonal unit roots at most of the seasonal frequencies (Annex Table A-4.5.1).[25] The results are similar to those obtained by Nachane and Lakshmi (2000).

Specification of Unrestricted Difference VARs

Having established the I(1) nature of the series, we have run the differenced VAR in two forms, *viz.*, annualised first difference as well as first difference:

$$X_t = G_0 + \sum_{i=1}^{N} g_i X_{t-i} \qquad \text{(4.1A)}$$

25. A limitation of the exercise is negligence of seasonal cointegration. While detection of cointegration may not be relevant for a short data series, seasonal cointegration could have been useful. Nevertheless, the theoretical development of seasonal cointegration at monthly frequency has been somewhat limited (see Johansen and Schaumburg, 1999 for a likelihood based analysis of seasonal cointegration at quarterly frequency), and we choose to ignore this issue.

Where, the different choices of the vector X are as follows:[26]

VAR 1A: X = {Δ_{12}CRR, Δ_{12}LAD, Δ_{12}LY, Δ_{12}LP};

VAR 2A: X = {Δ_{12}CRR, Δ_{12}LBC, Δ_{12}LY, Δ_{12}LP};

VAR 3A: X = {Δ_{12}CRR, Δ_{12}LINVA, Δ_{12}LY, Δ_{12}LP};

As the first differences of all the variables have been found to be I(0), we have also run a VAR in the first differences,

(4.1B) $$X_t = G_0 + \sum_{i=1}^{N} g_i X_{t-1} + \sum_{i=1}^{11} c_i D_i$$

where, the different choice of the vector X is as follows:

VAR 1B: X = {ΔCRR, ΔLAD, ΔLY, ΔLP};

VAR 2B: X = {ΔCRR, ΔLBC, ΔLY, ΔLP};

VAR 3B: X = {ΔCRR, ΔLINVA, ΔLY, ΔLP};

As per the AIC values, the orders of all the VARs are found to be two.

Impulse Responses

Care needs to be taken while interpreting the impulse responses in the difference VAR. After all a CRR shock in these models is really a shock in incremental CRR, annualised or monthly. Thus, an impulse response in ΔCRR, actually means a perturbation of CRR by 0.027 points. Similarly, an impulse response in Δ_{12}CRR, actually means a perturbation of CRR by 0.038 points. Instead of reporting all the impulse responses Figure 4.7 reports the impulse of one standard deviation shock in Δ_{12}CRR, or ΔCRR on the three balance sheet variables for VAR 4.1A and 4.1B, respectively. Interestingly, both for deposits and credit, the impact is one of north-bound in the first few months after which it gets tapered off. The results under the difference VAR are, thus, broadly in tune with the results obtained under the level VAR.

Variance Decomposition

How far does a change in CRR explain the balance sheet variables? Towards this end Table 4.5 below reports the forecast error variance

26. Note that since we have taken the variable in annualised first difference form, we have not incorporated the monthly seasonal dummies in the VAR.

Figure 4.7

Select Impulse Responses of Balance Sheet Variable to Changes in CRR in the Difference VAR Models

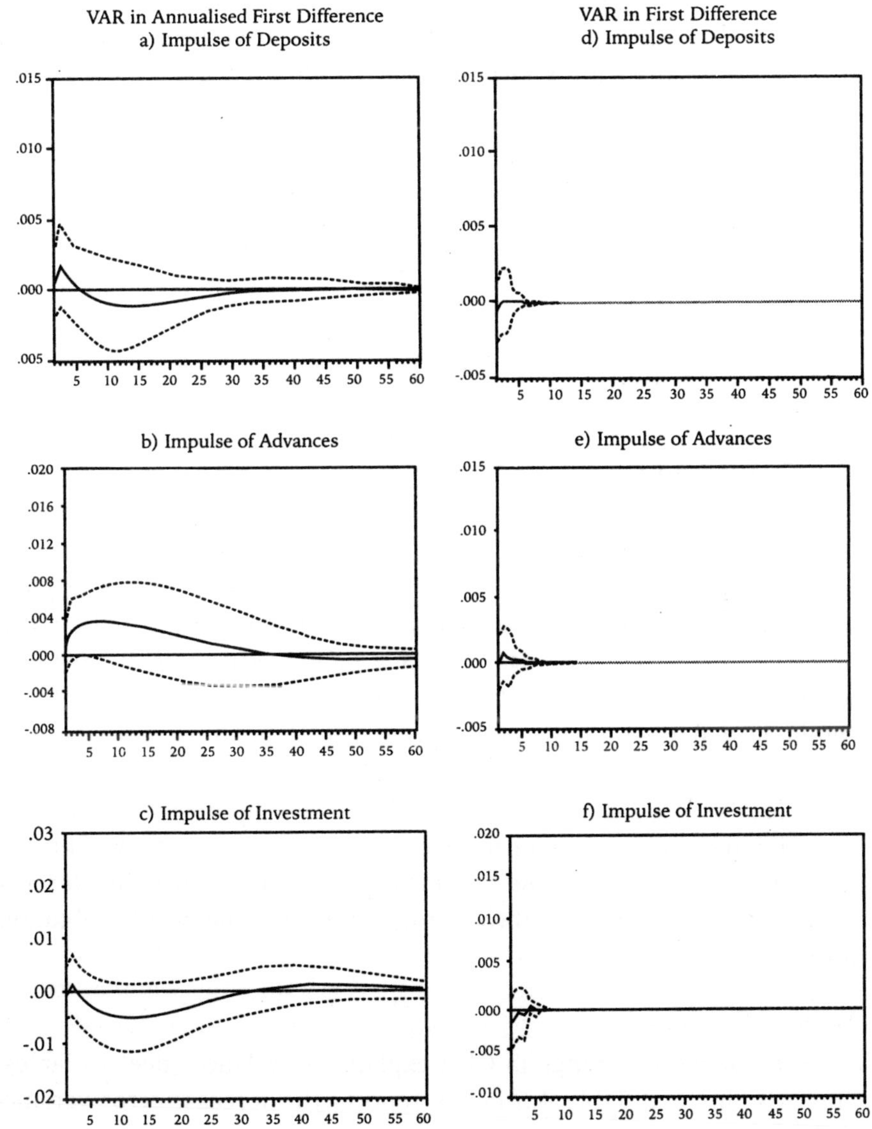

Table 4.5

Proportion of Variance of Balance Sheet Variable Explained by CRR: Results from Forecast Error Variance Decomposition in the Difference VAR

Steps (Months)	*VAR with Annualised Differenced Data*			*VAR with First Differenced Data*		
	VAR 1A with Deposits	*VAR 2A with Credit*	*VAR 3A with Investment*	*VAR 1B with Deposits*	*VAR 2B with Credit*	*VAR 3B with Investment*
(1)	(2)	(3)	(4)	(5)	(6)	(7)
1	0.10	0.02	0.10	0.29	0.01	1.00
12	1.84	11.63	5.77	0.35	0.49	1.17
24	3.33	12.23	9.94	0.35	0.49	1.17
36	3.35	11.49	9.26	0.35	0.49	1.17
48	3.36	11.35	9.59	0.35	0.49	1.17
60	3.38	11.36	9.71	0.35	0.49	1.17

decompositions (FEVD) of the three balance sheet variables that are explained by CRR. Two points deserve a mention. First, as far as VAR in annualised differences is concerned, CRR explains very little of the FEVD of aggregate deposits, as against that of credit or investment. Secondly, in the first difference VAR, the proportions of FEVD that are explained by balance sheet variables undergo drastic reduction. Nevertheless, the relative magnitudes of FEVD indicate that monetary policy shocks matter more for credit and investment than for deposits; this is similar to the pattern obtained in level VARs.

4.5.3 Results with Alternative Choice of Policy Variable

So far we have measured the stance of the monetary policy by the CRR. As already pointed out, as a part of the financial sector reform agenda, CRR was on a secular south-bound trajectory during the period under consideration. Hence, one can question the choice of monetary policy as measured by CRR. Consequently, we adopted an alternative variable, namely, growth of reserve money (GRM) as a proxy of monetary stance.[27]

27. Ideally we should have taken adjusted reserve money (adjusted for CRR changes); however, the series is not available.

The impulse responses of an expansionary monetary policy stance as measured by a unit standard deviation shock in GRM on the three balance sheet variables are reported in Figure 4.8. Both advances as well as deposits are found to be following a mild north-bound path as a result of expansionary monetary policy. The trajectory of investment turns out to be following a south-bound path—this is of course in consonance with the secular reduction in SLR over the period under consideration. If one considers the later period, *viz.*, 2003-04, there was an increase in commercial banks' holdings of Government securities indicating holding of Government securities in excess of the SLR requirement.

4.5.4 Results in a Five Variable VAR

So far, we have treated credit and investment separately in the VARs. What happens if they are considered together? Towards this end, we have estimated a five variable VAR with CRR, credit, and investment, along with output and prices. Impulse responses (with standard error bands) as given in Figure 4.9 indicate that bank credit continues to show an upward trend despite a CRR shock during the first month. This upward trend continues and takes nearly a year to taper off. Investments, on the other hand, seemed to have followed a south-bound movement with respect to a CRR shock. The broad pattern, thus, is in consonance with the impulse responses obtained earlier. Furthermore, considering the fact that correlation between the errors from credit and investment equation was as low as 0.0003, the placement of credit and investment variable would not have mattered materially in the impulse responses.

4.5.5 Results with Quarterly GDP

So far we have used IIP as an activity variable. Considering the fact that industries accounted for roughly 25 per cent of GDP during the period under reference, one may justifiably question the representativeness of IIP as the activity variable. The choice of the activity variable in our case, as already been pointed out, was dictated by considerations relating to availability of data.

Specifically, since for bulk of the period, GDP was available at an annual frequency, there was simply no way we could have run a VAR

Figure 4.8

Select Impulse Responses with Alternative Policy Variable

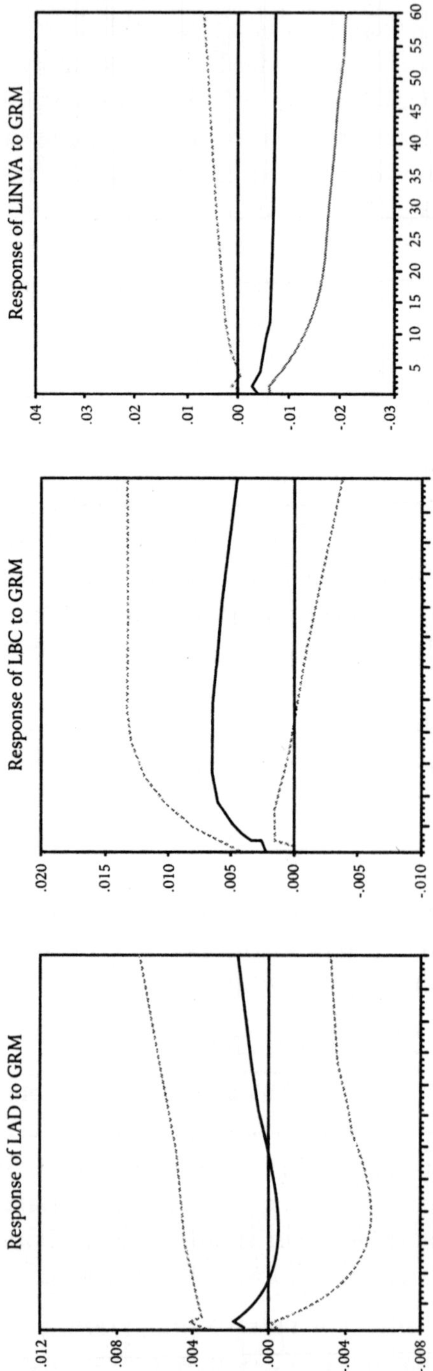

Figure 4.9

Impulse Responses in the Five Variable VAR

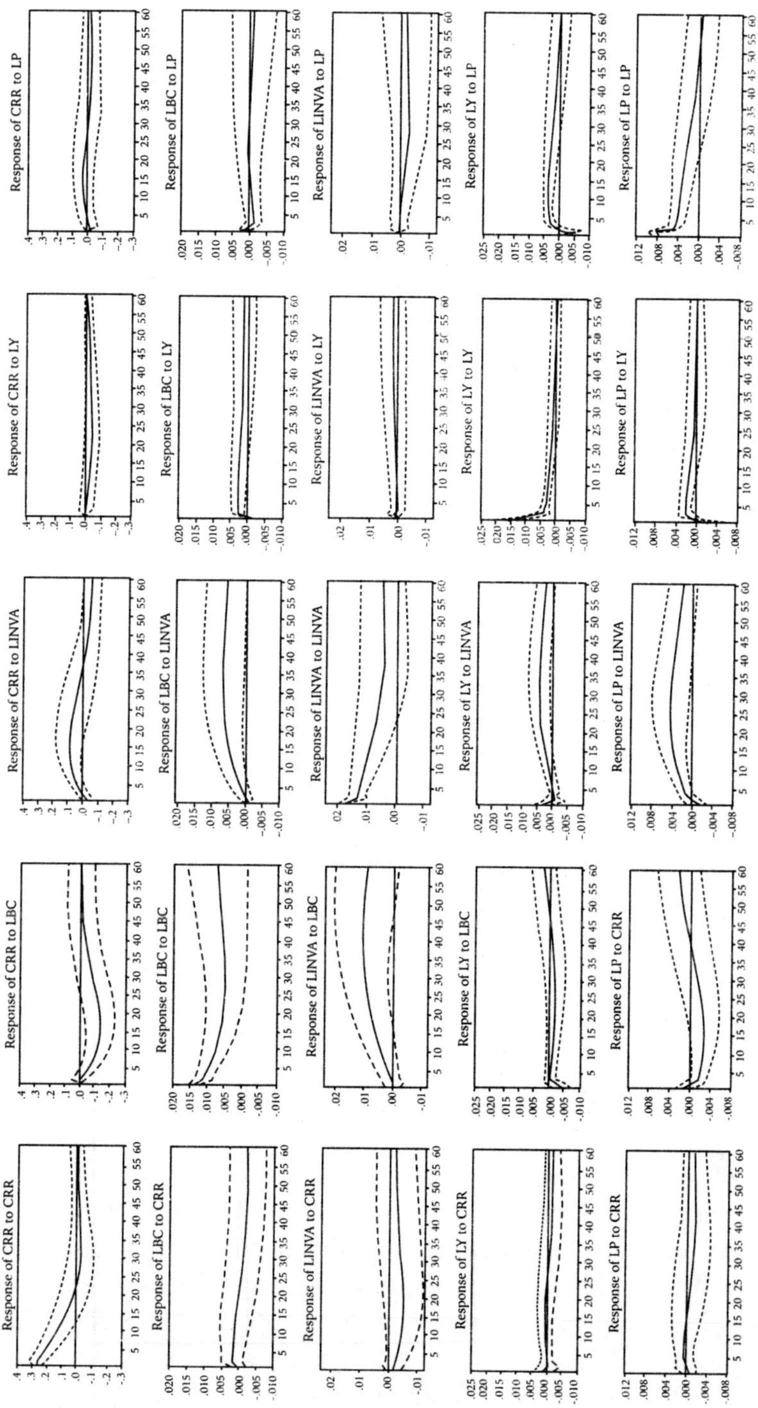

with 12 years of annual data. However, the Central Statistical Organisation (CSO) has started publishing quarterly estimates of national income since 1996-97. Thus, we have quarterly GDP data from 1996-97 Q1 to 2003-04 Q4, i.e., 32 quarters during the sample period. Hence, in order to check the robustness of our results we have run a quarterly VAR with CRR, balance sheet variables, quarterly GDP and prices from 1996-97 Q3 to 2003-04 Q4 in levels with 2 lags of the following form:

$$\text{(4.1C)} \qquad X_t = G_0 + \sum_{i=1}^{2} g_i X_{t-i} + \sum_{i=1}^{3} c_i D_i$$

with X_t = {CRR_t, $\log(B)_t$, $\log(GDP)_t$, $\log(P)_t$}; where B_t is one of the balance sheet variables, *viz.*, aggregate deposits (AD), aggregate bank credit (BC) and aggregate investment (INVA), and D_i's are the three monthly dummies so as to take care of seasonality pattern of the data.

The impulses of a monetary shock on the balance sheet variables, *viz.*, deposits, credit, and investment from the four variable VAR (i.e., treating deposits, credit, and investment separately) are reported in Figure 4.10. While credit follows an upward trend in the initial period in response to a CRR shock, investment follows a downward trend. This shows the robustness of the results arrived at with IIP as an activity variable earlier.

As earlier, we also ran the quarterly VAR with both credit and investment together. The impulse responses (reported in Figure 4.11) of credit and investment with respect to a CRR shock show a similar pattern.

4.5.6 Results with Interest Rate as an Additional Variable

As we did not include any interest rate in the variable vector in the VAR, questions may be raised about the veracity of the results in the presence of the interest rate. After all, the VAR results for the US have been found to be sensitive to inclusion of interest rates (Litterman and Weiss, 1985). Hence, we have rerun the VARs after including the weighted average call money rates (r) in the variable vector of the form: $\mathbf{X}_t$ = {CRR_t, r, B_t, Y_t, P_t}, with the balance sheet variable, B = BC, AD or INVA. Select impulse responses of an increase in CRR on

Figure 4.10

Impulse Responses of Balance Sheet Variables to a CRR Shock in the Quarterly Four-Variable VARs

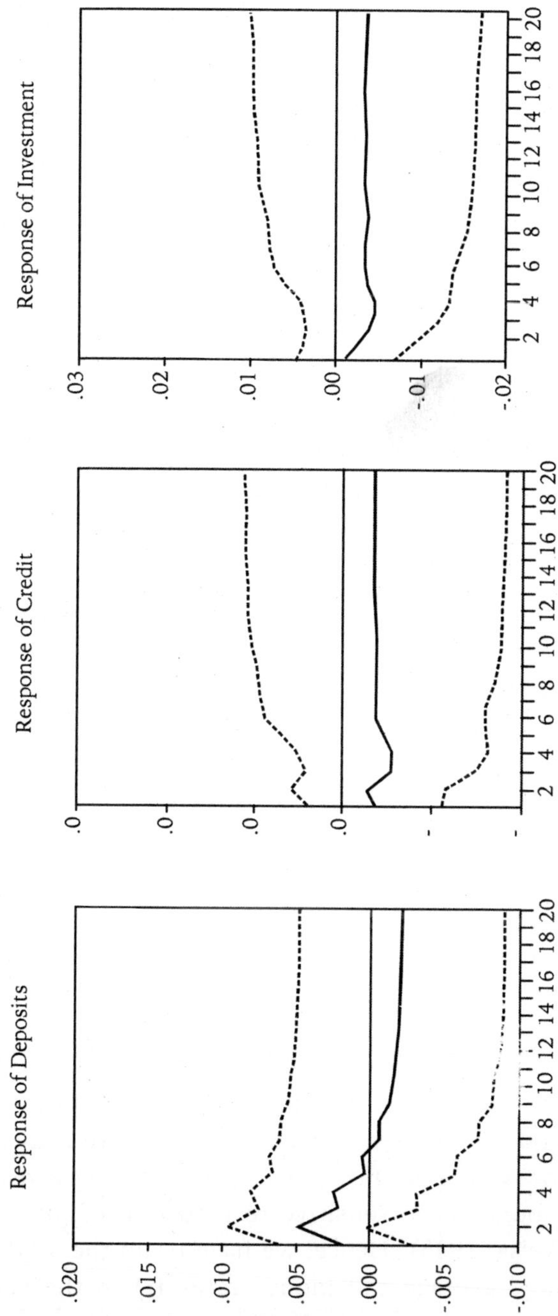

Figure 4.11

Impulse Responses of Balance Sheet Variables to a CRR Shock in the Quarterly Five-Variable VARs

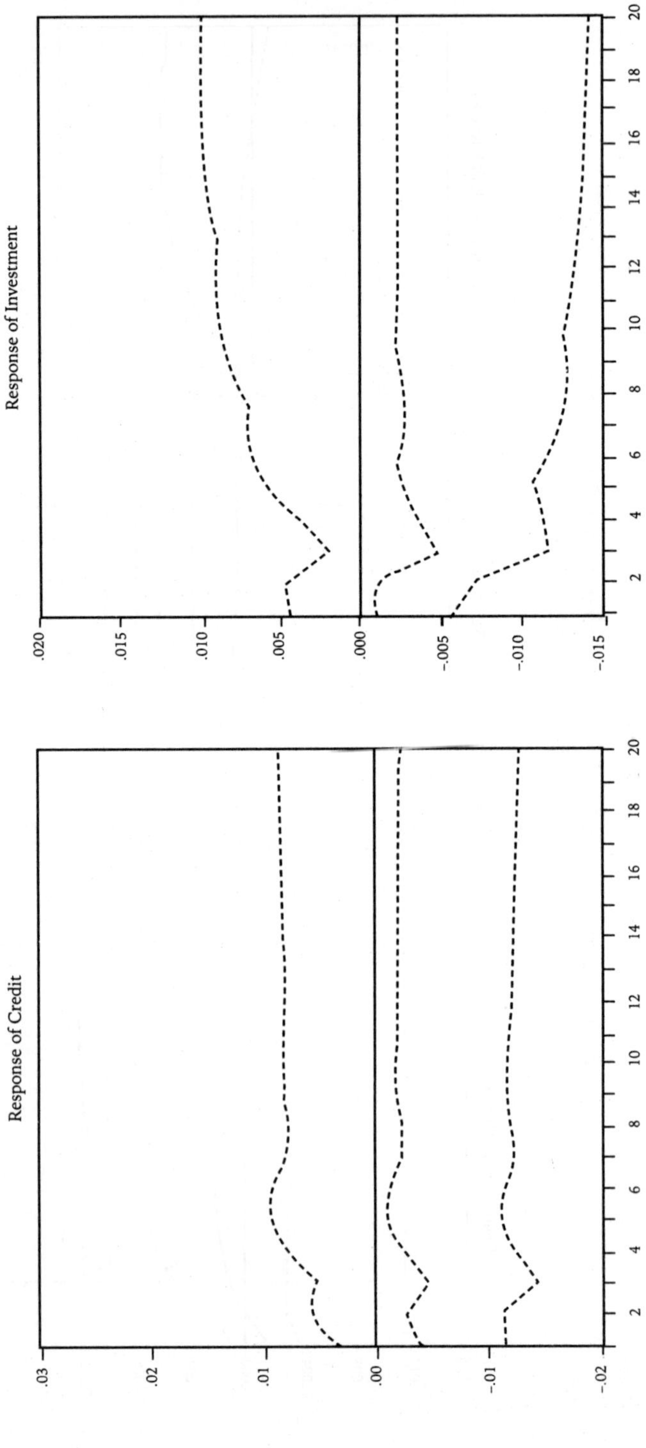

Figure 4.12

Select Impulse Responses in the VAR with Interest Rates

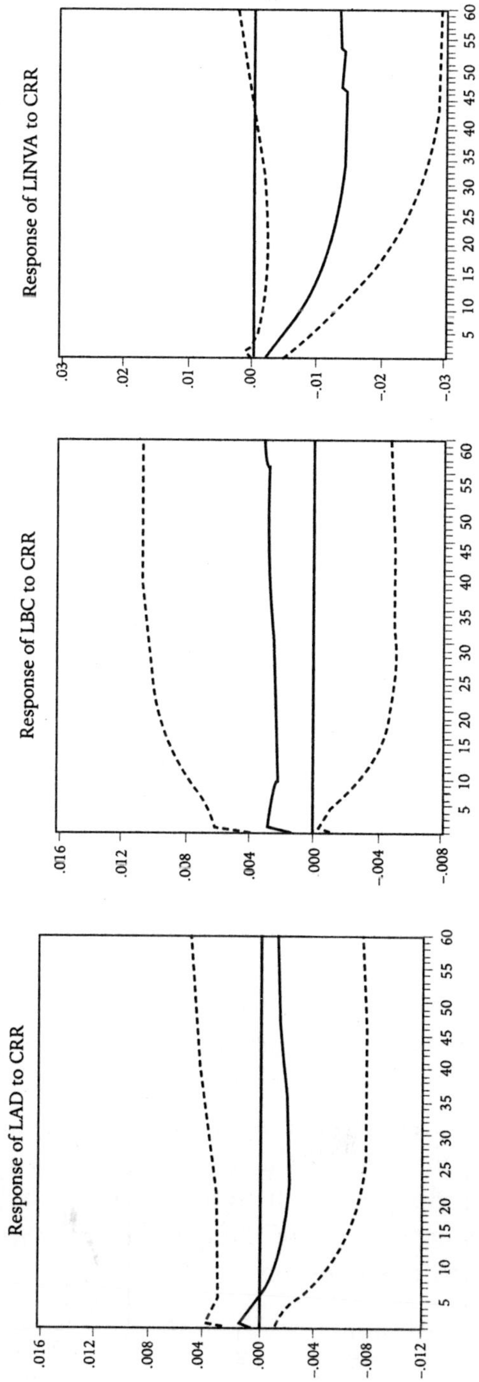

the three balance sheet variables are reported in Figure 4.12. These are similar to what was observed earlier.

4.6 Conclusion

How does the central bank's policy action influence commercial bank behaviour? Consider a situation where the central bank adopts a policy of monetary tightening. As Kashyap and Stein (1995) have argued, the impact of monetary tightening can be countered by any bank in one of the three possible ways, *viz.*, (i) reducing loans, (ii) selling securities (like Treasury bills) or (iii) raising non-deposit resources.

What has been the evidence of the aggregate commercial bank behaviour in this context? The results presented in this chapter allow us to discern the following broad trend. There seems to be a mild perverse impact of a contractionary monetary policy on bank advances, in the sense that a positive shock in CRR actually results in 'higher' bank advances during the initial period. This is fairly uniform and robust across various specifications of the models. Impact of a CRR shock on investment, however, are not perverse across various models. Does this mean that commercial banks have largely bypassed the impact of a contractionary monetary policy?

Such a phenomenon can be explained in terms of access of non-deposit resources like CDs. However, in the Indian case, CDs failed to have emerged as a viable alternative source of non-deposit resources and is a small fraction of aggregate deposits (less than 1 per cent of aggregate deposits for most of the years during the sample period). Illustratively, in March 2004, the outstanding amount of CDs was Rs. 4,461 crore as against an outstanding aggregate deposits of Rs. 15,04,416 crore.

There is, however, another angle to this result—*viz.*, the extent of heterogeneity in the behaviour across various types and sizes of banks. In other words, this perverse behaviour may not be true for all types of banks. As an explanation of the observed aggregative behaviour of banks, we turn to this question of heterogeneity in the next chapter.

Annex A-4.1

Vector Autoregression Model: A Methodological Digression

Let $\mathbf{Y}_t$ be the (nx1) vector of variables one is interested in, then the structural form of the model can be written as,

(A4.1.1) $AY_t = B_0 + C(L)\ Y_{t-1} + Bu_t$

where, u_t is a white noise error process that is serially uncorrelated, i.e., $E(u_t)=0$, $E(u_tu_t')=I$, i.e., $E(u_{it}u_{it}')=0$, and $E(u_{it}u_{is}')=0$ for $s \neq t$, and $C(L)$ is a lagged polynomial operator of order N, i.e., $C(L) = 1+L+L^2+ \ldots + L^N$, with $L^kY_t=Y_{t-k}$.

Two distinct issues have been thrown up by the literature in this context, *viz.*, (a) the process of identification of the above structural form VAR, and (b) time series properties of the variables and the appropriateness of the reduced form VAR. These two issues are taken separately.

Issues Relating to Identification of the Structural Form

The structural model (A4.1.1) is not directly observable; hence, a VAR in its reduced form can be estimated in the following form,

(A4.1.2) $Y_t = A^{-1}B_0+A^{-1}C(L)\ Y_{t-1}+A^{-1}Bu_t= G_0+G(L)\ Y_{t-1}+e_t$

Where, $G_0 = A^{-1}\ B_0$, $G(L) = A^{-1}C(L)$, and $e_t=A^{-1}Bu_t$.

From the relation between structural innovation (u) and reduced form residual (e), one can find out the relationship between the variance-covariance matrix of the respective residuals, *viz.*,

(A4.1.3) $\Sigma = E(e_te_t') = A^{-1}B\ E(u_t\ u_t')\ BA^{-1} = A^{-1}B\ I\ BA^{-1}$

Note that, if n be the number of variables in the VAR, we need to estimate $n^2 + n(n+1)/2$ distinct elements, whereas Σ has $n(n+1)/2$ distinct elements, which gives the maximum number of identifiable parameters in matrices A and B. Hence we need at least n^2 identifying restrictions.

The VAR literature suggests a number of identification restrictions. Originally suggested by Sims (1980), Choleski decomposition is the most traditional form of restriction in VAR models. Under the Choleski decomposition, A and B take the following form:

$$\text{(A4.1.4)} \qquad A=\begin{bmatrix} 1 & 0 & 0 & . & . & 0 \\ a_{21} & 1 & 0 & . & . & 0 \\ a_{31} & a_{32} & 1 & . & . & 0 \\ . & . & . & . & . & . \\ . & . & . & . & . & . \\ a_{n1} & a_{n2} & a_{n3} & . & . & 1 \end{bmatrix} \quad B=\begin{bmatrix} b_{11} & 0 & 0 & . & . & 0 \\ 0 & b_{22} & 0 & . & . & 0 \\ 0 & 0 & b_{33} & . & . & 0 \\ . & . & . & . & . & . \\ . & . & . & . & . & . \\ 0 & 0 & 0 & . & . & b_{nn} \end{bmatrix}$$

It may be noted that the identifying restriction on A follows a recursive scheme, and hence it is sensitive to the ordering. Normally, in such a scheme the most endogenous variable is ordered last. The transmission mechanism is, then, traced in terms of the trajectory of the impulse response functions out of a unit standard deviation shock in the variables. In fact, it is its sensitiveness to ordering which has invited most of the critiques to this particular form of modelling strategy. However, if the correlation coefficients between e_{it} and e_{jt} are small then the impulse responses will not be very sensitive to the ordering.

As an alternative to the above scheme of Choleski decomposition, a large literature had emanated in recent years on imposing economically meaningful identifying restrictions. Generically these models are called structural VAR. Starting with Bernanke (1986), the recent literature on monetary transmission channels is full with examples on such identifying restrictions [e.g., Christiano, Eichenbaum and Evans (1996), or Bernanke and Mihov (1998)]. One may note two such restrictions, *viz.*, (a) contemporaneous, and (b) long-run. As for example, in the first kind of model it is often assumed that macro variables, like GDP or price level, do not simultaneously react to monetary variables, like federal funds rate or non-borrowed reserves. Alternatively, restrictions are imposed on the monetary block of the model so as to reflect the operating procedure of the central bank. In the second class of models, restrictions of long-run nature are imposed [e.g., Blanchard and Quah (1989)] on the cumulative impulse response functions.

It may be noted that much of the debate behind "structural VAR" *versus* "reduced form VAR", adopting Choleski-type decomposition, is in line with the earlier Lucas-critique of imposing "incredible identifying restriction", on the large macro models. After all, VAR model came into existence precisely to get rid of the bias imposed from "too much theory', in an empirically estimable macro model. In fact, much of the Sims type work on reduced-form VAR also postulates a structure underlying the model, which is not necessarily mechanical. What matters, however, is to see the robustness of the impulse responses subject to the adoption of a particular ordering or recursive structure.

Time Series Properties of Variables and the Form of VAR

There is much debate in VAR literature on whether the researcher has to ensure stationarity of the variables before modelling them in a VAR. As many of the economic variables are I(1), the choice often arises as to whether to take the variables in level form or in difference form. Furthermore, if the I(1) variables like GDP, price level and monetary aggregates are cointegrated (possibly in conjunction with some I(0) variables like interest rates, or spreads) then, as Engle and Granger (1987) have shown, the first difference reduced form VAR (of the form, $\Delta Y_t = G_0 + G(L)\ \Delta Y_{t-1}$, where G(L) is a polynomial lagged operator of order N) is a mis-specification; instead one needs to have the VAR in vector error-correction model (VECM) of the form, $\Delta Y_t = H_0 + H(L)\ \Delta Y_{t-1} + \Pi Y_{t-N}$ (where H(L) is polynomial lagged operator of order N-1). In that case, the transmission mechanism has to be discerned from the impulse responses of the relevant VECM (e.g., Lutkepohl and Reimers, 1992).

The applied work in this context has progressed in three directions, *viz.*, (a) level VARs (without any checking of stationarity), (b) difference VAR (ensuring stationarity but not cointegration), and finally, (c) VECM (ensuring both stationarity and cointegration). In fact, justifications exist for all the three types and the message from literature in this context is that adopting one approach over the other is not exactly straight-forward.

For example, almost all works by Sims and his associates (like Sims, 1992) can be clubbed under the first category, whereby a reduced form VAR is run in terms of the level variables. The justification came from Sims, Stock and Watson (1990) who, in developing Fuller (1976)'s results, showed that coefficients were consistently estimated, independent of the order of integration of the variables. Furthermore, as Hamilton (1992) has pointed out, even if the true model is a VAR in differences, certain functions of the parameters and hypotheses tests based on VAR in levels have the same asymptotic distribution based on differenced data. Finally, as Sims and Ulhig (1991) has shown, one may give a Bayesian interpretation to the usual t or F distribution, even when the asymptotic theory for these statistics is non-standard. All these results show that VAR in difference form (if the variables are non-cointegrated) or in VECM form is by no means the only standard procedure; there is ample justification for running a VAR in levels.

Thus, because of the ambiguous stance of the literature, in the present chapter, following Hamilton (1992)'s suggestion, we follow a rather eclectic approach, whereby we employ the first two approaches, *viz.,* (a) level VAR, (b) differenced VAR (when the variables are I(1)).

We have purposefully avoided considering the third approach, *viz.,* a cointegrated VAR (in its ECM form). There are two reasons for this.

First, the primary reason behind neglecting the presence of cointegration is the short period (i.e., twelve years spanning from 1992-93 through 2003-04) of our analysis. While the data for the present exercise being available at monthly frequency, we did not have any degree of freedom problem for estimation, it is increasingly believed that increasing frequency is not exactly a substitute for increasing time span (Chambers, 2001). We, thus, refrained from finding any long-run relationship based on twelve years data.

Second, it may be noted that the specification of a dynamic model in levels has proved sufficient to remove the spurious regression problem and that the VECM representation of a VAR model in levels is just a reparamterisation, before the rank reduction restrictions are imposed (Fevaro, 2001). In fact, Sims, Stock and Watson (1990), argue that a VAR model in levels in the presence of cointegration is over-parameterised and, therefore, leads to inefficient but consistent estimates of parameters of interest. The loss of efficiency has to be weighted against the risk of inconsistency of estimates which occurs when the wrong cointegrating restrictions are imposed. Sims, Stock, and Watson (1990) show that standard distributions can be applied when doing an inference in a VAR model which involves variable admitting stationary linear combinations, reverting to non-standard distributions only when the subsets of variables on which inference is performed do not admit any stationary linear combination. It is instructive to turn to Fevaro (2001) in this context,

> Imposing the wrong cointegrating parameters will make the system converge to the wrong long-run equilibria but will also bias the short-run dynamics, as the system is pulled in the wrong direction. For this reason the recent research has taken a defined line and *VARs in levels rather than cointegrated VARs are used when the issue of economic interest is related to the short-run rather than to the long-run*" (p.80; emphasis added).

Annex A-4.2

Lag Selection in the VAR Model

Annex Table A-4.2.1

AIC Values for Selecting the Order of the VAR Model

Order	*VAR 1* *CRR, AD, Y, P*	*VAR 2* *CRR, BC, Y, P*	*VAR 3* *CRR, INVA, Y, P*
(1)	*(2)*	*(3)*	*(4)*
12	1239.2	1198.8	1167.4
11	1222.1	1188.5	1160.5
10	1221.2	1191.3	1161.9
9	1223.6	1191.5	1158.0
8	1230.9	1198.6	1162.3
7	1231.8	1199.5	1164.0
6	1228.7	1196.7	1168.6
5	1239.8	1202.8	1178.1
4	1241.7	1207.1	1184.9
3	1238.2	1212.7	1187.0
2	1243.1	1216.1	1187.8
1	1238.7	1211.9	1178.5
0	237.5	235.5	195.0

Annex A-4.3

Generalised Impulse Response Function: A Digression

A major critique against orthogonalised Impulse Reponse Functions (IRFs) is that these are sensitive to ordering. It is in this context that Pesaran and Shin (1998) proposed a generalised impulse response function, which is invariant to ordering.

Pesaran and Shin (1998) considered the *augmented* vector autoregressive model,

(A4.3.1) $$x_t = \sum_{i=1}^{p} \Phi_i x_{t-i} + \Psi w_t + \varepsilon_t, \quad t=1,2,\ldots,T$$

where $x_t = (x_{1t}, x_{2t}, \ldots, x_{mt})'$ is an $m\times 1$ vector of jointly determined dependent variables, w_t is an $q\times 1$ vector of deterministic and/or exogenous variables, and $\{\Phi_i, i=1, 2,\ldots,p\}$ and ψ are $m\times m$ and $m\times q$ coefficient matrices.

Under the standard assumptions, the above equation can be rewritten as the infinite moving average representation,

(A4.3.2) $$x_t = \sum_{i=0}^{\infty} A_i \varepsilon_{t-i} + \sum_{i=0}^{\infty} G_i w_{t-i}, \quad t=1,2,\ldots,T$$

where, the $m\times m$ coefficient matrices $\mathbf{A}_i$ can be obtained using a recursive relations of the form: $A_i = \sum \Phi_i A_{t-1}$, $i=1,2, \ldots$ with $\mathbf{A}_0 = \mathbf{I}_m$ and $\mathbf{A}_i = 0$ for $i<0$, and $\mathbf{G}_i = \mathbf{A}_i \psi$.

These assumptions are as follows:

- Assumption 1: $E(\varepsilon_t) = 0$, $E(\varepsilon_t \varepsilon_t') = \Sigma$ for all t, where $\Sigma = \{\sigma_{ij}$, $i, j=1, 2,\ldots,m\}$ is an $m \times m$ positive definite matrix, $E(\varepsilon_t \varepsilon_{t}') = 0$ for all $t = t'$ and $E(\varepsilon_t | w_t) = 0$.
- Assumption 2: All the roots of $\left| I_m - \Sigma_i \Phi_i z^i \right| = 0$ fall outside the unit circle.
- Assumption 3: $x_{t''1}, x_{t''2}, \ldots, x_{t''p}, w_t$, $t = 1, 2,\ldots,T$, are not perfectly collinear.

Since, an impulse response function measures the time profile of the effect of shocks at a given point in time on the (expected) future values of variables in a dynamical system, according to Pesaran and Shin (1998), the best way to describe an impulse response is to view it as the outcome of a 'conceptual' experiment in which the time profile of the effect of a hypothetical $m\times 1$ vector of shocks of size

$\delta=(\delta_1,...,\delta_m)'$, say, hitting the economy at time *t* is compared with a base-line profile at time *t*+*n*, given the economy's history.

Pesaran and Shin (1998) pointed out three main issues in this regard:

- The types of shocks hitting the economy at time *t*;
- the state of the economy at time *t*–1 before being shocked; and
- the types of shocks expected to hit the economy from *t*+1 to *t*+*n*.

Denoting the known history of the economy up to time *t*–1 by the non-decreasing information set Ω_{t-1}, the generalised impulse response function of $\boldsymbol{x}_t$ at horizon *n* is defined by (Koop *et al*, 1996)

$$\text{(A4.3.3)} \qquad GI_x(n,\delta,\Omega_{t-1})=E(x_{t+n}|\varepsilon_t=\delta,\Omega_{t-1})-E(x_{t+n}|,\Omega_{t-1})$$

Using (A4.3.3) in (A4.3.2), we have $GI_x(n,\delta,\Omega_{t-1})=A_n\delta$, which is independent of Ω_{t-1}, but depends on the composition of shocks defined by δ.

It will be pertinent to compare the approach of the orthogonalised and the generalised impulse response function. The traditional approach, *a la* Sims (1980) is to resolve the problem surrounding the choice of δ by using the Cholesky decomposition of $\Sigma, PP'=\Sigma$, where **P** is an *m*×*m* lower triangular matrix. Then, (A4.3.2) can be rewritten as,

$$\text{(A4.3.4)} \quad x_t=\sum_{i=0}^{\infty}(A_iP)(P^{-1}\varepsilon_{t-i})+\sum_{i=0}^{\infty}G_iw_{t-i}=\Sigma(A_iP)\xi_{t-i}+\sum_{i=0}^{\infty}G_iw_{t-i}\ t=1,2,...,T$$

such that $\xi_t=P^{-1}\varepsilon_t$ are orthogonalised; namely, $E(\xi_t\xi_t'=I_m$. Hence, the m×1 vector of the orthogonalised impulse response function of a unit shock to the jth equation on $\mathbf{x}_{t+n}$ is given by,

$$\text{(A4.3.5)} \qquad \Psi_j^o=A_nPe_j, n=0,1,2,.$$

where e_j is an *m*×1 selection vector with unity as its *j*th element and zeros elsewhere.

An alternative approach would be to use (A4.3.3) directly, but instead of shocking all the elements of ε_t we could choose to shock only one element, say its *j*th element, and integrate out the effects of other shocks using an assumed or the historically observed distribution of the errors. In this case we have:

$$\text{(A4.3.6)} \qquad GI_x(n,\delta_j,\Omega_{t-1}) = E(x_{t+n}|\varepsilon_t = \delta_j,\Omega_{t-1}) - E(x_{t+n}|\Omega_{t-1})$$

Assuming that ε_t has a multivariate normal distribution, Pesaran and Shin (1998) has proved that:

$$\text{(A4.3.7)} \qquad E(\varepsilon_t|\varepsilon_{jt} = \delta_j) = (\sigma_{1j},\sigma_{2j},.....\sigma_{mj})'\sigma_{jj}^{-1}\delta_j = \Sigma e_j\sigma_{jj}^{-1}\delta_{jj}$$

In such a set-up the $m\times 1$ vector of the (unscaled) generalised impulse response of the effect of a shock in the *j*th equation at time *t* on x_{t+n} is given by

$$\text{(A4.3.8)} \qquad \frac{A_n\Sigma e_j}{\sqrt{\sigma_{jj}}}\left(\frac{\delta_j}{\sqrt{\sigma_{jj}}}\right), n = 0,1,2,........$$

If we setting $\delta_j=(\delta_{jj})^{-1/2}$, the scaled generalised impulse response function, which measures the effect of one standard error shock to the jth equation at time t on expected values of **x** at time t+n, is given by,

$$\text{(A4.3.9)} \qquad \Psi_j^g(n) = \sqrt{\frac{1}{\sigma_{jj}}}A_n\Sigma e_j; \quad n = 0,1,2,.........$$

Annex A-4.4

Time Series Properties of the Variables

Annex Table A-4.4.1

Time Series Properties of the Level Variables

	CRR	*AD*	*BC*	*INVA*	*Y*	*P*
	Includes an intercept but not a trend					
(1)	(2)	(3)	(4)	(5)	(6)	(7)
DF	0.100	-0.250	0.234	0.613	-1.083	-2.221
ADF(1)	-0.015	-0.264	0.243	0.797	-0.367	-2.309
ADF(2)	-0.038	-0.300	0.214	0.915	-0.206	-2.388
ADF(3)	-0.056	-0.440	0.227	0.752	-0.282	-2.472
ADF(4)	0.012	-0.552	0.270	0.698	-0.193	-2.629
ADF(5)	-0.114	-0.612	0.361	0.725	-0.033	-2.774
ADF(6)	-0.463	-0.260	0.356	0.742	0.031	-2.917
ADF(7)	-0.512	-0.319	0.393	0.921	0.096	-3.215
ADF(8)	-0.588	-0.403	0.555	0.953	0.197	-3.461
ADF(9)	-0.475	-0.426	0.567	1.008	0.149	-3.759
ADF(10)	-0.478	-0.547	0.442	0.866	0.101	-4.196
ADF(11)	-0.552	-0.599	0.435	0.856	-0.804	-5.118
ADF(12)	-0.429	-0.527	-0.001	0.890	-0.599	-1.371
	Includes an intercept and a trend					
	(8)	(9)	(10)	(11)	(12)	(13)
DF	-2.081	-4.069	-2.916	-1.798	-7.486	-3.582
ADF(1)	-2.247	-3.869	-2.864	-1.392	-5.242	-3.476
ADF(2)	-2.288	-3.621	-3.363	-1.151	-4.995	-3.379
ADF(3)	-2.322	-2.544	-3.301	-1.502	-5.718	-3.292
ADF(4)	-2.242	-1.997	-2.971	-1.652	-5.685	-3.169
ADF(5)	-2.408	-1.806	-2.452	-1.600	-4.550	-3.097
ADF(6)	-2.962	-3.297	-3.326	-1.582	-4.109	-3.019
ADF(7)	-3.097	-3.133	-2.741	-1.144	-3.529	-2.875
ADF(8)	-3.295	-2.783	-2.095	-1.077	-2.513	-2.820
ADF(9)	-3.164	-2.757	-2.083	-0.937	-1.839	-2.799
ADF(10)	-3.231	-2.256	-2.348	-1.338	-1.666	-2.823
ADF(11)	-3.440	-2.052	-2.388	-1.383	-0.359	-2.974
ADF(12)	-3.294	-2.352	-3.363	-1.260	-1.277	-2.097

Note: : (1) Excepting CRR all variables are in log. (2) For the level variables, the 95 per cent critical values for the ADF are -2.88 and -3.44 for the regressions with an intercept and with an intercept and trend, respectively.

Annex Table A-4.4.2

Time Series Properties of the Annualised First Difference Variables

	Δ_{12} CRR	Δ_{12} AD	Δ_{12} BC	Δ_{12} INVA	Δ_{12} Y	Δ_{12} P
	Includes an intercept but not a trend					
(1)	(2)	(3)	(4)	(5)	(6)	(7)
DF	-10.701	-3.743	-2.453	-3.052	-4.646	-2.502
ADF(1)	-7.769	-3.175	-2.493	-2.530	-3.187	-2.779
ADF(2)	-6.378	-3.366	-3.131	-2.200	-2.8[illegible]4	-2.790
ADF(3)	-5.899	-2.988	-3.282	-2.583	-2.776	-2.718
ADF(4)	-4.782	-3.198	-3.653	-2.814	-2.494	-2.775
ADF(5)	-3.451	-3.772	-3.529	-3.296	-2.663	-2.767
ADF(6)	-3.197	-4.852	-4.540	-3.702	-2.568	-2.891
ADF(7)	-2.933	-4.472	-4.591	-3.581	-2.633	-3.033
ADF(8)	-3.045	-4.227	-4.590	-3.441	-2.612	-3.008
ADF(9)	-2.934	-4.634	-4.805	-2.866	-2.679	-3.142
ADF(10)	-2.711	-4.096	-4.678	-3.390	-2.486	-3.031
ADF(11)	-2.841	-4.388	-4.771	-4.047	-2.745	-2.649
ADF(12)	-2.797	-3.033	-2.877	-2.112	-2.202	-2.494
	Includes an intercept and a trend					
	(8)	(9)	(10)	(11)	(12)	(13)
DF	-10.691	-3.745	-2.403	-3.202	-4.662	-2.476
ADF(1)	-7.770	-3.166	-2.442	-2.683	-3.213	-3.025
ADF(2)	-6.385	-3.362	-3.113	-2.353	-2.921	-3.083
ADF(3)	-5.913	-2.985	-3.273	-2.738	-2.803	-2.988
ADF(4)	-4.792	-3.196	-3.669	-2.977	-2.524	-3.139
ADF(5)	-3.439	-3.770	-3.547	-3.479	-2.687	-3.170
ADF(6)	-3.181	-4.850	-4.634	-3.912	-2.592	-3.464
ADF(7)	-2.909	-4.483	-4.721	-3.805	-2.655	-3.824
ADF(8)	-3.028	-4.246	-4.763	-3.679	-2.633	-3.868
ADF(9)	-2.915	-4.652	-5.057	-3.089	-2.697	-4.253
ADF(10)	-2.684	-4.127	-4.988	-3.648	-2.506	-4.224
ADF(11)	-2.824	-4.423	-5.152	-4.346	-2.752	-3.562
ADF(12)	-2.780	-3.075	-3.160	-2.403	-2.223	-3.329

Note : For the differenced variables, the 95 per cent critical values for the ADF are -2.88 and -3.44 for the regressions with an intercept and with an intercept and trend, respectively.

Annex A-4.5

Presence of Seasonal Unit Roots in the Data

A seasonal series is one which has a spectrum with distinct peaks at the seasonal frequencies, q =(2pj/s), j = 1, 2, ..., s-1, where s is the number of seasons in the year. If data are quarterly, then the frequencies of interest are at 0, ¼, ½, and ¾ cycles, or q=0, p/2, p, and 3p/2. An integrated series is one that has an infinite mass in its spectrum at some frequency, q. In contrast, the spectrum of a stationary series is finite, but non-zero, at all frequencies. If a seasonal series has a unit root at 'all' of its frequencies, it is said to be 'seasonally integrated', or SI(s), and it needs to be s-differenced to make it stationary.

Beaulieu and Miron (1993) extended, for monthly data, the approach developed by Hylleberg, Engle, Granger and Yoo (1990), for finding out the presence for seasonal unit roots in the quarterly data. In order to appreciate the Beaulieu and Miron (1993) methodology, we may note that the polynomial $(1\text{-}B)^{12}$ has the following 12 roots, *viz.*, ± 1, $\pm i$, $-\frac{1}{2}(1 \pm \sqrt{3i})$, $\frac{1}{2}(1 \pm \sqrt{3i})$, $-\frac{1}{2}(\sqrt{3} \pm i)$, $\frac{1}{2}(\sqrt{3} \pm i)$ corresponding to the frequencies 0, π, $\pm\pi/2$, $\pm 2\pi/3$, $\pm\pi/3$, $\pm 5\pi/6$, and $\pm\pi/6$. It may be noted that while out of all these 12 roots, only the root +1 corresponds to the conventional unit root, all others are seasonal unit root.

The procedure computes seasonal unit roots for any series Y_t from the following regression equation, *viz.*,

(A4.5.0) $$\phi(L)Y_{13,t} = a + \sum_{k=1}^{12} \pi_k Y_{k,t-1} + \text{Trend} + \text{Seasonal Dummies}$$

where, $\phi(L)$ is chosen such that the residuals are white noise, and Y_1, ..., Y_{13} are defined as follows where (with L is the lag operator, i.e., $L^k X_t = X_{t-k}$):

(A4.5.1) $$Y_{1,t} = (1+L+L^2+L^3+L^4+L^5+L^6+L^7+L^8+L^9+L^{10}+L^{11})Y_t$$

(A4.5.2) $$Y_{2,t} = -(1-L+L^2-L^3+L^4-L^5+L^6-L^7+L^8-L^9+L^{10}-L^{11})Y_t$$

(A4.5.3) $$Y_{3,t} = -(L-L^3+L^5-L^7+L^9-L^{11})Y_t$$

(A4.5.4) $$Y_{4,t} = -(1-L^2+L^4-L^6+L^8-L^{10})Y_t$$

(A4.5.5) $Y_{5,t} = -\frac{1}{2}(1+L-2L^2+L^3+L^4-2L^5+L^6+L^7-2L^8+L^9+L^{10}-2L^{11})\ Y_t$

(A4.5.6) $Y_{6,t} = (\sqrt{3}/2)\ (1-L+L^3-L^4+L^6-L^7+L^9-L^{10})Y_t$

(A4.5.7) $Y_{7,t} = \frac{1}{2}\ (1-L-2L^2-L^3+L^4+2L^5+L^6-L^7-2L^8-L^9+L^{10}+2L^{11})Y_t$

(A4.5.8) $Y_{8,t} = -(\sqrt{3}/2)\ (1+L-L^3-L^4+L^6+L^7-L^9-L^{10})Y_t$

(A4.5.9) $Y_{9,t} = -\frac{1}{2}\ (\sqrt{3}-L+L^3 - \sqrt{3}\ 3L^4+2L^5 - \sqrt{3}L^6+L^7-L^9+\sqrt{3}L^{10}-2L^{11})Y_t$

(A4.5.10) $Y_{10,t} = \frac{1}{2}(1-\sqrt{3}L+2L^2 - \sqrt{3}L^3+L^4-L^6 + \sqrt{3}L^7-2L^8+\sqrt{3}L^9 - L^{10})Y_t$

(A4.5.11) $Y_{11,t} = \frac{1}{2}(\sqrt{3} + L-L^3 - \sqrt{3}L^4-2L^5 -\sqrt{3}L^6-L^7+L^9+\sqrt{3}L^{10}+L^{11})Y_t$

(A4.5.12) $Y_{12,t} = -\frac{1}{2}(1 + \sqrt{3}L+2L^2 + \sqrt{3}L^3+L^4-L^6 - \sqrt{L}^7-2L^8 - \sqrt{3}L^9-L^{10})Y_t$

(A4.5.13) $Y_{13,t} = (1-L^{12})Y_t$

Depending upon the data generating process one can include a time trend and seasonal dummies in the above regression equation. Figures given in Annex Table A-4.5.1 reports the t and F statistics associated with coefficients $\pi_1, \ldots \pi_{12}$. Comparing them with the critical values provided by Beaulieu and Miron (1993) the presence of seasonal unit roots is rejected for all the series for almost all the frequencies. Thus, on the whole we reject the presence of seasonal unit roots at most of the seasonal frequencies.

Annex Table A-4.5.1

Seasonal Unit Root Tests: Results from Beaulieu-Miron Tests

Roots	*CRR*	*AD*	*BC*	*INVA*	*Y*	*P*
(1)	*(2)*	*(3)*	*(4)*	*(5)*	*(6)*	*(7)*
$t(\pi_1)$	-5.53	-3.34	-4.83	-3.84	-2.26	-8.57
$t(\pi_2)$	-2.98	-1.42	-1.42	-1.86	-2.38	-2.48
$t(\pi_3)$	-3.76	-2.36	-3.98	-3.81	-3.85	-2.93
$t(\pi_4)$	-3.52	-3.52	-2.84	-3.4	-1.09	-2.75
$t(\pi_5)$	-3.76	-1.94	-2.79	-3.16	-3.67	-3.09
$t(\pi_6)$	1.42	0.83	0.62	1.62	0.43	2.01
$t(\pi_7)$	-3.05	-1.94	-1.47	-4.48	-3.11	-3.19
$t(\pi_8)$	-3.56	-1.75	-2.43	-3.04	-1.35	-4.19
$t(\pi_9)$	-4.70	-3.4	-4.79	-3.79	-2.96	-3.32
$t(\pi_{10})$	2.02	-0.23	-0.32	1.07	0.39	0.36
$t(\pi_{11})$	-3.37	-2.54	-2.17	-2.07	-1.07	-5.43
$t(\pi_{12})$	-4.09	-4.84	-3.99	-3.64	-3.99	-3.33
$F(\pi_3, \pi_4)$	13.33	10.54	14.32	15.51	8.13	8.91
$F(\pi_5, \pi_6)$	7.75	2.30	4.12	6.58	6.84	7.35
$F(\pi_7, \pi_8)$	11.46	3.70	4.23	18.18	6.10	15.68
$F(\pi_9, \pi_{10})$	13.84	5.81	11.57	7.76	4.48	5.60
$F(\pi_{11}, \pi_{12})$	14.49	14.23	10.02	8.06	8.11	22.33

Note : (1) Auxiliary regressions include a constant, trend and seasonal dummies.

(2) For 240 observations, at 1 per cent, the critical values from the distribution of test statistics for seasonal unit roots, as given in Beulieu and Miron (1993), p. 325 are as follows: $t(\pi_1) = -3.85$, $t(\pi_2) = -3.40$, $t(\pi_j) = -3.85$ for j = 3, 5, 7, 9, 11; $t(\pi_j) = -2.66$ for j = 4,6,8,10, 12; $F(\pi_i, \pi_j) = 8.79$ for i = 3, 5, 7, 9, 11, and j = 4, 6, 8, 10, 12.

5

The Impact of Monetary Policy

Does Ownership Matter?

5.1 Introduction

The aggregative evidence presented in Chapter 4 indicates that while a restrictive monetary policy seems to have contractionary effects on investments, its effect on credit is somewhat perverse during the initial period. But what could be the possible reason? In search of an explanation, this chapter, as well as the next, investigates the response of banks in a disaggregated context. The disaggregated context of banks is often couched in terms of some specific attributes of banks, such as, size, presence of liquid assets or degree of capitalisation. The theoretical and empirical literature finds that bank characteristics like size, liquidity, capitalisation, and ownership structure determine their loan supply response after a restrictive monetary policy action. These characteristics reflect the informational frictions that a bank faces when trying to attract new funds to finance its loan supply. Thus, the literature seeks to answer the following question: Is there any significant difference in the impact of monetary policy among different types of banks depending upon the attributes?

Given the time period (i.e., 1990s onwards) and techniques employed (i.e., VAR models), it is not possible to handle these attributes in a coherent framework in terms of their role in determining the bank-specific impact of monetary policy. It is important to note that the VAR models are handled within a span of fourteen years and, thus, high frequency data are required to take care of any problems relating to degrees of freedom for estimating economically meaningful relationships. These attributes could be revealed from a bank-wise data set, which in India is available only in the balance sheets, and, therefore, available at annual frequency.[1] Hence for the sake of feasibility the available level of disaggregation in the high-frequency data with respect to ownership had been explored here.

The basic source of high frequency data relating to commercial banks is a fortnightly return collected by the Reserve Bank of India (RBI) from all scheduled commercial banks under section 42(2) of the Reserve Bank of India Act, 1934 relating to maintenance of cash reserve ratio by all scheduled commercial banks. While the RBI collects the data from all scheduled commercial banks for the purpose of calculating the CRR balance that is to be maintained by the bank, the published data is, however, aggregative in nature.

Fortunately, a recent RBI publication (*Selected Banking Indicators, 1981-2002*) has published the fortnightly data relating to scheduled commercial banks with respect to a specific level of disaggregation, namely, ownership. Thus, data relating select items of assets and liabilities of the scheduled commercial banks are available for the following four groups of banks separately, *viz.*, (a) State Bank of India and its associates, (b) other public sector banks, (c) foreign banks, and (d) Indian private banks.

This chapter seeks to address the following question: does the impact of monetary policy differ across different bank groups (based on ownership)? While the immediate motivation for pursuing this issue has come from the availability of data, one may argue in the Indian context that apart from attributes like size or liquidity, the ownership profile of banks (i.e., whether public, private or foreign) may matter in determining the impact of monetary policy on banks' portfolio. After all, there could be differences between these types of banks in terms of sources of funds (including non-deposit resources). Illustratively, the State Bank of India, by virtue of undertaking Government business, has access to sizeable 'float funds'. The nationalised banks, likewise, are able to access low cost deposits owing to an extensive branch network, contrary to foreign banks,

1. Of late, banks started publishing quarterly financial results. There are, however, no standard data-base covering these quarterly results, which are typically un-audited in nature.

many of which being located in select urban centres, face stiff competition for deposits There is also a sizeable literature in India on whether or not ownership of banks is an important determinant of their efficiency and profitability.[2] Accordingly, the present chapter looks into the question of differential impact of monetary policy across bank groups, in terms of the broad aggregate balance sheets of the four types of commercial banks.

The rest of the chapter is organised as follows. Section 5.2 gives a brief survey of the relevant literature. Some related stylised facts of Indian banking are given in section 5.3. Section 5.4 is devoted to the impact of monetary policy on banks with varying ownership types and section 5.5 discusses some of the robustness exercise. Conclusions are presented in section 5.6.

5.2 Heterogeneity in Impact of Monetary Policy on Banks: A Select Review of Literature

Investigating the heterogeneity of the impact of central bank's policy actions on banks' balance sheet is largely an offshoot of the lending channel. The differential impact is often related to the size of the bank. After all, one of the basic pre-conditions for existence of credit channel of monetary transmission, *viz.*, absence of non-deposit resources like Certificates of Deposit (CDs), is likely to be true for a small bank than a large bank. In this context, the basic question that is put forward in the literature is: "Are banks ... Modigliani/Miller creatures whose lending is unaffected by changes in their deposit liabilities" (Kashyap and Stein, 1995)? In other words, the basic issue is whether the banks can alter their financing mix in response to a change in bank reserves and ultimately can avoid the contractionary impact on lending.

Kashyap and Stein (1995), in an influential paper on this issue, developed a two period model of bank portfolio behaviour in which banks have two assets, *viz.*, loans and securities, and two liabilities, *viz.*, deposits and non-deposit external finance. The key difference between loans and securities in their model is that unlike loans, securities can be costlessly liquidated in the second period. This, in

2. See Sarkar *et al.* (1998) on this issue.

essence, captures the notion that faced with a monetary contraction banks do have alternative sources of raising funds and that they need not necessarily cut loans or securities. However, the basic difference between small and large banks in their framework is that due to some informational asymmetry and related adverse selection problem, the marginal cost of external financing is an increasing function of the amount raised.[3] They have, thus, assumed that banks face a quadratic cost of raising non-deposit resources. In such a set-up, if there exists a homogenous loan market, then they have demonstrated that in response to a given contraction in deposits, lending volume of the small banks declines more rapidly than that of the large banks. Furthermore, in their two-period story, since any fall in securities holding in the first period would have to be made up from external finance in the second period, securities holding of a small bank declines more slowly than that of the large banks in response to a given contraction in deposits. However, when the postulate of a homogenous competitive loan market is replaced by a heterogenous loan demand, a number of complications arise. In such a set-up, depending on certain conditions, the loan rate for small banks could be more sensitive or less sensitive to monetary policy than the same for large banks. Thus, one can, no longer, get straightforward relative comparability of the loan supply effects of monetary policy across different sizes of banks.

In order to empirically test these predictions of their model, Kashyap and Stein (1995) used quarterly data (1976 Q1 to 1992 Q2) from the statutory reports submitted by the banks to the Fed, popularly known as the "Call Reports". They constructed asset grouping for big (those in 99 percentile) and small banks (those at or below 75, 90, 95 and 98 percentile). Measuring monetary policy by the changes in the federal funds rate, their basic result may be summarised as follows: While a contractionary monetary policy has similar effects on deposits across size-classes, such a policy actually increases lending by the large banks in the short run. However, in the case of securities holding by the banks the evidence is not as clear as it is in the case of loans.

3. The basic result as demonstrated in Stein (1998) is discussed in Chapter 2.

Kashyap and Stein (1997) looked at the European experience in this regard. They reviewed four different variables, *viz.*, (a) importance of small banks, (b) availability of non-bank finance, (c) bank health, and (d) importance of small firms, and assessed their cumulative effect on the predictive potency of the lending channel. Based on these qualitative evidence they found sufficient country-specificity in the role of banks in monetary policy. While Italy emerged as the country where strong lending effects were observed, for the United Kingdom this appeared to be the least.

Kashyap and Stein (2000) extended their analysis further to incorporate two more measures of monetary policy, *viz.*, (i) Boschen-Mills (1995) index of US monetary policy stance, and (ii) a Bernanke-Mihov (1998)—type of VAR based measure of monetary policy. Investigating the cross-sectional differences in the response of monetary policy, they stressed the importance of liquidity or 'buffer stock' held by each bank. Their principal finding was that monetary policy exerted a more powerful impact on banks with lower ratios of cash and securities to assets. They, however, pointed out that such buffer stocks would not be able to fully offset the effects of a contractionary monetary policy.

5.2.1 Ownership and Monetary Policy Impact on Banks

A recent strand of the literature extended the number of attributes of a bank that influence the impact of monetary policy actions. In this regard, there had been attempts to look into the ownership structure of the banking system.

In an interesting study, Agung (1998) assessed the implication of Kashyap-Stein (1995) predictions for Indonesia. Using monthly data for the period 1983 through 1995, Agung (1998) classified banks into three categories, *viz.*, (i) state banks which are large and foreign exchange licensed banks, (ii) private forex licensed banks, comprising domestic and foreign/joint banks, and (iii) private non-forex licensed banks. For each type of bank, a level VAR was constructed with the following variables: monetary policy indicator (proxied by one-month inter-bank interest rate), exchange rate, balance sheet variables, output, and prices. Comparing the response of balance sheet variables (to a monetary shock) significant differences were observed.

In particular, a monetary contraction failed to influence the lending by the state banks; however, small banks' lending declined. A similar pattern emerged even when the loans were disaggregated into investment and working capital loans.

The VAR analysis of Bank of Korea (1998) arrived at similar results. It considered a VAR for Korea over January 1987 through May 1994 with the following variables: changes in monetary base (monetary policy indicator), industrial production index, consumer price index, and a balance sheet variable (*viz.*, bank loans, cash and security holdings separately). Considering the six largest commercial banks under the 'large' category, and all other banks under 'medium and small sized' category, the impulse responses from the VARs revealed that a one per cent decrease in the monetary base seemed to have greater dampening effect on the lending volume and securities holdings of small and medium sized banks than those of the six largest banks.

But why would the response of banks vary depending on ownership? Pill (1997) argued that after an increase in domestic interest rates the incentive to raise funds abroad to finance domestic lending increases. Banks with better access to foreign sources of funds will enjoy a comparative advantage over banks that are dependent on domestic non-deposit funding. Foreign-owned banks are therefore likely to gain a larger market share in credit. Using the data for Spanish banks for the period, 1985-1996, Pill (1997) found that foreign-owned banks increased their lending to Spanish residents following an unanticipated rise in official interest rates.

de Bondt (1999) subdivided the sample of Dutch banks between foreign and domestic-owned banks, putting forward the hypothesis that foreign-owned banks might have better access to the international capital markets and other foreign sources of funds than much larger wholly domestic-owned banks. Monetary policy contractions may be tempered by the ability of international banks to borrow funds offshore. His study found stronger evidence for a lending channel when foreign banks are dropped from the sample.

Ashcraft (2001) discussed the importance of ownership structure for the working of the lending channel. He argued that affiliated banks tended to react less sensitively to increases in the monetary policy interest rate because of the fact that the presence of international capital markets tended to weaken the influence of the financial constraint faced by the subsidiary banks. He finds evidence for this hypothesis in an analysis of U.S. banking data on affiliated and non-affiliated banks.[4]

Arena, Reinhart, and Vazques (2006) presented interesting cross-country evidence in this regard. Based on a dataset comprising 1,565 banks in 20 Asian and Latin American countries during 1989-2001 and comparing the response of the volume of loans, deposits, and bank-specific interest rates on loans and deposits, to various measures of monetary conditions, they looked for systematic differences in the behaviour of domestic and foreign banks. Using differences in bank ownership as a proxy for financial constraints on banks, the paper found some evidence (though weak) that foreign banks have a lower sensitivity of credit to monetary conditions relative to their domestic competitors, with the differences driven by banks with lower asset liquidity and/or capitalisation. At the same time, the lending and deposit rates of foreign banks tended to be smoother during periods of financial distress. However, the differences of the foreign banks with domestic banks did not appear to be strong.

In terms of specifics, the present chapter is close in spirit to Agung (1998) or Bank of Korea (1998). In analytical terms, the Chapter constructs an Agung-type VAR model for India and tries to observe the differences in the impact of monetary policy on balance sheet variables like deposits or advances of different types of banks.

5.2.2 Indian Literature on Ownership of Banks

There is a large literature relating efficiency of Indian banks to their ownership. Empirical evidence from emerging markets suggests that the foreign banks, on average, perform better than the domestic banks and contribute to the improvement of operative efficiency of the banking sector as a whole. For India, Sarkar *et al.* (1998) found that while there was some evidence of private and foreign banks to be

4. Altunbas *et al.* (2002), using a variety of approaches, for different ownership types in the German banking market, found little evidence to suggest that privately owned banks are more efficient than their mutual and public-sector counterparts.

more efficient than their counterparts in the public sector, there had been improvements in the efficiency of public sector banks following their listing on the stock exchanges. Kumbhakar and Sarkar (2003) analysed the relationship between deregulation and total factor productivity (TFP) growth in Indian banking using a generalised shadow cost function approach. Decomposing TFP growth into a technological change, a scale, and a miscellaneous component, and using a disaggregated panel data analysis of public and private banks over 1985-1996 they found that despite a significant decline in regulatory distortions, the anticipated increase in TFP growth had not yet materialised. While private sector banks had improved their performance mainly due to the freedom to expand output, public sector banks did not respond well to the deregulation measures.

Ram Mohan (2003) evaluated the performance of public sector banks (PSBs) consequent to disinvestment by comparing the performance to stocks of PSBs with performance of the Sensex. Computing the relative returns of private sector banks with respect to the Sensex and using these to compare public and private sector bank performance, he found that PSB stocks' performance on an average was not significantly different from that of the Sensex or from that of private sector bank stocks. He, thus, concluded that listing on the exchanges, a profit orientation and a measure of autonomy could together produce improvements in performance.

Bhaumik and Piesse (2004), using bank-level data from India, for six years (1995-96 to 2000-01), have shown that while foreign banks had high credit-deposit ratios, the domestic banks had experienced much greater improvements in technical efficiency in the context of credit. The most significant improvements in technical efficiency were registered by the new domestic private sector banks. There was weak evidence that foreign banks' bullishness varied only with respect to blue chip borrowers. Together with recent literature on the Indian banking system, these results emphasise the dominance of competition rather than changes in ownership-mix as a policy objective for banks in an emerging market economy (Bhaumik and Dimova, 2004).

More recently, Mohan (2006a) found substantial Improvements in efficiency of the banking system reflected, *inter alia,* in a reduction in operating expenditure, interest spread and cost of intermediation in general. Interestingly, intermediation cost (i.e., the ratio of operating expense to total assets) witnessed a gradual reduction across various bank groups barring foreign banks during 1992-2004.

What then is the upshot of the discussion? Does private ownership lead to better firm performance than public ownership? The theoretical literature and the empirical evidence indicate that agency problems may affect the performance of publicly owned firms. At the same time, competition and hard budget constraints can induce state-owned firms to operate efficiently.

In India, banking sector reforms and deregulation were initiated in 1992. Accordingly, would the private banks be in a better position to cushion their portfolio from monetary policy actions? In fact, it is found that the improvement in profitability has been fairly broad-based cutting across bank groups. If we define 'Government-owned PSBs' as the set of select PSBs (Chapter 3), which were fully Government-owned at end-March 2002, and 'divested PSBs' as the set of select PSBs, which have accessed the capital market and consequently, lowered the Government holding in them, then an important highlight of the entire process has been the sharp improvement in the performance of divested public sector banks. This suggests that the issue of ownership is not as strong a factor in bank performance as is often made out to be. Rather, competition induced public-sector banks to reduce the performance gap that existed between them and both domestic private and foreign banks. Existing empirical evidence indicates, thus, that the ownership effect in Indian banking is at best weak.[5]

5.3 Some Stylised Facts

A digression on the different types of banks is in order at this juncture. As far as the taxonomy is concerned, attention is confined to four types of banks, *viz.*, 1) SBI and its Associates, 2) Nationalised Banks, 3) Foreign Banks, and 4) Other Scheduled Commercial Banks (private banks). The taxonomy is both from a functional viewpoint as well as dictated by availability of data.

---

5. See RBI (2003a) for details.

It should be noted that despite the differences in ownership, until the reforms, the private sector as well as the foreign banks were under a similar regulatory regime as the public sector banks. A key control variable in this connection was the RBI guidelines on branch expansion, which was allowed only as a percentage of total number of branches of a bank. Nevertheless, the thrust of the extent of social banking was relatively less on the private and foreign banks than on the public sector banks; consequently the number of rural branches was quite low both for these banks.

5.3.1 Public Sector Banks

After the nationalisation of 14 major commercial banks in 1969, banking had largely been a state-dominated activity in India. Subsequently in 1980, six more banks were nationalised. Of these public sector banks, State Bank of India (SBI) and seven of its associate banks, with earlier history of state control, are perhaps a class by itself.[6] Together they constituted the state controlled public sector banks accounting for more than three-fourth of total assets, in which the share of SBI alone was one-fourth. Apart from the SBI and its associates, other nationalised banks differ largely in size—at one end of the size spectrum, there are the large banks like Punjab National Bank or Bank of Baroda, and at the other end there are small banks like Vijaya Bank.

An interesting feature of these public sector banks needs to be taken into consideration. Over the 1990s, many of the public sector banks had been listed in the stock exchanges with a number of them having accessed the equity market more than once (Table 5.1). The initial infusion of capital by the Government in public sector banks, was followed by expanding the capital base with equity participation by the private investors. Nevertheless, the reduction in the share of the public sector banks in the aggregate assets of the banking sector during the last fifteen years had not been insignificant—from 90 per cent in 1991 to around 75 per cent in 2004. Furthermore, the share of wholly Government-owned public sector banks (i.e., seven banks where no diversification of ownership has taken place) sharply

6. The Imperial Bank of India was nationalised in 1955 to create the State Bank of India.

declined from about 90 per cent to 10 per cent of aggregate assets of all scheduled commercial banks during the same period (Reddy, 2005). As a result, the public sector banks in India are not fully Government owned and there are elements of private ownership in them. This mixed ownership aspect is an important feature of bank governance in India (Mohan, 2006a).

Table 5.1

Ownership Structure of Listed Public Sector Banks

(As at end-March 2004, per cent)

Bank	*Date of first trading in NSE*	*Government's/ RBI's Share (%)*	*Share of Others (%)*
(1)	*(2)*	*(3)*	*(4)*
State Bank of India	October 24, 1994	59.7	40.3
Oriental Bank of Commerce	February 8, 1995	66.5	33.5
Dena Bank	January 22, 1997	71.0	29.0
Bank of Baroda	February 26, 1997	66.8	33.2
Bank of India	May 7, 1997	69.5	30.5
Corporation Bank	December 5, 1997	57.2	42.8
State Bank of Bikaner & Jaipur	February 4, 1998	75.0	25.0
State Bank of Travancore	March 3, 1998	75.0	25.0
Syndicate Bank	December 27,1999	73.5	26.5
Indian Overseas Bank	December 13, 2000	61.2	38.8
Vijaya Bank	January 10, 2001	53.9	46.1
Andhra Bank	April 4, 2001	62.5	37.5
Punjab National Bank	April 26, 2002	80.0	20.0
Union Bank of India	September 24, 2002	60.9	39.2
Allahabad Bank	November 29, 2002	71.2	28.8
Canara Bank	December 23, 2002	73.2	26.8
UCO Bank	October 9, 2003	75.0	25.0
Bank of Maharashtra	April 12, 2004	76.8	23.2

Note: The Associate Banks of SBI which are yet to access the capital market are not included.

Source: Mohan (2005) and RBI. *Report on Trends and Progress of Banking in India*, various issues.

5.3.2 *Foreign Banks*

Foreign banks operate more than 200 branches in India. The entry of foreign banks is based on reciprocity, bilateral economic and political relations. An inter-departmental committee in the Central Government with a RBI representative approves applications for entry and expansion of foreign banks.

Based on the duration and the extent of their presence, there are two kinds of foreign banks in India. The first type, Citi Bank, Standard Chartered Bank or ABN Amro has a long history and reasonably large retail base. Illustratively, the ABN Amro Bank in India has more than 75 years of experience and is traditionally known as 'Diamond Financing Bank' with its first branch in India opened in 1920. The Citi Bank started its operation in India as early as in 1902. The Standard Chartered Bank, one of the oldest foreign banks in India, opened its first overseas branch in India in Calcutta in 1858. The second category of foreign banks started their operation much later and catered to specialised clientele. As for example, the first Indian branch of Dresdner Bank was opened in 1995 at Mumbai. Similarly, the Oman International Bank started its Indian operations at Mumbai in 1985. Subsequently it opened a branch at Cochin in 1994. These are typically a few branches bank catering to the trade-finance requirement of the home country.

Foreign banks in India are broadly subject to the same regulations as scheduled banks. They are permitted to accept deposits and provide credit in accordance with banking laws and RBI regulations. Currently nearly 30 foreign banks are licensed to operate in India. Foreign bank branches in India finance trade through their global networks. Foreign banks, however, are not required to open branches in rural areas, or to make loans to the agricultural sector.

5.3.3 Private Sector Banks

Apart from the public sector and foreign banks, there are a large number of private sector banks in India. After the nationalisation of 14 commercial banks in 1969, no new private banks were licensed by the RBI in the country until the early 1990s though there was no legal barrier on the entry of private sector banks. However, since 1993, following the financial sector reform programme, a number of new private sector banks have come into existence. While share of private banks had experienced a steady decline over the post-nationalisation period up to the early 1990s, expectedly their share increased since the mid 1990s with the initiation of financial liberalisation in India. Thus, within the Indian private banks, technically there are two types of banks; while the first type is the old private sector banks (like Federal Bank or Sangli Bank), the second type would be the new private banks (like ICICI Bank or IndusInd Bank) which came into being as a result of liberalisation of the branch licensing policy in the mid-1990s.[7]

5.3.4 Old Generation Private Sector Banks

Old generation private banks started out and continue to function as community banks. To begin with they were nurtured and developed by particular communities. The source of their business was also largely from their linkages to such communities. The exception here is Jammu and Kashmir Bank, which has grown largely because of the fact that the State Government's business has been conducted almost entirely through this bank. A major feature of these banks is the regional concentration. Most of these banks have nearly 75 per cent of their branches in the State they were founded in. A large number of them were founded in Tamil Nadu and Kerala; 10 such banks operate in both these States.

5.3.5 New Generation Private Sector Banks

New private sector banks have not been allowed to be set up in India till 1993. The Narasimham Committee Report of 1991 has envisaged a larger role for private sector banks in recognition of the need to introduce greater competition with a view to achieving higher productivity and efficiency of the banking system in India.

In order to introduce greater competition in the banking system, the RBI issued guidelines in January 1993 for the establishment of new banks in the private sector. The important guidelines in respect of the entry of new banks in the private sector apart from the required minimum paid-up capital of Rs.100 crore and the prudential accounting norms and the capital adequacy are:

- The banks should list of their shares on stock exchanges within a stipulated time frame of operations.

7. Since the aggregative data does not give the break-up between the old and new private banks, this chapter is unable to handle this bifurcation empirically.

- Their management set-up or liquidity requirements are to be governed by the provisions of the Reserve Bank of India Act, 1934, and the Banking Regulation Act, 1949, and also the directives, instructions/guidelines and advice given by the Reserve Bank.
- They would observe directions in regard to priority sector lending with modification allowed in the composition of such lending for an initial period of three years.
- The new banks shall not be allowed to set up a subsidiary or mutual fund for at least three years after its establishment.
- The banks shall make use of modern infrastructural facilities to provide good customer service as also institute a high powered customer grievances cell to handle customer complaints.
- They would maintain CRR on a continuous basis as stipulated by the regulatory requirement.

In 1994-95 out of 10 banks applied, 6 new private banks *viz.*, UTI Bank, Induslnd Bank, ICICI Bank, Global Trust Bank, Centurion Bank, and HDFC Bank, commenced banking business. Subsequently, in 1995-96, three more new private banks *viz.*, Times Bank, Bank of Punjab, and lDBI Bank became operational taking the total to 9. Two more 'in principle' approvals were granted over this period, both of which, *viz.*, Yes Bank and Kotak Mahindra Bank have been operational. The new private sector banks had been very aggressive in business expansion and were reporting higher profit levels. In certain areas, these banks had even outpaced the foreign banks. Owing to mergers, their numbers presently stand at 9.

The big player in this segment is ICICI Bank. The ICICI, originally established as a Development Finance Institution in 1955 at the initiative of the World Bank, the Government of India and representatives of Indian industry, promoted the ICICI Bank in 1994 as its wholly-owned subsidiary. Subsequently, in October 2001, the Boards of Directors of ICICI and ICICI Bank approved the reverse merger of ICICI and two of its wholly-owned retail finance subsidiaries, ICICI Personal Financial Services Limited and ICICI Capital Services Limited, with ICICI Bank. The merger was approved by shareholders of ICICI and ICICI Bank in January 2002, and by the

Reserve Bank of India in April 2002. Consequent to the merger, the ICICI group's financing and banking operations, both wholesale and retail, have been integrated into a single entity and it has emerged as the second largest bank in India.

5.3.6 Relative Shares of the Bank Groups

What has been the importance of the different bank groups? Towards this, Table 5.2 reports the relative share in three basic indicators, *viz.*, deposits, investments, and bank credit.

Table 5.2

Share of Different Bank Groups

(Per cent)

Variables	*Year*	*SBI Group*	*Nationalised Banks*	*Public Sector Banks*	*Private Banks*	*Foreign Banks*
(1)	(2)	(3)	(4)	(5)	(6)	(7)
Deposits	1970	26.1	58.9	85.1	6.1	8.8
	1980	27.1	64.9	92.0	5.2	2.8
	1990	28.8	63.8	92.5	3.9	3.5
	2000	28.1	54.5	82.6	5.9	11.4
	2004	26.7	50.2	76.8	5.0	18.2
Advances	1970	29.5	54.3	83.8	5.6	10.6
	1980	32.2	59.9	92.1	4.5	3.3
	1990	32.9	59.8	92.7	3.5	3.8
	2000	28.3	51.0	79.3	8.4	12.2
	2004	24.8	47.9	72.7	7.1	20.2
Investment	1970	28.8	57.5	86.3	5.7	8.0
	1980	29.5	62.3	91.8	4.7	3.5
	1990	30.2	62.5	92.7	3.9	3.4
	2000	32.2	50.8	83.0	6.1	10.8
	2004	32.4	46.6	79.0	5.1	15.8

Source: RBI. *Statistical Tables relating to Banks in India*, various issues.

Some broad trends emerge from all these indicators. First, over the twenty year period 1970-1990, there has been a steady increase in the extent of public ownership in the banking sector. Second, in line with the liberalisation programme and divesture in ownership of banks over the 1990s, there has been a reduction in the share of public sector banks. Third, *per contra*, the share of both private and foreign banks increased over the 1990s. Finally, notwithstanding the dilution of public ownership, public sector banks continue to account for more than three-fourths in all these basic banking variables.

5.3.7 Performance Indicators of the Bank Groups

As a prelude to the performance assessment of the Indian banking sector, one may note that the policy environment in the 1990s has been dominated by two primary concerns. First, in the first half of the decade, the focus of reforms was on deregulation and liberalisation of the banking sector which was guided primarily by the recommendations of the Committee on Financial System (Chairman: M. Narasimham) (1991). The measures aimed at deregulation could broadly be categorised under three heads: (a) lowering of statutory pre-emptions, (b) deregulation of interest rates, and (c) greater operational autonomy. Second, in the wake of incidents like those of the Barings Bank and the bank failures during the South-East Asian crisis, the second half of the 1990s saw increased awareness on regulation and supervision of banks. Hence there has been a greater concern with prudential norms for banks and risk management. Marking the second phase of reforms in the foreground of the banking crisis in South-East Asia, the *Committee on Banking Sector Reforms* (the Narasimham Committee II; Government of India, 1998) submitted its report in April 1998 and emphasised prudential measures like the increase in the capital to risk-weighted assets ratio (CRAR) to 10 per cent within a stipulated time period, introduction of market risk on Government securities, stricter norms for non-performing assets (NPAs) and provisioning requirements, and the introduction of asset-liability management and risk management guidelines. The focus consequently has shifted to enhancement of levels of transparency and standards of disclosure in respect of financial information provided by the banking sector.

What has been the relative performance of these bank groups? In terms of profitability parameters, there is very little doubt that the profitability of the banking system has improved during the 1990s (Table 5.3). The net profits of the scheduled commercial banks (SCBs) climbed steadily from 0.2 per cent of total assets as at end-March 1996 to 0.8 per cent as at end-March 2002. This increase in profitability was achieved despite a narrowing of spreads and higher provisions for non-performing loans.

Table 5.3

Important Parameters of Select Bank Groups

(Per cent)

Bank Group	*1995-96*	*1996-97*	*1997-98*	*1998-99*	*1999-00*	*2000-01*	*2001-02*	*2002-03*	*2003-04*
(1)	*(2)*	*(3)*	*(4)*	*(5)*	*(6)*	*(7)*	*(8)*	*(9)*	*(10)*
Operating Expenses/Assets									
SCBs	2.9	2.9	2.6	2.7	2.5	2.6	2.2	2.3	2.2
Public Sector Banks	3.0	2.9	2.7	2.7	2.5	2.7	2.3	2.3	2.2
Old Private Sector Banks	2.6	2.5	2.3	2.3	2.2	2.0	2.1	2.0	2.0
New Private Sector Banks	1.9	1.9	1.8	1.7	1.4	1.8	1.1	2.0	2.1
Foreign Banks	2.8	3.0	3.0	3.6	3.2	3.1	3.0	2.8	2.8
Spread/Assets									
SCBs	3.1	3.2	3.0	2.8	2.7	2.9	2.6	2.8	2.9
Public Sector Banks	3.1	3.2	2.9	2.8	2.7	2.9	2.7	3.0	3.1
Old Private Sector Banks	3.1	2.9	2.6	2.2	2.3	2.5	2.4	2.5	2.5
New Private Sector Banks	2.8	2.9	2.2	2.0	2.0	2.1	1.2	1.6	1.9
Foreign Banks	3.7	4.1	3.9	4.4	3.9	3.6	3.2	3.4	3.5
Net Profit/Assets									
SCBs	0.2	0.7	0.8	0.5	0.7	0.5	0.8	1.0	1.2
Public Sector Banks	-0.1	0.6	0.8	0.4	0.6	0.4	0.7	1.0	1.2
Old Private Sector Banks	1.1	0.9	0.8	0.5	0.8	0.6	1.1	1.2	1.2
New Private Sector Banks	1.9	1.7	1.6	1.0	1.0	0.8	0.4	0.9	1.1
Foreign Banks	1.6	1.2	1.0	0.7	1.2	0.9	1.3	1.6	1.7
Gross NPAs to Gross Advances									
SCBs	N.A.	15.7	14.4	14.7	12.7	11.4	10.4	10.5	9.0
Public Sector Banks	18.0	17.8	16.0	15.9	14.0	12.4	11.1	11.0	9.5
Old Private Sector Banks	N.A.	10.7	10.9	13.1	10.8	10.9	11.0	11.6	9.4
New Private Sector Banks	N.A.	2.6	3.5	6.2	4.1	5.1	8.9	10.4	8.8
Foreign Banks	N.A	4.3	6.4	7.6	7.0	6.8	5.4	5.5	5.2
Net NPAs to Net Advances									
SCBs	N.A.	8.1	7.3	7.6	6.8	6.2	5.5	5.2	3.8
Public Sector Banks	8.9	9.2	8.2	8.1	7.4	6.7	5.8	5.4	3.9
Old Private Sector Banks	N.A.	6.6	6.5	9.0	7.1	7.3	7.1	7.5	5.5
New Private Sector Banks	N.A.	2.0	2.6	4.5	2.9	3.1	4.9	5.0	3.9
Foreign Banks	N.A.	1.9	2.3	2.9	2.4	1.8	1.9	1.9	1.5
CRAR									
SCBs	N.A.	10.4	11.5	11.3	11.1	11.4	12.0	12.7	12.9
Public Sector Banks	8.7	10.0	11.6	11.3	10.7	11.2	11.8	12.6	13.2
Old Private Sector Banks	10.7	11.7	12.3	12.1	12.4	11.9	12.5	12.8	13.7
New Private Sector Banks	N.A.	15.3	13.2	11.8	13.4	11.5	12.3	11.3	10.2
Foreign Banks	N.A	N.A	10.3	10.8	11.9	12.6	12.9	15.2	15.0

Source: RBI. *Report on Trends and Progress of Banking in India*, various issues.

How was this increase in profitability made possible? While one expects that the competitive forces during a period of financial sector reforms will drive the profits down, competitive forces also resulted in making a firm more conscious about its cost structure, so as to improve its bottom line. In fact, in the Indian case, the improvement in profitability was primarily due to a combination of larger trading incomes and a curtailment in operating expenses, including the wage bill.

Expectedly, there were differences in profitability or efficiency indicators between these banks. As for example, in 1994-95, while the foreign banks employed 1.4 per cent of the total staff employed in the banking sector, with a 0.3 per cent of the total bank branches, their share in deposits was nearly 7 per cent. Similar trends exist for private sector banks too.

The improvement in the profitability of the banking system has been reinforced by an improvement in its health. The CRAR of the banking system, as at end-March 2004, worked out to 13.2 per cent of risk weighted assets, well above the stipulated 9 per cent. The ratio of net non-performing assets to net advances declined to 3.8 per cent as at end-March 2004 from 8.1 per cent as at end-March 1997. Admittedly, the improvement in CRAR partly reflected the recapitalisation of banks by the Government. At the same time, it is also true that a number of banks had been accessing the capital market for funds since the mid-1990s.

5.3.8 Portfolio Pattern

As the basic thrust of this chapter is to see whether the different bank groups react differently to a monetary shock, a discussion of the portfolio pattern of the different types of banks will be in order. To begin with, one may note that two major uses in the asset side are credit and investment, while bank credit consists of food and non-food credit, bank investments comprise investment in government securities, bonds/debentures/shares issued by public sector undertakings (PSUs), and private corporate sector and commercial paper. While the choice between the two alternative assets, credit and investment, depends on their relative risk and return, with the deregulation of interest rates on loans, and gradual reduction in CRR and SLR requirements, one would expect banks to alter their asset portfolios in favour of loans. However, there are views that the trends in credit and investment during 1992-93 through 2003-04 suggest otherwise (Tables 5.4, 5.5 and Annex Table A-5.1).

Table 5.4

Composition of Assets and Liabilities of Various Bank Groups

(As per cent of total assets/liabilities)

Bank Group	*Year*	*Capital and Reserves*	*Deposits*	*Borrowings*	*Other Liabilities and Provisions*	*Cash and Other Liquid Assets*	*Investments*	*Advances*	*Fixed Assets*
(1)	(2)	(3)	(4)	(5)	(6)	(7)	(8)	(9)	(10)
SBI and Associates	1992	1.7	65.7	8.2	24.4	11.9	25.7	46.7	15.7
	1995	3.6	72.1	6.7	17.7	14.9	33.5	41.2	10.3
	2000	4.6	76.2	3.2	16.0	17.0	36.0	38.4	8.7
	2004	5.1	78.8	3.1	13.1	9.7	45.1	40.1	5.0
Nationalised	1992	3.2	85.7	4.6	6.5	14.5	30.5	48.3	6.8
	1995	7.3	83.6	3.4	5.8	15.5	34.7	40.1	9.7
	2000	5.5	86.7	1.6	6.2	14.1	38.3	40.2	7.4
	2004	5.6	86.1	1.5	6.8	9.6	41.0	44.7	4.8
Private	1992	2.1	86.3	3.7	7.9	20.9	28.6	45.2	5.3
	1995	5.7	76.1	5.7	12.6	19.5	27.0	41.3	12.1
	2000	6.1	83.2	5.2	5.5	15.6	37.2	40.8	6.4
	2004	6.1	73.1	11.0	9.8	10.0	36.7	46.5	6.7
Foreign	1992	3.7	68.5	16.1	11.7	21.3	32.2	37.0	9.5
	1995	9.6	74.1	8.9	7.4	15.6	31.9	40.3	12.3
	2000	9.8	59.5	22.7	8.0	11.9	35.8	43.0	9.3
	2004	10.9	58.5	18.6	12.0	12.4	30.5	44.4	12.7

Source: RBI. *Report on Trends and Progress of Banking in India*, various issues.

Table 5.5

Portfolio Choice of Different Bank Groups: Growth Rates

(Per cent)

Variables	*Year*	*SBI Group*	*Nationalised Banks*	*Foreign Banks*	*Private Banks*
(1)	(2)	(3)	(4)	(5)	(6)
Deposits	1991-92	27.8	12.4	58.4	25.3
	1995-96	14.8	10.0	10.0	16.4
	2000-01	24.9	15.1	5.8	23.9
	2003-04	10.9	16.5	27.7	29.3
Credit	1991-92	7.0	5.4	29.2	20.5
	1995-96	23.1	13.1	43.4	36.0
	2000-01	16.4	15.4	21.9	23.5
	2003-04	15.9	15.0	15.2	21.5
Investment	1991-92	21.3	18.8	14.9	25.4
	1995-96	9.4	11.0	14.2	21.4
	1996-97	16.5	9.7	13.1	27.0
	2000-01	15.2	18.1	13.1	8.7
	2003-04	17.1	24.9	16.9	43.9

Source: RBI. *Report on Trends and Progress of Banking in India*, various issues.

Notwithstanding the year to year variations, the increasing importance of the private sector banks comes out clearly from all the indicators. Before we proceed further, it should be noted that the above aggregation in terms of the four-type classification camouflage any intra group heterogeneity. Illustratively, it may be noted that while these 27 state-owned banks faced similar policy parameters, there were significant size differentials. SBI alone accounted for more than one-fourth nearly of all the banking variables. Next to SBI, there are four to five large banks like Central Bank of India, Bank of India, Punjab National Bank, Bank of Boroda or Canara Bank, each of which accounts for nearly 5 per cent or more of the major banking variables. Most of the associates of SBI, when treated separately, are quite small. On the other hand, within the private sector banks, ICICI Bank accounts for a large share.

5.4 Impact of Monetary Shock on Different Types of Banks

5.4.1 Methodology and Data Base

In order to assess the impact of monetary policy on commercial bank balance sheet, the model used in Chapter 4 is adopted with one major modification, *viz.*, incorporation of bank-specific variables. Thus, to gauge the impact of monetary policy on balance sheet variables, we run a VAR of the following form:

$$(5.1)\quad X_t = G_o + \sum_{i=1}^{N} g_i X_{t-1} + \sum_{i=1}^{11} c_i D_i$$

with X_t = {MP_t, B^j_t, Y_t, P_t}; where MP_t is a measure of monetary policy stance, B^j_t is a balance sheet variable for the jth bank group (j= 1, .. , 4), and Y_t, P_t are real activity and prices, respectively. As already indicated, the focus was on B^j, *viz.*, deposits, advances and investment. Thus, a VAR is run corresponding to each choice of bank group (4 groups), and (ii) balance sheet variable (*viz.*, deposits, advances and investment), with all together 12 VAR models. The impact of MP_t on B^j_t has been sought to be described in terms of the impulse response (from a Choleski decomposition) of B^j from MP. The policy variable is placed first, followed by the balance sheet variables, and finally by the real GDP and prices.[8]

Data Base

As far as the banking data for the four types of banks (i.e., SBI and Associates, Public Sector Banks, Indian Private Banks and Foreign Banks) are concerned, these are culled out from *Selected Banking Indicators, 1981-2002,* published by the Reserve Bank of India. Subsequent data has been taken from the RBI website. As in the earlier chapter, the frequency of the data is monthly and the time period is 1990-91 through 2003-04, i.e., 14 years. However, for the purpose of running the VAR models, we have concentrated on the 12 year period 1992-93 through 2003-04.

---

8. However, in view of the fact that the correlation coefficients between the errors of various equations turned out to be low the ordering may not be of much significance.

5.4.2 Impulses from the Level VARs

The level VARs of the form (5.1), have been run for all the four types of banks, and for three banking variables, *viz.*, deposits, advances and investment. These 12 VARs generated 192 impulse responses functions (i.e., 16 IRFs from each VARs). Of these we confine our attention to an impulse of MP on B^j, and accordingly, the Figures below report a specific impulse response of a CRR shock on the balance sheet variable of a particular bank group, *viz.*, a) Figure 5.1 (with bank-group specific deposits), b) Figure 5.2 (with bank-group specific advances), and c) Figure 5.3 (bank-group-specific investments). In visual terms, we ask the following question: *is the impact of a CRR shock same/different across different bank groups?*

Figure 5.1

Impulse Reponses on Deposits of a CRR Shock

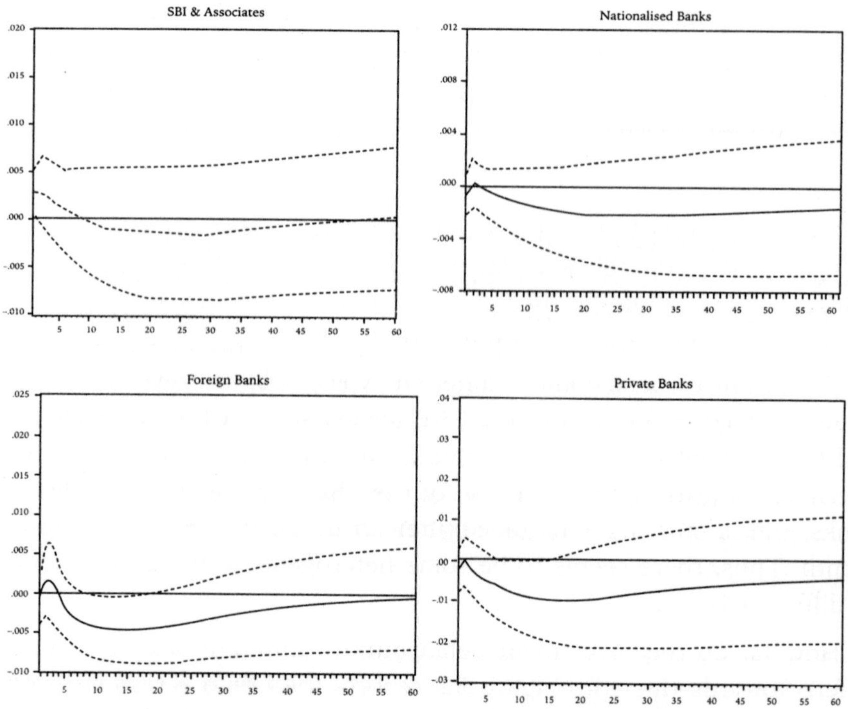

Figure 5.2

Impulse Reponses on Advances of a CRR Shock

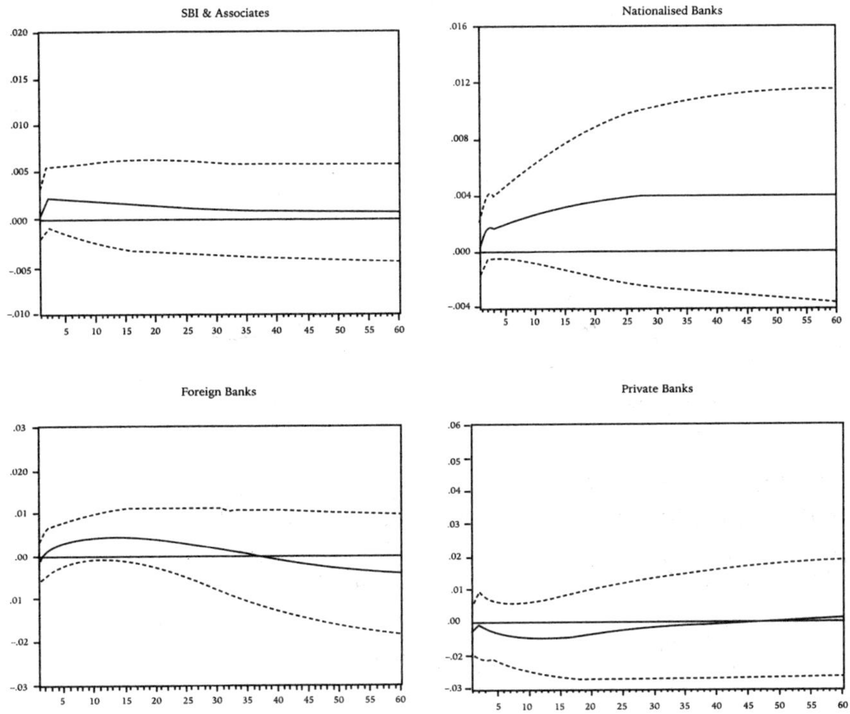

Figure 5.1 reports the impact of a CRR shock on the deposits of various types of banks. All the four Figures show a mild contractionary tendency in deposits. That is to say, the deposits behaviour was found to be reasonably invariant across bank groups.

The advances behaviour of different types of banks revealed more interesting patterns. In case of a CRR shock, advances of nationalised and foreign banks actually exhibited an increasing pattern during the initial 12 months horizon. In case of the SBI group as well as private banks, the impulses get flattened after an initial increase in the first month. Thus, there seems to be some heterogeneity in the behaviour of different banks.

How far do the investment behaviours of different sizes of banks differ? Towards this end, Figure 5.3 reports the impulse responses of

Figure 5.3

Impulse Reponses on Investment of a CRR Shock

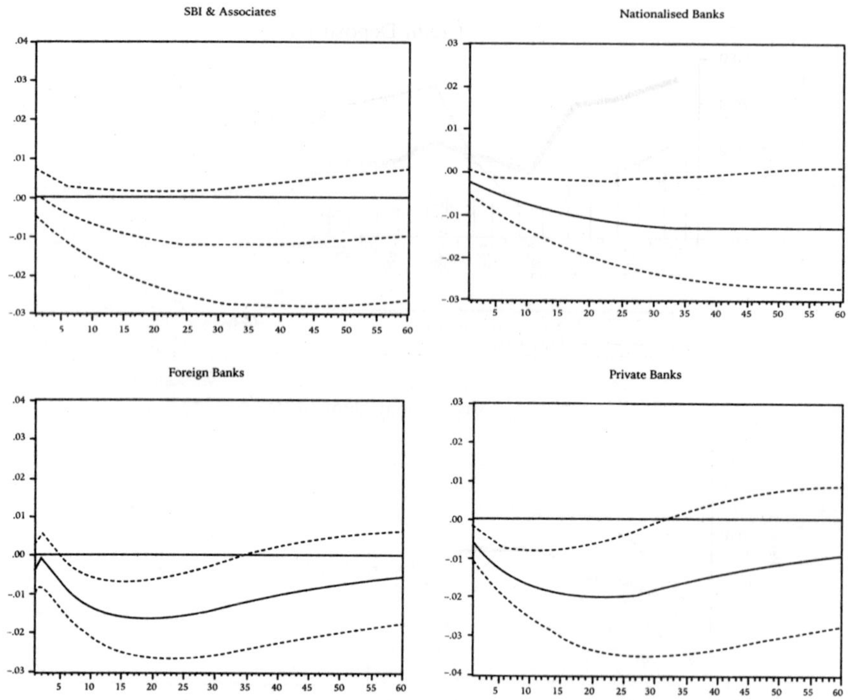

a CRR shock on investments of different types of banks. In general, the investment behaviour exhibited a downward trend.

How do we explain the differences in the impulses of advances and investment across bank groups? In this context, Figure 5.4 reports the credit-deposit ratios and investment-deposits ratios of SCBs. Note that SBI has experienced a steady decline in its credit-deposit ratio and almost an equally steady increase in its investment-deposit ratio. Almost a similar trend is noticeable for the nationalised banks as well. The same is not necessarily true for foreign and private banks.

But why had the investment portfolios experienced an upsurge? It may be noted that since 1996-97 there was an uniform downward trend in interest rates in G-Sec market—the weighted average of interest rate on Central Government securities came down from 12. 01 per cent in 1996-97 to 5.71 per cent in 2003-04 (Figure 5.5).

Figure 5.4

Credit-Deposit and Credit-Investment Ratios of SCBs

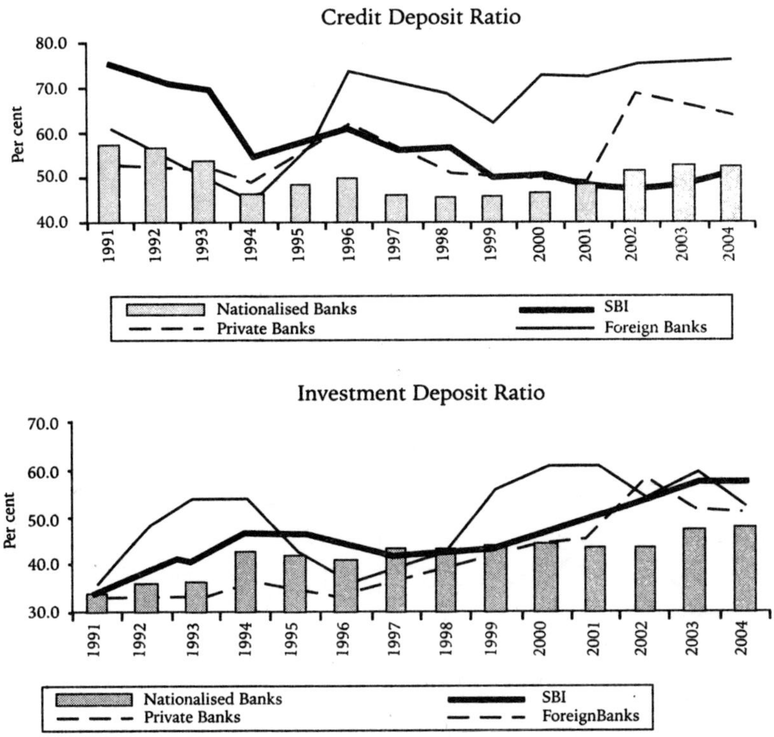

Figure 5.5

Weighted Average of Interest Rates on Central and State Govt. Dated Securities

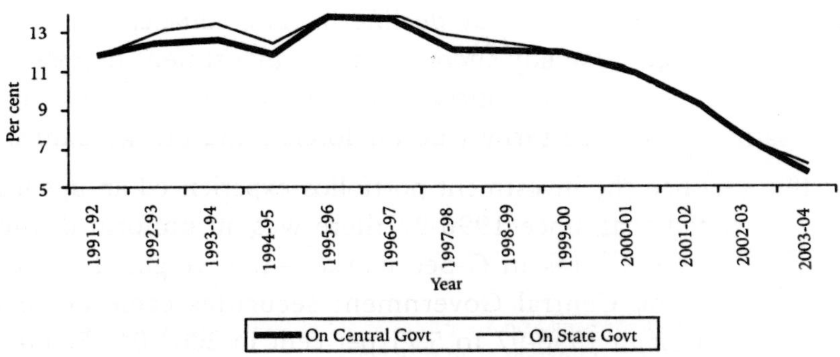

This, coupled with the adoption of the prudential norms, whereby G-Secs have zero risks as against the various credit risks associated with advances, could have given a positive impetus to the banks to hold G-Secs in a big way.

This does not mean all banks reacted in the same way to the twin factors of a downward interest rate cycle and prudential norms. To see this purely in the context of return profile of banks' portfolio, let us refer to the income of the banks to these two sources, *viz.*, advances and investment. We take the ratio of 'interest on advances' to 'advances' and the ratio of 'income on investment' to 'investment' as the relevant incomes from these two sources.[9] Figure 5.6 depicts these sources of

Figure 5.6

Operating Income from Advances and Investment

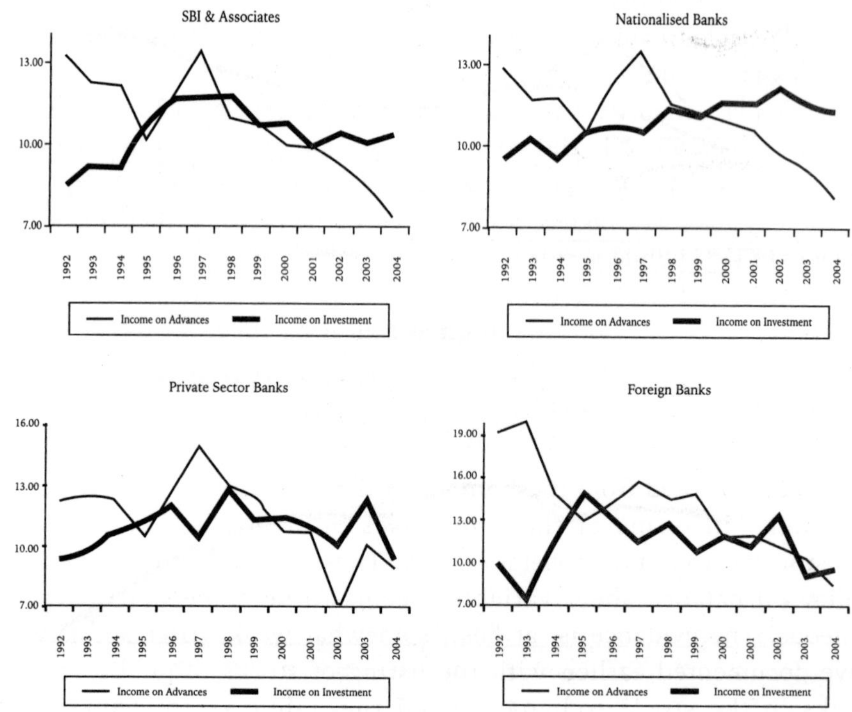

9. The income from investment has been taken net of profit/loss on sale of investments and profit/loss on revaluation of investments.

income for the four bank groups separately. While for nationalised banks, income from investment registered a steady increase and dominated the income on advances since 1998, for SBI and associates it is a much recent trend. It is only for the foreign banks that income on advances continued to dominate over that on investment even in recent years. This phenomenon, in some sense, is consistent with Banerjee, Cole, and Duflo (2004)'s hypothesis of credit squeeze on the part of the public sector banks or Mohan (2002)'s hypothesis of lazy banking; however, such hypothesis is not true for all types of banks. Furthermore, if one considers the investment portfolio of the SBI and its associates, by its sheer size (with nearly one-third of the total investment of all SCBs), the SBI group would not be able to off-load its Government without possibly a crash in the G-Sec market.

How do we interpret of bank group—specific advances behaviour? To begin with, it may be noted that there is some wedge between the behaviour of the private banks with other banks, which is dominated by smaller sized banks, notwithstanding the emergence of banks like ICICI Bank or HDFC Bank in recent years. How do the large banks differ *vis-à-vis* small banks in the Indian context? While no definitive answer can be offered in this connection, several conjectures may be put forward. First, it could be that the extent of non-deposit resources with the larger banks was higher. Secondly, by virtue of being the banker of many cash-rich public sector units large banks like SBI had access to a large amount of float funds. Thirdly, in non-metropolitan areas (i.e., where RBI is absent) SBI used to act as a clearing house for the banking sector in that area. Hence at any point of time SBI would have large surplus funds. Finally, due to its large export credit, larger banks had its refinance facilities from the Exim Bank, IDBI or RBI.

It may be noted from these impulses that there exists some group-specificity in terms of these impulses on deposits, advances or investments from any monetary shock. Thus, the impact of monetary policy on balance sheet variables seems to be somewhat heterogeneous. The evidence is, at best, somewhat weak. After all, as we have documented earlier, with the listing of stocks of public sector banks in the stock exchanges, even the public sector banks are exposed to market discipline. Besides, on the basis of size it could be difficult to distinguish between the ownership patterns. As the literature in this context has emphasised the role of capital and liquidity in this context, Figure 5.7 reports the trends in capital and cash in hand (as a proxy of liquidity), both as a percentage of assets.[10] The differences between bank groups are much more glaring in case of capital than liquidity.

Figure 5.7

Trends in Capitalisation and Liquidity

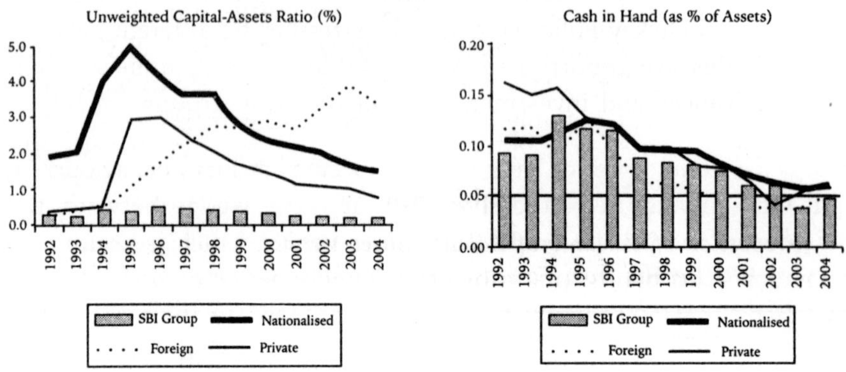

5.4.3 Variance Decomposition

Table 5.6 below reports the FEVD patterns, namely, the proportion of the three balance sheet variables, *viz.*, deposits, credit and investment that are explained by CRR shock for each of the four types of banks. The numbers reveal some heterogeneity—particularly in case of investment, where CRR shocks explains a large chunk of the forecast error variance of investment.

5.5 How Robust are these Results?

5.5.1 Sensitiveness of the VARs with respect to Ordering

As already pointed out, VAR impulses could be sensitive to ordering of variables. Annex Table A-5.2-A reports the correlation structure of the error processes of all the 12 VAR models. In general, the correlation between the balance sheet variable and CRR is found to be low. Hence,

10. This is merely the ratio of capital to assets, and hence is unweighted. Hence, it differs from CRAR.

it is unlikely that the impulse responses that we have discussed above will be influenced by the ordering of the variables.

5.5.2 Impulses from the Difference VAR

Time Series Properties of the Variables

The results reported so far corresponded to level VARs. In the earlier chapter, we have argued that the results of a VAR model are quite sensitive to the degree of difference. That is to say, a level VAR and a difference VAR may give distinct results.[11] Results from Dickey-Fuller and augmented Dickey-Fuller statistics for size-specific different balance sheet variables are reported in Annex Table A-5.3. It appears that deposits, advances and investments for all the bank groups are I(1).

Table 5.6

Proportion of Variance of Balance Sheet Variable Explained by CRR: Results from Forecast Error Variance Decomposition

Balance Sheet Variable	*Period*	*SBI Group*	*Nationalised Banks*	*Foreign Banks*	*Private Banks*
(1)	(2)	(3)	(4)	(5)	(6)
Deposits	1	3.45	0.35	0.09	0.64
	12	1.30	2.06	6.01	8.49
	24	1.47	5.76	12.85	15.54
	36	1.61	7.86	13.01	16.53
	48	1.44	8.55	11.56	15.63
	60	1.23	8.51	10.15	14.43
Credit	1	0.04	0.10	0.23	0.18
	12	2.25	5.66	4.04	1.46
	24	2.31	9.87	5.88	2.06
	36	2.12	12.80	3.89	1.78
	48	1.88	14.62	2.96	1.47
	60	1.65	15.63	3.22	1.31
Investment	1	0.00	1.59	0.97	5.52
	12	4.14	17.25	18.24	37.34
	24	13.64	31.02	42.59	52.62
	36	21.22	40.18	50.80	55.45
	48	25.61	45.40	51.82	53.57
	60	27.65	48.21	50.41	50.52

11. Note that while Agung (1998) took a level VAR, the variables in Kashyap and Stein (1995, 1997)'s various regression exercises were in first difference.

Impulses from the Difference VAR

Having established the order of integration of the variables, we ran VARs of the following form:

$$(5.2)\quad \Delta X_t = G_0 + \sum_{i=1}^{N} g_i\, \Delta X_{t-i} + \sum_{i=1}^{11} c_i D_i$$

With $\mathbf{X}_t$ = {CRR_t, B^j_t, Y_t, P_t}; where B^j_t is a balance sheet variable (i.e., deposits, advances and investment) for the jth bank group (j= 1, .. , 4), and Y_t, P_t are real activity and prices, respectively. As earlier we confine our attention to impact on ΔB^j out of a unit standard deviation shock in ΔCRR for all the four bank-groups. Figures 5.8, 5.9, and 5.10 report the impulse responses relating to deposits, advances, respectively for all the four bank groups.

Figure 5.8

Impulse Responses on Deposits of a CRR Shock in the Difference VAR

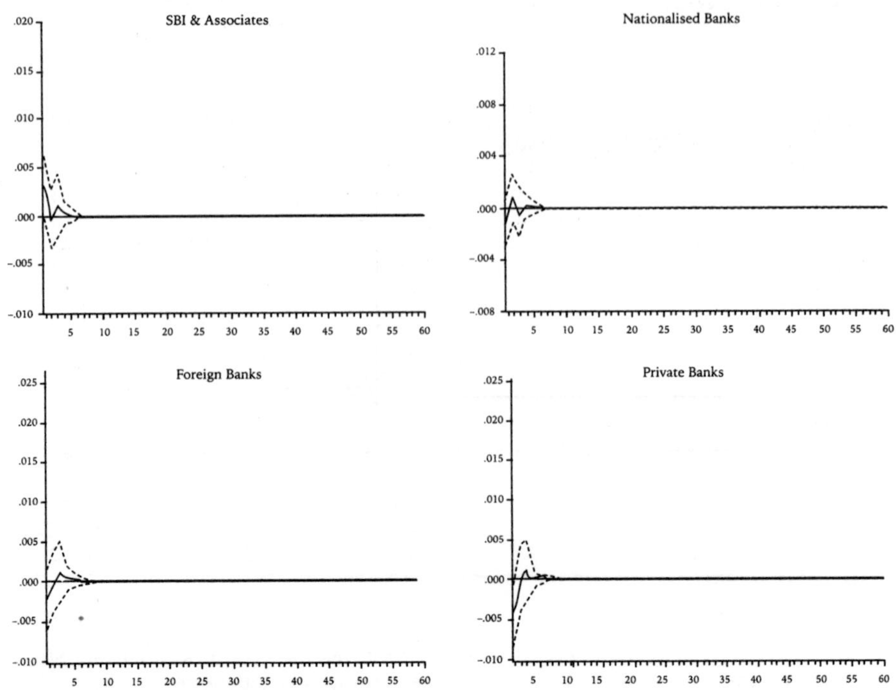

Figure 5.9

Impulse Responses on Advances of a CRR Shock in the Difference VAR

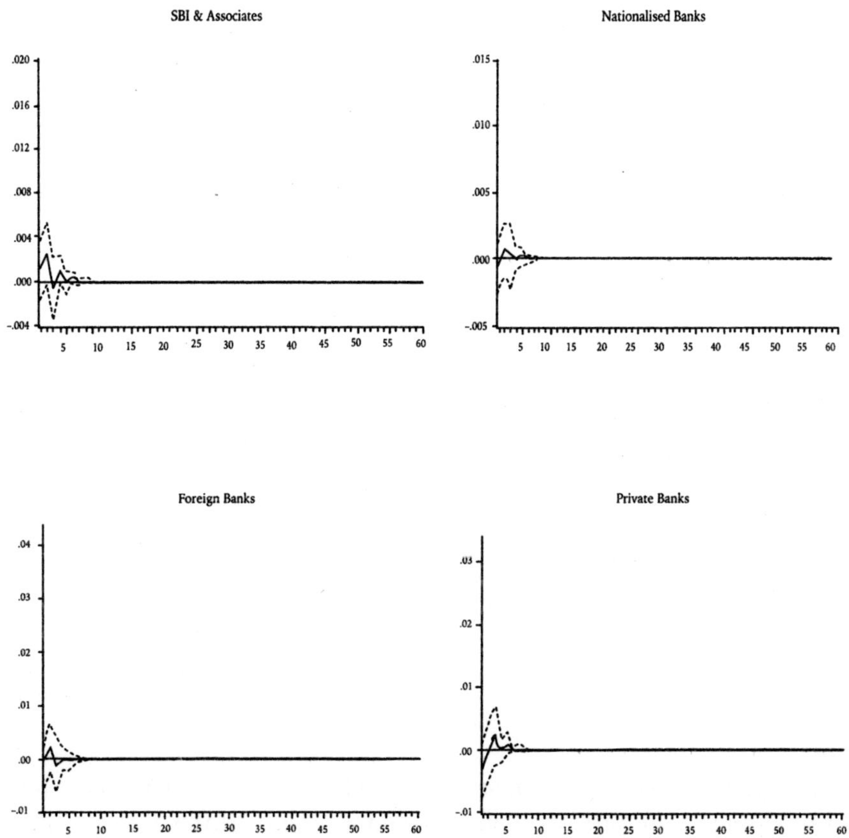

Figure 5.10

Impulse Responses on Investment of a CRR Shock in the Difference VAR

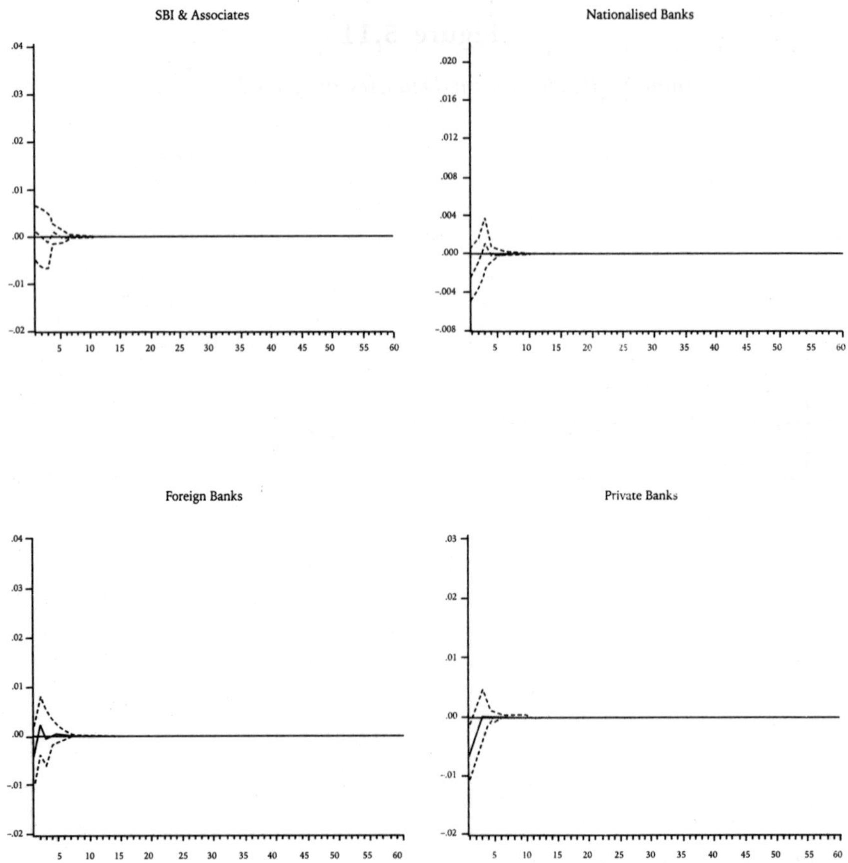

In general the perturbation in CRR seemed to have been smoothened out within a year's span. Some limited evidence of differential impact of monetary policy on banks' balance sheet is found in these impulses as well. As far as deposits are concerned, for all types of banks (excepting SBI and Associates), the impact is expansionary. For advances it is uniformly expansionary for all types of banks at least during the initial six months. The response of investment is dissimilar for the SBI and associates.

Figure 5.11

Impulse Responses on Deposits of a GRM Shock

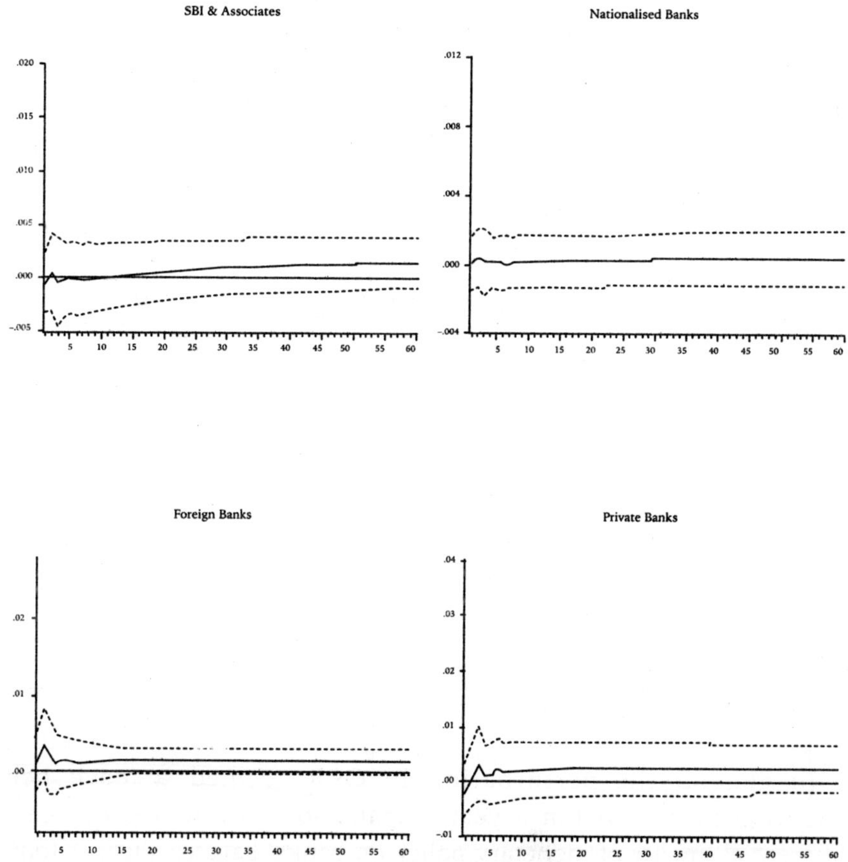

Figure 5.12

Impulse Responses on Advances of a GRM Shock

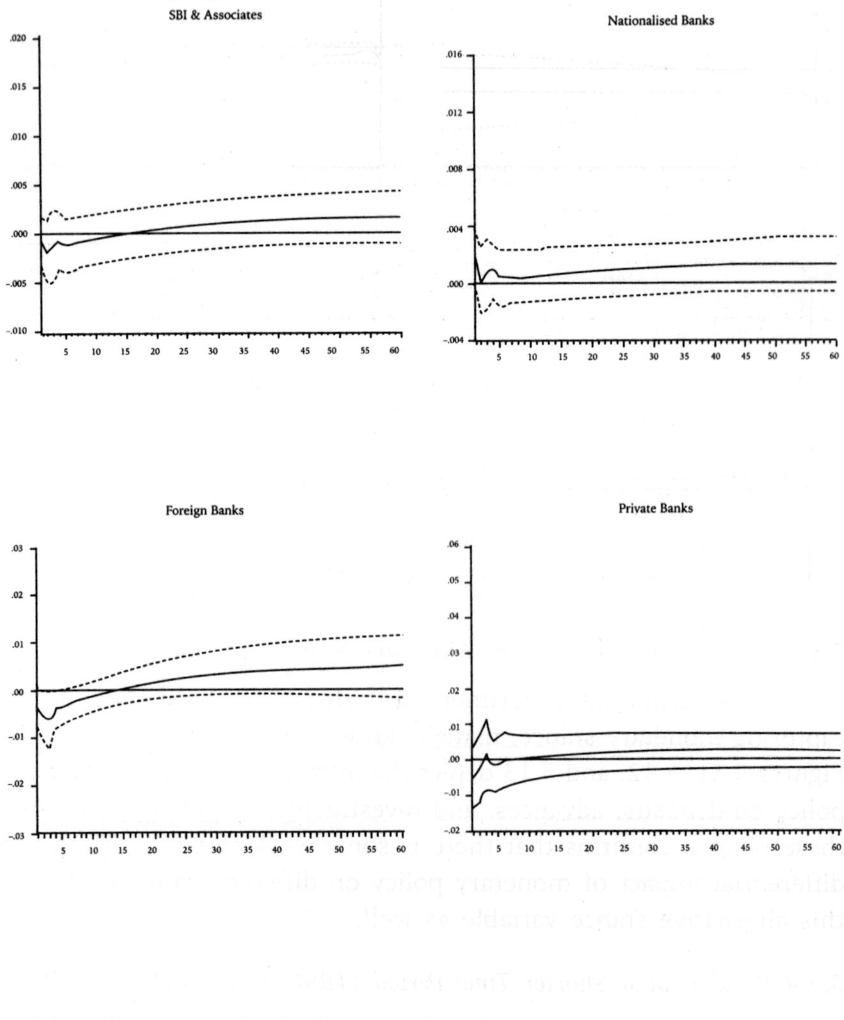

Figure 5.13

Impulse Responses on Investments of a GRM Shock

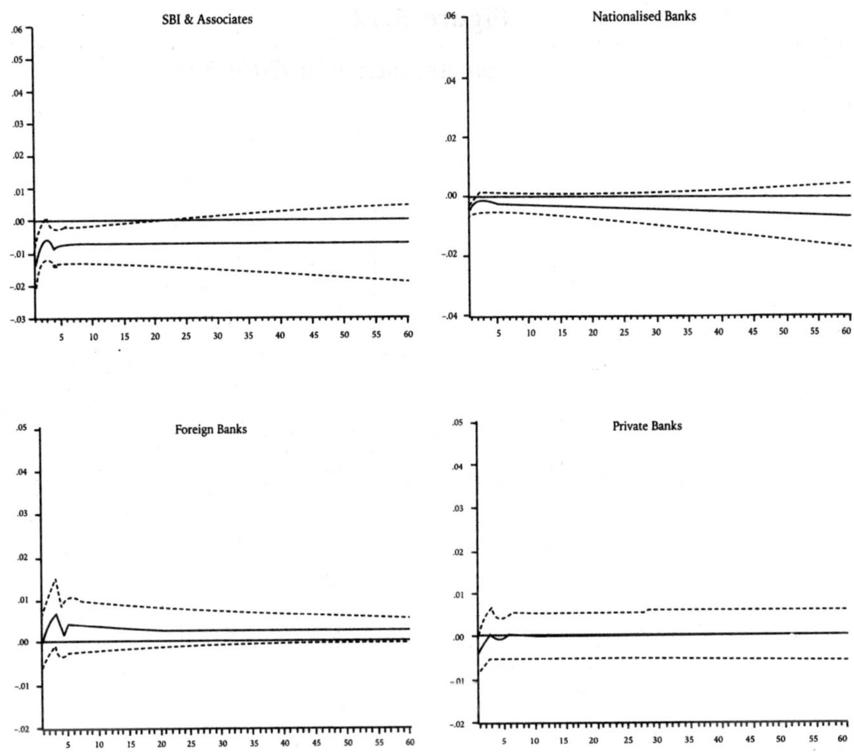

5.5.3 Results with Alternative Monetary Stance Variables

As earlier we experimented with an alternative variable for capturing monetary stance, namely, growth of reserve money (GRM). Figures 5.11, 5.12, and 5.13 depict the impulse responses of monetary policy on deposits, advances, and investments, respectively. A look at these Figures confirms that there is some weak evidence in favour of differential impact of monetary policy on different bank groups with this alternative stance variable as well.

5.5.4 Results for a Shorter Time Period (1996-97 through 2003-04)

So far we have run VARs for the period 1992-93 through 2003-04. Since the new private banks came into existence much later, we tried

Figure 5.14

Impulse Responses on Deposits of a CRR Shock: 1996-97 through 2003-04

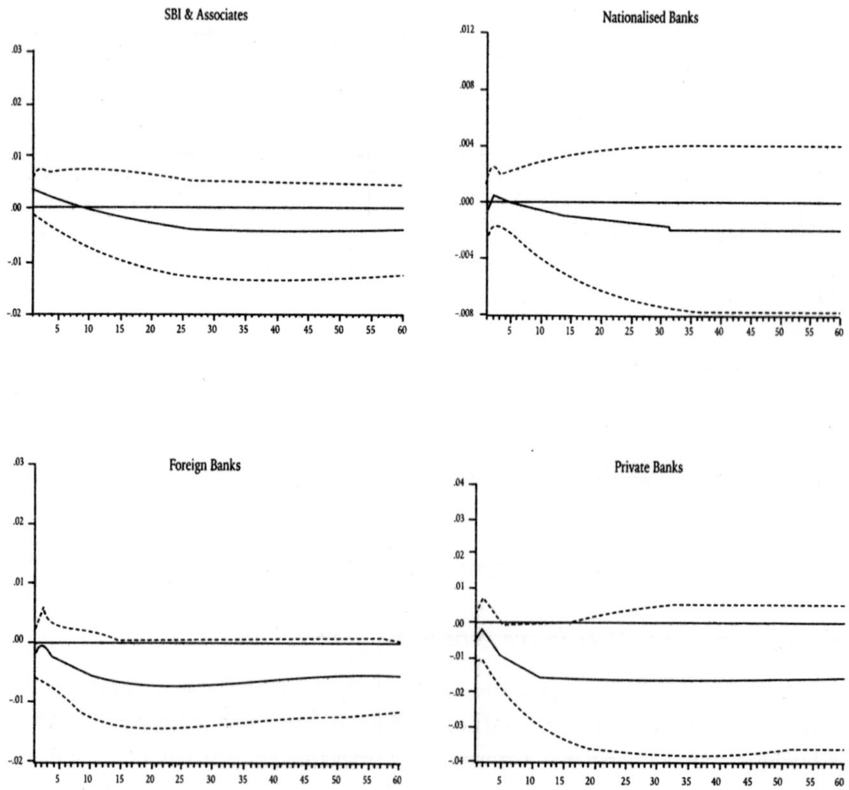

Figure 5.15

Impulse Responses on Advances of a CRR Shock: 1996-97 through 2003-04

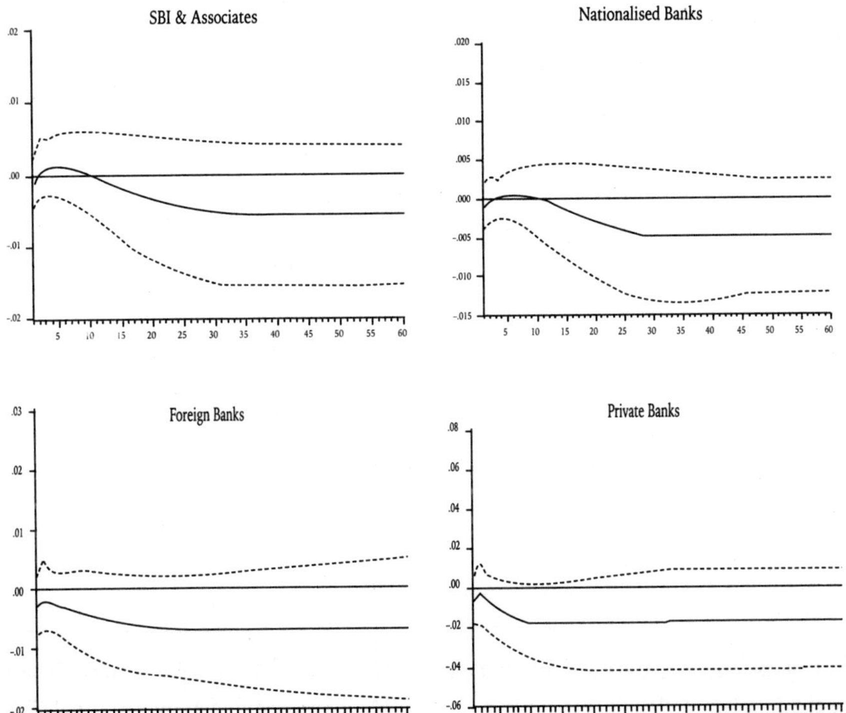

Figure 5.16

Impulse Responses on Investment of a CRR Shock: 1996-97 through 2003-04

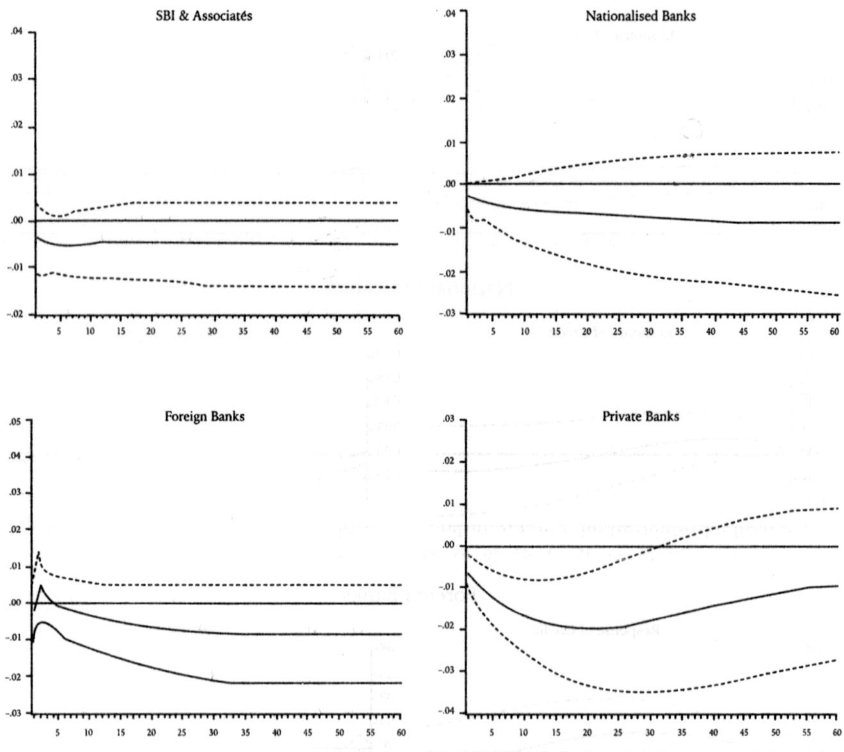

to check the robustness of our results by running a VAR for a shorter period, *viz.*, 1996-97 through 2003-04. Figures 5.14, 5.15, and 5.16 below present the IRFs of the CRR shocks on deposits, credits and advances. These confirm the heterogeneity in the bahaviour of the different bank groups in response to the central bank's policy actions.

5.5.5 Results from a Five Variable VAR

We have so far treated deposits, advances and investment separately. In order to check the robustness of the results, in the spirit

Figure 5.17

Impulse Reponses on Advances and Investment of a CRR Shock

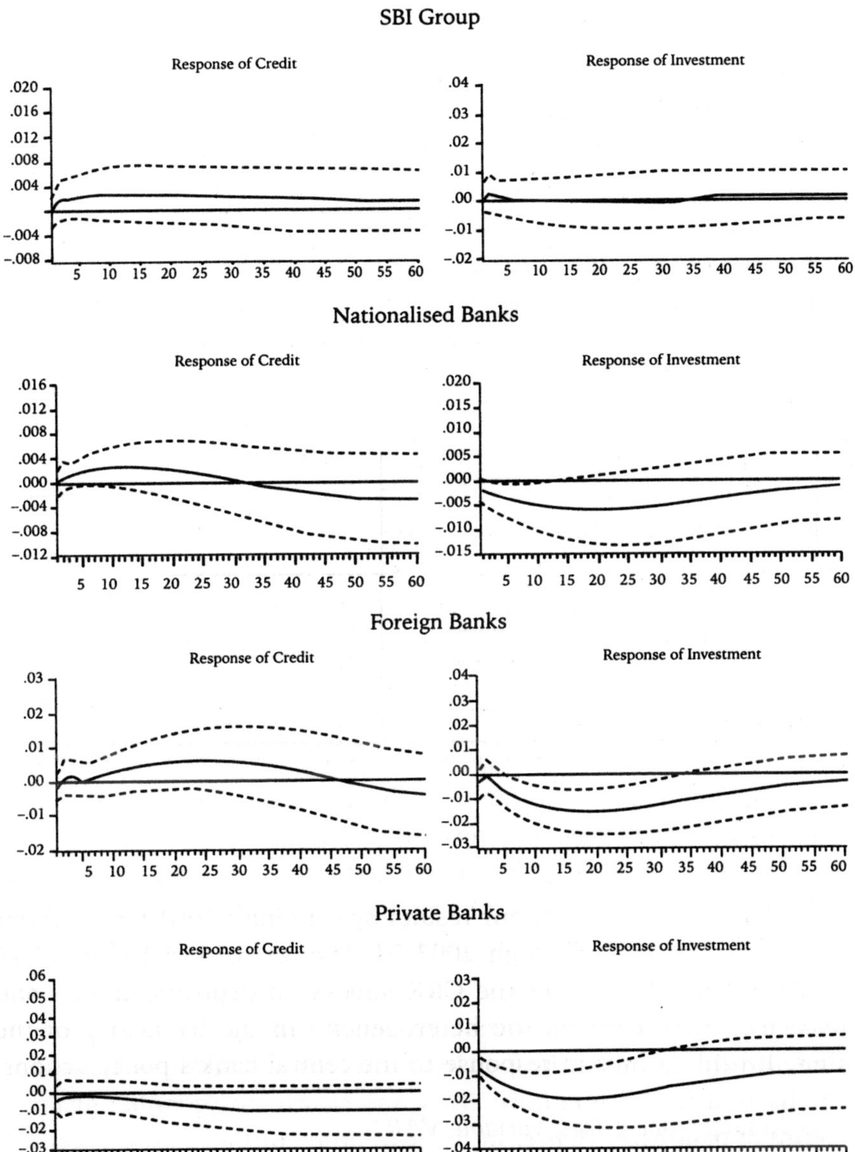

of Bernanke and Blinder (1992) we have included advances and investments of each bank group simultaneously in the VAR and run a five variable VAR of the following form:

$$(5.3)\quad X_t = G_1 + \sum_{i=1}^{N} g_i' X_{t-i} + \sum_{i=1}^{11} c_i' D_i$$

with $\mathbf{X}_t$ = {CRR_t, ADV_t, INV_t, Y_t, P_t}. As earlier, four VARs are run corresponding to each of the four bank groups.

The impulse responses of a CRR shock on deposits, advances, and investment for each of the four bank groups are depicted in Figure 5.17. The IRFs exhibit some heterogeneity among the different bank groups. The correlation pattern of the error series seems to indicate that the impulses are reasonably insensitive to ordering (Annex Table A-5.2B).

5.6 Conclusion

In discerning the somewhat perverse impulse of aggregate credit, this chapter looked into disaggregated bank behaviour. While we get some support in favour of differential impact of monetary policy on different types of banks (based on ownership), the evidence is at best weak. In fact, insofar as the validity of the Kashyap-Stein propositions are concerned, we find some weak evidence on the differential impact of monetary policy on bank advances.

The monthly nature of the data is ill-equipped to capture the differences in lendable resources of large (defined in terms of aggregate balance sheet size) *versus* small banks. Empirical evidence for the US (Kashyap and Stein, 1994) and elsewhere (Farinha and Marquez, 2001) have demonstrated that the impact of a contractionary monetary policy is likely to vary across bank size. By aggregating data across bank size, the monthly data was not able to take adequate cognizance of the 'marginal' impact of monetary policy change across bank groups.

There could be various explanations of the weak evidence presented in this chapter. After all, ownership cannot be a proxy for size, liquidity or capitalisation—the three variables have been emphasised in the literature. This was clearly not possible given the nature of data base. Hence, in order to probe further into the question of differential impact of monetary policy across different banks, we turn to individual bank behaviour in the next chapter.

Annex Table A-5.1-A

Composition of Assets and Liabilities of Various Bank Groups: State Bank of India and its Associates

(As per cent of total assets/liabilities)

Year	Capital & Reserves	Deposits	Borrowings	Other Liabilities and Provisions	Cash and Liquid Assets	Investments	Advances	Fixed Assets
(1)	(2)	(3)	(4)	(5)	(6)	(7)	(8)	(9)
1992	1.7	65.7	8.2	24.4	11.9	25.7	46.7	15.7
1993	1.8	68.4	10.5	19.4	11.4	28.2	47.3	13.1
1994	3.4	70.7	4.9	21.0	15.8	33.2	38.1	12.9
1995	3.6	72.1	6.7	17.7	14.9	33.5	41.2	10.3
1996	3.8	68.6	7.9	19.6	17.5	29.8	41.8	10.9
1997	4.8	72.4	3.9	18.9	17.9	30.2	40.6	11.3
1998	5.2	74.6	3.8	16.4	17.9	31.2	41.9	9.0
1999	4.6	76.7	3.6	15.1	21.9	33.3	37.9	6.9
2000	4.6	76.2	3.2	16.0	17.0	36.0	38.4	8.7
2001	4.3	77.5	2.8	15.4	17.7	39.0	37.3	5.9
2002	4.5	78.1	2.2	15.2	16.7	41.3	36.6	5.4
2003	4.7	79.2	2.3	13.8	11.0	45.2	38.3	5.5
2004	5.1	78.8	3.1	13.1	9.7	45.1	40.1	5.0

Source: RBI. *Report on Trends & Progress of Banking in India*, various issues.

Annex Table A-5.1-B

Composition of Assets and Liabilities of Various Bank Groups: Nationalised Banks

(As per cent of total assets/liabilities)

Year	Capital and Reserves	Deposits	Borrowings	Other Liabilities and Provisions	Cash and Liquid Assets	Investments	Advances	Fixed Assets
(1)	(2)	(3)	(4)	(5)	(6)	(7)	(8)	(9)
1992	3.2	85.7	4.6	6.5	14.5	30.5	48.3	6.8
1993	3.3	85.3	4.5	7.0	14.5	31.1	45.3	9.1
1994	6.0	85.6	2.1	6.3	14.3	36.2	39.2	10.3
1995	7.3	83.6	3.4	5.8	15.5	34.7	40.1	9.7
1996	6.7	82.3	4.9	6.2	16.2	33.5	40.6	9.7
1997	6.7	85.7	1.5	6.1	15.4	36.7	39.0	8.8
1998	6.9	86.0	1.2	5.9	15.9	37.1	39.0	8.1
1999	5.9	86.2	1.7	6.2	15.9	37.5	39.0	7.6
2000	5.5	86.7	1.6	6.2	14.1	38.3	40.2	7.4
2001	5.2	87.3	1.4	6.1	13.0	37.8	42.2	7.1
2002	5.3	87.5	1.5	5.8	10.8	38.0	44.8	6.5
2003	5.4	87.0	1.4	6.3	8.6	40.7	45.5	5.2
2004	5.6	86.1	1.5	6.8	9.6	41.0	44.7	4.8

Source: RBI. *Report on Trends and Progress of Banking in India*, various issues.

Annex Table A-5.1-C

Composition of Assets and Liabilities of Various Bank Groups: Indian Private Banks

(As per cent of total assets/liabilities)

Year	Capital and Reserves	Deposits	Borrowings	Other Liabilities and Provisions	Cash and Liquid Assets	Investments	Advances	Fixed Assets
(1)	(2)	(3)	(4)	(5)	(6)	(7)	(8)	(9)
1992	2.1	86.3	3.7	7.9	20.9	28.6	45.2	5.3
1993	2.5	86.3	4.4	6.8	20.4	28.4	44.8	6.4
1994	3.0	88.2	2.5	6.2	19.4	31.6	43.1	5.9
1995	5.7	76.1	5.7	12.6	19.5	27.0	41.3	12.1
1996	7.4	79.3	7.8	5.5	17.3	25.8	49.0	8.0
1997	6.8	84.3	3.5	5.4	14.9	30.4	47.3	7.5
1998	6.5	85.8	2.6	5.1	16.8	32.8	43.7	6.7
1999	5.7	83.5	5.3	5.4	16.6	35.1	41.2	7.1
2000	6.1	83.2	5.2	5.5	15.6	37.2	40.8	6.4
2001	5.4	83.6	5.2	5.7	14.3	38.0	41.7	6.1
2002	6.0	63.3	21.2	9.4	12.6	37.0	43.5	6.9
2003	6.2	70.1	14.0	9.8	9.3	36.1	46.7	8.6
2004	6.1	73.1	11.0	9.8	10.0	36.7	46.5	6.7

Source: RBI. *Report on Trends and Progress of Banking in India*, various issues.

Annex Table A-5.1-D

Composition of Assets and Liabilities of Various Bank Groups: Foreign Banks

(As per cent of total assets/liabilities)

Year	Capital and Reserves	Deposits	Borrowings	Other Liabilities and Provisions	Cash and Liquid Assets	Investments	Advances	Fixed Assets
(1)	(2)	(3)	(4)	(5)	(6)	(7)	(8)	(9)
1992	3.7	68.5	16.1	11.7	21.3	32.2	37.0	9.5
1993	5.7	67.2	20.2	6.9	17.1	36.4	33.6	12.9
1994	7.0	77.5	7.0	8.5	11.2	41.8	34.7	12.3
1995	9.6	74.1	8.9	7.4	15.6	31.9	40.3	12.3
1996	10.7	64.3	17.7	7.4	17.4	23.5	47.2	11.9
1997	11.4	66.9	14.2	7.5	14.6	25.8	47.8	11.7
1998	11.5	65.7	15.1	7.8	16.1	28.2	44.9	10.8
1999	9.4	61.9	21.3	7.3	17.6	34.4	38.5	9.6
2000	9.8	59.5	22.7	8.0	11.9	35.8	43.0	9.3
2001	8.8	58.1	26.3	6.7	14.1	35.1	42.2	8.5
2002	9.4	57.5	26.5	6.5	17.5	31.3	43.4	7.8
2003	11.5	59.6	19.7	9.3	9.4	35.1	44.8	10.8
2004	10.9	58.5	18.6	12.0	12.4	30.5	44.4	12.7

Source: RBI. *Report on Trends and Progress of Banking in India*, various issues.

Annex Table A-5.2-A

Correlation Matrix of the Errors in the 4 Variable VARs

VAR with Bj	*Banks*	*Variables*	*CRR*	*Bj*	*LY*	*LP*
(1)	(2)	(3)	(4)	(5)	(6)	(7)
1. Bj = Deposits	1.1 SBI & Associates	CRR	1.000	0.186	0.045	0.041
		Bj		1.000	-0.141	0.016
		LY			1.000	-0.476
		LP				1.000
	1.2 Nationalised Banks	CRR	1.000	-0.059	0.042	0.043
		Bj		1.000	-0.162	0.066
		LY			1.000	-0.472
		LP				1.000
	1.3 Foreign Banks	CRR	1.000	-0.030	0.038	0.035
		Bj		1.000	0.013	-0.086
		LY			1.000	-0.465
		LP				1.000
	1.4 Private Banks	CRR	1.000	-0.080	0.045	0.029
		Bj		1.000	-0.003	0.029
		LY			1.000	-0.499
		LP				1.000
2. Bj = Advances	2.1 SBI & Associates	CRR	1.000	0.020	0.050	0.025
		Bj		1.000	-0.121	0.097
		LY			1.000	-0.473
		LP				1.000
	2.2 Nationalised Banks	CRR	1.000	0.031	0.045	0.041
		Bj		1.000	-0.340	0.363
		LY			1.000	-0.473
		LP				1.000
	2.3 Foreign Banks	CRR	1.000	-0.048	0.057	-0.002
		Bj		1.000	-0.083	0.097
		LY			1.000	-0.471
		LP				1.000
	2.4 Private Banks	CRR	1.000	-0.042	0.068	0.032
		Bj		1.000	-0.005	0.107
		LY			1.000	-0.480
		LP				1.000
3. Bj = Investment	3.1 SBI & Associates	CRR	1.000	0.001	0.040	0.036
		Bj		1.000	0.133	-0.127
		LY			1.000	-0.474
		LP				1.000
	3.2 Nationalised Banks	CRR	1.000	-0.126	0.019	-0.059
		Bj		1.000	-0.129	0.023
		LY			1.000	-0.485
		LP				1.000
	3.3 Foreign Banks	CRR	1.000	-0.098	0.056	0.023
		Bj		1.000	0.072	-0.019
		LY			1.000	-0.479
		LP				1.000
	3.4 Private Banks	CRR	1.000	-0.235	0.032	0.022
		Bj		1.000	0.051	-0.064
		LY			1.000	-0.485
		LP				1.000

Annex Table A-5.2-B

Correlation Matrix of the Errors in the 5 Variable VAR

Bank	*Variables*	*CRR*	*LBC*	*LINV*	*LY*	*LP*
(1)	(2)	(3)	(4)	(5)	(6)	(7)
SBI & Associates	CRR	1.000	0.005	0.059	0.049	0.008
	LBC		1.000	-0.083	-0.138	0.067
	LINV			1.000	0.136	-0.134
	LY				1.000	-0.476
	LP					1.000
Nationalised Banks	CRR	1.000	0.010	-0.119	0.022	0.010
	LBC		1.000	-0.221	-0.371	0.346
	LINV			1.000	0.172	-0.205
	LY				1.000	-0.518
	LP					1.000
Foreign Banks	CRR	1.000	-0.072	-0.102	0.069	-0.004
	LBC		1.000	-0.148	-0.065	0.112
	LINV			1.000	0.078	-0.025
	LY				1.000	-0.474
	LP					1.000
Private Banks	CRR	1.000	-0.079	-0.276	0.064	0.015
	LBC		1.000	0.245	-0.009	0.081
	LINV			1.000	0.083	-0.073
	LY				1.000	-0.484
	LP					1.000

Annex Table A-5.3

Time Series Properties of the Variables: Results from Dickey-Fuller (DF) and Augmented Dickey-Fuller (ADF) Statistics

Model	Statistic	AD1	AD2	AD3	AD4	BC1	BC2	BC3	BC4	INV1	INV2	INV3	INV4
(1)	(2)	(3)	(4)	(5)	(6)	(7)	(8)	(9)	(10)	(11)	(12)	(13)	(14)
Level:	DF	-0.38	-0.15	-3.84	-0.50	0.01	1.46	-1.64	-0.81	-0.34	-0.66	-2.03	0.72
With an	ADF(1)	-0.37	-0.14	-3.41	-0.54	0.01	1.65	-1.55	-0.80	-0.26	-0.74	-2.18	0.74
Intercept	ADF(2)	-0.35	-0.14	-3.05	-0.56	-0.07	1.52	-1.40	-0.77	-0.16	-0.74	-2.06	0.76
& not a	ADF(3)	-0.33	-0.13	-2.86	-0.75	-0.05	1.52	-1.45	-0.81	-0.29	-0.74	-2.05	0.77
Trend	ADF(4)	-0.31	-0.10	-2.76	-0.82	-0.02	1.68	-1.52	-0.87	-0.24	-0.73	-1.98	0.80
	ADF(5)	-0.32	0.01	-2.76	-0.77	0.02	2.15	-1.58	-0.97	-0.27	-0.70	-1.98	0.84
	ADF(6)	-0.32	-0.34	-2.57	-0.67	0.02	1.67	-1.37	-0.81	-0.13	-0.70	-1.91	0.79
	ADF(7)	-0.34	-0.31	-2.72	-0.67	0.01	1.93	-1.52	-0.92	-0.03	-0.68	-1.93	0.81
	ADF(8)	-0.35	-0.26	-2.95	-0.67	0.02	2.54	-1.74	-1.11	-0.03	-0.66	-1.91	0.90
	ADF(9)	-0.25	-0.27	-2.78	-0.66	0.04	2.58	-1.73	-1.09	-0.01	-0.66	-1.90	0.87
	ADF(10)	-0.26	0.03	-2.81	-0.65	0.03	2.13	-1.75	-1.04	-0.12	-0.62	-1.83	0.93
	ADF(11)	-0.24	0.17	-3.01	-0.64	0.03	2.12	-1.66	-1.06	0.01	-0.58	-1.93	1.02
	ADF(12)	-0.23	-0.02	-3.01	-0.69	-0.19	1.47	-1.41	-1.26	-0.02	-0.60	-2.08	0.87
Level:	DF	-2.92	-5.23	-3.57	-2.05	-2.85	-2.67	-1.48	-1.18	-2.76	-2.79	-3.07	-3.00
With an	ADF(1)	-3.15	-4.60	-3.50	-1.81	-2.95	-2.45	-1.65	-1.22	-2.26	-2.42	-2.97	-3.00
Intercept	ADF(2)	-2.70	-4.13	-3.50	-1.68	-3.64	-2.68	-1.87	-1.34	-1.84	-2.45	-3.09	-3.03
& Trend	ADF(3)	-2.34	-3.18	-3.56	-0.97	-3.65	-2.69	-1.78	-1.15	-2.39	-2.43	-3.10	-3.10
	ADF(4)	-2.21	-2.53	-3.60	-0.75	-3.34	-2.44	-1.61	-0.89	-2.26	-3.05	-3.19	-3.03
	ADF(5)	-2.30	-1.79	-3.59	-0.92	-3.03	-1.85	-1.47	-0.60	-2.42	-2.67	-3.17	-2.88
	ADF(6)	-2.50	-3.07	-3.68	-1.48	-3.38	-2.57	-1.90	-1.19	-2.06	-2.73	-3.45	-3.49

contd...

contd...

Model	*Statistic*	*AD1*	*AD2*	*AD3*	*AD4*	*BC1*	*BC2*	*BC3*	*BC4*	*INV1*	*INV2*	*INV3*	*INV4*
(1)	*(2)*	*(3)*	*(4)*	*(5)*	*(6)*	*(7)*	*(8)*	*(9)*	*(10)*	*(11)*	*(12)*	*(13)*	*(14)*
	ADF(7)	-2.77	-3.05	-3.55	-1.62	-3.01	-1.99	-1.64	-0.81	-1.78	-2.39	-3.29	-3.34
	ADF(8)	-2.92	-2.99	-3.47	-1.41	-2.90	-1.48	-1.33	-0.29	-1.82	-2.01	-3.36	-2.99
	ADF(9)	-2.49	-3.05	-3.47	-1.42	-2.84	-1.43	-1.32	-0.31	-1.81	-2.01	-3.36	-3.16
	ADF(10)	-2.58	-2.67	-3.45	-1.37	-2.96	-1.70	-1.28	-0.47	-2.27	-2.23	-3.40	-2.98
	ADF(11)	-2.58	-2.56	-3.44	-1.28	-3.04	-1.69	-1.36	-0.80	-1.91	-2.72	-3.40	-2.78
	ADF(12)	-2.62	-2.70	-3.42	-1.60	-4.54	-2.38	-2.10	-1.31	-2.08	-2.65	-3.39	-
First	DF	-10.99	-13.92	-9.68	-12.55	-11.16	-12.52	-10.26	-11.22	-14.04	-13.05	-12.67	-11.60
Difference:	ADF(1)	-9.43	-10.25	-6.17	-8.89	-6.66	-7.52	-6.70	-7.47	-10.76	-8.60	-7.31	-8.22
With an	ADF(2)	-8.54	-10.06	-4.78	-9.47	-5.96	-6.26	-6.02	-6.85	-6.23	-6.97	-6.03	-6.58
Intercept	ADF(3)	-7.30	-9.68	-4.08	-8.05	-5.96	-6.07	-5.78	-6.59	-5.82	-4.86	-4.89	-5.86
and not a	ADF(4)	-5.90	-10.86	-3.79	-6.04	-5.96	-7.09	-5.47	-6.50	-4.96	-5.18	-4.51	-5.42
Trend	ADF(5)	-4.93	-3.93	-3.23	-4.19	-4.88	-4.01	-3.88	-4.23	-5.24	-4.66	-3.64	-3.69
	ADF(6)	-4.11	-3.81	-3.38	-3.74	-5.17	-4.75	-4.16	-4.67	-5.37	-4.97	-3.80	-3.74
	ADF(7)	-3.75	-3.75	-3.60	-3.91	-4.98	-5.92	-4.66	-5.60	-4.83	-5.40	-3.48	-4.18
	ADF(8)	-4.16	-3.49	-3.15	-3.69	-4.77	-5.15	-4.25	-4.91	-4.48	-4.87	-3.33	-3.65
	ADF(9)	-3.84	-4.26	-3.03	-3.63	-4.28	-3.64	-3.98	-3.98	-3.52	-4.02	-2.99	-3.77
	ADF(10)	-3.68	-4.36	-3.12	-3.64	-3.99	-3.38	-3.44	-2.84	-3.85	-3.20	-3.08	-3.98
	ADF(11)	-3.47	-3.53	-2.93	-2.96	-2.64	-2.14	-2.22	-1.87	-3.44	-3.21	-3.17	-2.85
	ADF(12)	-3.52	-2.76	-3.07	-2.50	-2.88	-2.02	-2.58	-1.61	-3.39	-3.01	-2.70	-2.77

contd...

contd...

Model	*Statistic*	*AD1*	*AD2*	*AD3*	*AD4*	*BC1*	*BC2*	*BC3*	*BC4*	*INV1*	*INV2*	*INV3*	*INV4*
(1)	*(2)*	*(3)*	*(4)*	*(5)*	*(6)*	*(7)*	*(8)*	*(9)*	*(10)*	*(11)*	*(12)*	*(13)*	*(14)*
First	DF	-10.94	-13.87	-10.12	-12.53	-11.12	-12.77	-10.35	-11.24	-13.98	-13.03	-12.82	-11..64
Difference:	ADF(1)	-9.39	-10.22	-6.52	-8.88	-6.64	-7.76	-6.79	-7.50	-10.72	-8.61	-7.44	-8.28
With an	ADF(2)	-8.51	-10.02	-5.09	-9.49	-5.94	-6.52	-6.13	-6.90	-6.20	-6.99	-6.18	-6.65
Intercept	ADF(3)	-7.27	-9.64	-4.39	-8.09	-5.94	-6.39	-5.93	-6.66	-5.79	-4.88	-5.05	-5.94
and Trend	ADF(4)	-5.87	-10.82	-4.12	-6.09	-5.94	-7.56	-5.66	-6.60	-4.94	-5.21	-4.68	-5.50
	ADF(5)	-4.91	-3.90	-3.52	-4.24	-4.86	-4.41	-4.04	-4.31	-5.21	-4.68	-3.81	-3.77
	ADF(6)	-4.09	-3.77	-3.75	-3.79	-5.15	-5.24	-4.37	-4.77	-5.35	-4.99	-3.98	-3.82
	ADF(7)	-3.73	-3.69	-4.06	-3.97	-4.96	-6.56	-4.94	-5.76	-4.80	-5.42	-3.66	-4.27
	ADF(8)	-4.15	-3.41	-3.58	-3.75	-4.75	-5.86	-4.56	-5.08	-4.45	-4.89	-3.52	-3.74
	ADF(9)	-3.83	-4.19	-3.48	-3.68	-4.27	-4.26	-4.32	-4.16	-3.49	-4.04	-3.17	-3.88
	ADF(10)	-3.67	-4.27	-3.67	-3.69	-3.98	-4.03	-3.77	-3.03	-3.82	-3.22	-3.30	-4.10
	ADF(11)	-3.46	-3.42	-3.48	-3.01	-2.63	-2.66	-2.46	-2.09	-3.41	-3.24	-3.44	-2.97
	ADF(12)	-3.51	-2.60	-3.75	-2.56	-2.87	-2.54	-2.83	-1.84	-3.36	-3.04	-2.92	-2.90

Note: (1) For the level variables, the 95% critical values for the ADF are -2.88 and -3.44 for the regressions with an intercept and with an intercept & trend, respectively; the same for the differenced data are -2.88, and -3.45, respectively.

(2) Groups 1, 2, 3 & 4 refer to SBI & associates, Nationalised banks, Foreign banks and Private Banks, respectively.

(3) AD: Aggregate Deposits; BC: Bank Credit; INV: Investment, so that AD1: Aggregate Deposits of SBI & Associates and so on.

6

Size, Liquidity and Capital

How do they Influence Bank Credit?

6.1 Introduction

In Chapter 5 we have seen that there is some limited evidence towards differential impact of monetary policy on credit extended by different groups of banks. But what are the factors that play an important role in determining differential impact of monetary policy across different (by whichever criterion) banks? In the literature along with size, the recent literature stressed the [illegible] capital.

What is the intuition behind such importance [illegible] a large bank like the State Bank of India or [illegible] the one who has larger liquidity, then size will be able to capture the liquidity aspect of the bank as well. However, this may not be [illegible] After all, the need for buffer stock could be larger for a smaller bank. In other words, the ability of shield credit from monetary policy could spring independently from size and liquidity. Hence, the lending channel should be more important for small banks (Kashyap and Stein, 1995). What are the distinguishing characteristics of small banks? These normally have a very simple capital structure and in the Indian context are financed almost exclusively [illegible] and lower access to non-deposit funding.

Admittedly, the impact of the bank lending channel should also be greater for banks with less liquid assets and less capital. Less liquid banks cannot protect their loan portfolio against monetary [illegible] simply by drawing down cash and securities (Stein, 1998; Kashyap and Stein, 2000; Kashyap *et al.*, 2002). Besides, poorly capitalised banks have less access to markets for uninsured funding, so their lending is

6

Size, Liquidity and Capital

How do they Influence Bank Credit?

6.1 Introduction

In Chapter 5 we have seen that there is some limited evidence towards differential impact of monetary policy on credit extended by different groups of banks. But what are the factors that play an important role in determining differential impact of monetary policy across different (by whichever criterion) banks? In this context along with size, the recent literature stressed the role of liquidity and capital.

What is the intuition behind such importance of these factors? If a large bank like the State Bank of India or ICICI Bank is also the one who has larger liquidity, then size will be able to capture the liquidity aspect of the bank as well. However, this may not be necessarily true. After all, the need for buffer stock could be large for a smaller bank. In other words, the ability to insulate credit from monetary policy could spring independently from size and liquidity. In fact, the lending channel should be more important for small banks (Kashyap and Stein, 1995). What are the distinguishing characteristics of the small banks? These normally have a very simple capital structure and in the Indian context, are financed almost exclusively with deposits and lower access to non-deposit funding.

Admittedly, the impact of the 'bank lending channel' should also be greater for banks with less liquid assets and less capital. Less liquid banks cannot protect their loan portfolio against monetary tightening simply by drawing down cash and securities (Stein, 1998; Kashyap and Stein, 2000; Kashyap *et al.*, 2002). Besides, poorly capitalised banks have less access to markets for uninsured funding, so their lending is more dependent on monetary policy shocks (Peek and Rosengren, 1995a; Kishan and Opiela, 2000).[1]

One might even consider a case where faced with a monetary contraction, a large bank may not reduce its lending due to its access to non-deposit resources, while a small bank may not decrease its credit due to its liquid assets. On the contrary, if a large bank has also higher liquid assets then during a period of monetary contraction the lending of a large bank may be maintained due to its access to both non-deposit resources as well as liquid assets. Thus, if a larger bank has higher liquidity, then during the time of monetary contraction, it might draw down such liquid assets so as to avoid any major cut in advances extended to the business sector. If one thinks of a two-way classification in terms of the attributes of size and liquidity, then the effect of a contractionary monetary policy will be felt most for those small banks with low liquidity, and least for those large banks which have high liquidity.

Similarly, capital constraint too can play a major role in influencing bank behaviour; particularly introduction of Basel-type capital requirement norms seemed to have affected the credit behaviour of banks in a number of countries (BIS, 1999; Santos, 2000). There could be various reasons behind the importance of bank capital in determining the effect of monetary policy, *viz.*, (a) its influence on banks' risk taking incentives, (b) its role promoting efficient corporate governance of the banking sector, and (c) its influence on the competitiveness of banks (Altunbas *et al.*, 2001).

In this context, the present chapter examines the importance of size, liquidity and capital in the relationship between the central bank's policy actions and bank credit behaviour. In reference to the earlier two empirical chapters the distinctive features of the chapter are three: (a) data base, (b) econometric technique, and (c) emphasis on three attributes of banks in determination of the relationship. Let us briefly look into each of the three issues.

1. All these studies on cross-sectional differences in the effectiveness of the "bank lending channel" refer to the US. The literature on European countries is instead far from conclusive (e.g., Altunbas *et al.*, 2002; Ehrmann *et al.*, 2003).

First, as far as data base is concerned, the analysis thus far utilised 'high frequency aggregative data'—monthly data for all banks in Chapter 4, and monthly data for ownership-wise classification of banks (i.e., public, private and foreign) in Chapter 5. The present chapter makes a departure from this data base and employs the bank-wise balance sheet at annual frequency. Given the fact that these are audited balance sheets as against the statutory fortnightly returns (maintained for the purpose of calculation of CRR), one would expect better coverage and reliability in the data.

Second, from the above data base we have generated a balanced panel of commercial banks for a 10 year period from 1994-95 to 2003-2004 and consequently employed the technique of estimating panel regressions. This also is a departure from the earlier chapters which employed the time series technique of VAR models.

Finally, unlike the earlier chapters, which aimed at primarily detection of patterns in the portfolio behaviour of the commercial banks, the present chapter examines the influence of three crucial variables, *viz.*, size, liquidity and capital for the credit behaviour of a panel of Indian banks in the recent period. In doing so, we included various cross product terms to account for the interdependence between the variables.

The rest of the Chapter is organised as follows. While section 6.2 gives a resume of the received literature, section 6.3 gives a description of the panel and some stylised facts of the recent trends in size, liquidity and capital of commercial banks in India. A brief description of econometric methodology as well as the model is given in section 6.4. Section 6.5 is devoted to the estimation of the credit behaviour of commercial banks in terms of three crucial variables, *viz.*, size, liquidity and capital. Some robustness tests are reported in section 6.6. Concluding observations are presented in section 6.7.

6.2 Received Literature

6.2.1 Size, Liquidity and Bank Credit

Reaction of commercial banks to the central bank's policy actions in a detailed dis-aggregative context has been studied in the credit channel literature at length. These (mainly US-based) studies have typically investigated the response of bank loan and other asset and deposit categories to changes in monetary policy stance as captured by changes in the federal funds rate. In addition, these studies also investigate whether monetary policy has a differential impact for banks of different characteristics: (a) asset size (*e.g.*, Kashyap and Stein, 1995), (b) asset size and liquidity (*e.g.*, Kashyap and Stein, 1997, Peek and Rosengren, 1995a and 1995b), (c) asset size and capital strength (*e.g.*, Kishan and Opiela, 2000). All these studies found that a bank lending channel existed and this was mainly transmitted through small banks. The bank lending channel also appeared to be strengthened when these small banks were either relatively illiquid or undercapitalised. In short, the evidence strongly suggested that a bank lending channel was present for balance sheet constrained small banks.

The idea that a monetary contraction may not lead to a fall in bank credit is crucial to the credit channel literature. The credit market is often regarded as a 'customer market', as against 'auction market', where prices do not clear the market automatically. Okun (1981) observed that banks forge an implicit contract to help the borrower in the event of a rainy day. A number of interview-based studies indicated that banks' immediate reaction to a monetary contraction is to reduce its security holding rather than loan portfolio.[2]

But the basic function of a bank is to accept deposits and sanction loans. Why do they then hold liquid assets? There is a large literature for explaining the holding of liquid assets by a bank.[3] The traditional portfolio management theory links holding of liquid asset by a particular bank to its degree of risk aversion (*e.g.*, Pyle, 1971). That is to say, banks which are more risk averse will hold relatively more liquid assets. The liquid asset held by a bank could be seen as a buffer stock. As Kashyap, Rajan and Stein (2002) had shown that the coexistence of lending and deposit acceptance by the banks could theoretically be seen as manifestations of the same primitive function: provision of liquidity on demand. Recent literature in this context emphasised the reasons for banks' difficulty to raise external finance.

---

2. See Kakes (2000) on this issue with particular reference to the Netherlands.
3. See Alger and Alger (1999) for a survey on the literature on liquid assets and loans.

Holmström and Tirole (1998) also stressed that a key function of a bank is provision of liquidity in the form of loan commitments.

In the context of the Kashyap and Stein (1995) model, the recent literature emphasised the role of bank capital and liquidity in determining the sensitiveness of bank loans to monetary policy. The intuition that had driven this literature is that the lending behaviour of liquidity/capital constrained banks would vary. Kashyap and Stein (1997) showed that due to the presence of buffer stocks with the banks, contractionary monetary policy might fail to lead to any reduction in loan supply. That is to say, the drawdown in deposits might be compensated by reduction in security holding (liquid bank asset) and not necessarily by decrease in loan supply (illiquid bank asset).

Evidence from various European studies was less decisive. Kashyap and Stein (1997) reviewed various indicators that may affect the bank lending channel in Europe. They concluded that the characteristics of the Italian system suggested that it was likely to be sensitive to the bank lending channel, whereas the lending channel was likely to be weak in the United Kingdom.

de Bondt (1998) was the first to use disaggregated bank data to test for evidence of the lending channel across various European countries. He tested whether there existed important differences in the way in which European banks with varying characteristics (in terms of balance sheet size and liquidity) respond to changes in the stance of monetary policy (short-term interest rates) during the 1990–1995 period. de Bondt (1998) used changes in money market rates (as a proxy for monetary policy stance) in his interactive regression models. Overall evidence supported the existence of a bank lending channel in Germany, Belgium and the Netherlands, while in the rest of the countries under study (France, Italy and the United Kingdom) no significant effect was found. However, when the stance of monetary policy is measured by a monetary conditions index, the bank lending channel also appears to exist in Italy and France. Subsequently, de Bondt (1999) adopted a different approach by using aggregate bank data to examine the main bank lending channels in the same six European countries. By including security holdings within a vector error correction model as a variable used to detect loan supply effects, he found evidence that credit constraints due to monetary policy are important in Italy, Germany and France, but not in the United Kingdom, Belgium and Netherlands.

de Bondt (2000) extended this idea empirically in terms of liquidity–constrained banks and looked into the role of liquidity along with size in influencing bank loans for a number of European countries. The sample in de Bondt (2000)'s empirical analysis consisted of the following EU countries, *viz.*, Germany, France, Italy, the United Kingdom, Belgium, and the Netherlands. He constructed an unbalanced panel for each country, consisting of individual banks' data for the years 1990-1995. He estimated panel regressions for change in bank loans in terms of the following independent variables, *viz.*, short-term interest rate (as a measure of monetary policy), liquidity available to the bank, bank size, and real growth rate of the economy under consideration, with interaction between the variables.[4] His empirical finding indicated a high degree of country specificity. In particular the empirical results provided strong evidence for Germany, and the Netherlands; on the contrary, for the UK the empirical support was found to be weak.

Favero *et al.* (1999) used individual bank balance sheet data to investigate the response of banks in France, Germany, Italy and Spain to monetary tightening during 1992. They found no evidence of the bank lending channel in any country although they did find that banks in different countries responded in different ways to protect the supply of loans from the liquidity squeeze. Small banks in Germany, Italy and (to a lesser extent) Spain maintained (or even increased) loan supply by raising new deposits, whereas banks in France used their excess capital to maintain lending levels.

Overall, the evidence of a bank lending channel in Europe was rather inconclusive. This is perhaps to be expected given the different methodologies and time periods adopted in the aforementioned literature.

In a larger cross country set up, using yearly bank-level data for 832 banks in 27 countries during 1986-1998, Vazquez (2001) found the following. First, the sensitivity of loan growth to monetary

4. Thus, the cross product terms between the independent variables were present.

conditions was larger for banks operating in developing countries. Second, bigger banks were more able to isolate loan growth from changes in monetary policy particularly in developing countries.

6.2.2 Capital Constraint and Bank Behaviour

The idea that capital constraints could be an important determinant of bank lending and to that extent could limit the efficacy of the credit channel of monetary transmission mechanism is originally due to Kashyap and Stein (1995). They considered a bank which has three assets, *viz.*, reserves, loans and bonds, and two liabilities, *viz.*, deposits and CDs. In their framework, the bank maximises profit, subject to the three constraints, *viz.*, balance sheet equality between assets and liabilities, reserve requirement (a relationship between reserves and deposits), and liquidity constraint (a relationship between reserves plus bonds to deposits). In this world, as a result of contractionary monetary policy shocks, a bank would not only sell securities but would also reduce loans. That is to say a bank's asset mix of loan and securities would represent an interior optimum of a portfolio choice problem.

Once risk-based capital requirement is introduced, Kashyap and Stein (1995) showed that the bank's ability to extend loans got intertwined to its level of equity capital. Thus, if a bank's lending was constrained by equity capital, then instead of adjusting loans, the bank would only adjust the volume of securities so that in the event of a contractionary monetary policy, lending for the capital constrained banks would not go down.

Peek and Rosenrgren (1995a) constructed a single period model of profit maximising banks and showed that insofar as lending behaviour was concerned the behaviour of capital–constrained and capital–unconstrained banks could be quite different. The bank in their model was assumed to have three assets, *viz.*, loans, securities, and reserves, and three liabilities, *viz.*, bank capital, transaction deposits, and non-transaction deposits. Apart from the reserve ratio, they introduced the 'required capital-to-asset' ratio as a crucial determinant of bank behaviour. In this set-up the comparative static exercises for the profit maximising banks indicated that while for the capital constrained banks a contractionary monetary policy left the deposits quantity unaltered, for the capital unconstrained banks, a contractionatry monetary policy reduced total deposits. Thus, they inferred that the impact of a change in monetary policy would be weaker when a majority of banks were capital constrained. Furthermore, they pointed out that loans of the constrained banks would respond positively to changes in federal funds rate, while for the unconstrained banks the response would be negative.[5] While this extreme form of the result might not be true, the basic message that came out from their work was that the impact of monetary policy on loan supply was greater for the unconstrained banks than that for the banks with a binding capital constraint. Peek and Rosenrgren (1995b) tested the validity of their predictions for banks in the New England district of the Fed for 1989:Q2 through 1994:Q4 (i.e., 23 quarters) separately for constrained and unconstrained banks.[6] This was done in terms of a regression equation relating loan growth to current and two lagged values of both the federal funds target rate and change in bank equity capital.[7] Though the sum of the coefficients for federal funds target rate was not significantly different from zero, yet their numerical values indicated limited support in favour of their basic proposition.

Kishan and Opiela (2000) looked into the question of bank size and bank capital in the context of bank lending channel for the US banks. Segregating banks by asset size and capital leverage ratio, they hypothesised that small and undercapitalised may not be able to offset the impact of a contractionary monetary policy by selling large time deposits. Consequently, the loan supply of these banks would be more responsive to monetary policy than that of large well-capitalised banks. Based on the observed capital-asset ratio (CAR), they subdivided the banks in their sample (for the U.S economy) into three groups: (a) undercapitalised (with CAR < 8 per cent), (b) adequately

5. To quote, "The model implies that an increase in the federal funds target rate should have a negative effects on loans in the unconstrained banks sample and a positive effect for constrained banks. Or, if taken less literally, the relative implication of the model is that unconstrained banks should reduce loans by more than constrained banks in response to a tightening of monetary policy" (Peek and Rosengreen, 1995b: 54-65).

6. They defined constrained banks as those under a formal regulatory action or having CAMEL 4 or CAMEL 5 rating.

7. The other regressors in the equations are: seasonal dummies, lagged inflation rates, yearly change in the New England employment rate.

capitalised (with 8 per cent < CAR < 10 per cent), and (c) well-capitalised (with CAR > 10 per cent). Small (assets less than $300 million) and undercapitalised banks were found to be the most responsive to monetary policy.

Altunbas, de Bondt, and Marqués-Ibánez (2004) examined bank-level panel data estimates for 1991-1999 for the Euro area and showed that the lending behaviour of the least-capitalised banks in France and Italy was more responsive to a change in monetary policy than that of better-capitalised banks. The degree of capitalisation seemed to have mattered for the monetary policy impact on lending of the key players in the German and euro area banking system. They interpreted their findings as suggestive of the potential influence that the new Basel capital requirements could have the monetary transmission channel through bank capital.

More recently, Gambacorta (2005), using a new quarterly data set of data for all Italian banks over the period 1986–2001, estimated a panel loan equation that had a number of new features. First, the data set included a new measure of capitalisation, the amount of capital that exceeds regulatory requirements, that was better able to capture the effects of capital constraints on loan supply. Besides, the data set disentangled banks' funds in core deposits (insured debt), CDs and deposits in bearer form (uninsured debt).[8] Second, heterogeneity in the monetary policy pass-through was tested taking simultaneously into account not only the bank specific characteristics of size, liquidity and capitalisation, but also affiliation with a group, to capture the effects of internal capital markets in bank holding companies. Third, there was a detailed comparison between results on the bank lending channel obtained using supervisory reports data and those based on Bank-Scope, a publicly available data set. The results indicated that the effects of monetary policy tended to differ among banks—after a tightening, the decrease in total deposits was more pronounced for less capitalised banks that have a lower ability to raise uninsured form of funds. This result was significant at conventional values only when an excess capital indicator was used, instead of the standard capital-

8. This should improve the understanding of the first step of the bank lending channel on deposits because distributional effects, if any, should be detected only with respect to funds that are not insured.

to-asset ratio (in order to capture the effect of the Basel capital requirements). As for lending, size did not affect the banks' reaction to a monetary policy impulse. This could be explained by a closer customer relationship, which provided an incentive for small banks, which were more liquid on average, to smoothen the effects of a tightening on supplied credit. Liquidity was a significant factor enabling banks to attenuate the effect of a decrease in deposits on lending. The drop in liquidity following a monetary tightening was indeed greater for small and poorly capitalised banks. The presence of internal capital markets in bank holding companies also contributed to isolating exogenous variations in the financial constraints faced by subsidiary banks.

6.2.3 Indian Evidence

Available literature in the Indian context has been primarily confined to behaviour of the various features of commercial banks in recent years. While size and liquidity have not attracted much attention, there are attempts to analyse, in particular, the influence of capital adequacy ratio (CAR) and behaviour of bank capital.

Nag and Das (2002) tried to assess the imposition of uniform capital requirements on the flow of credit to the business sector by public sector banks. Estimating a supply equation of bank credit they found that capital-adequacy ratio had a negative impact on credit supply in the sense that capital requirements enforced a "risk-averse mind-set on the overall risk taking appetite of the banks."

In exploring the factors influencing off-balance sheet (OBS) activities of public sector banks Nachane and Ghosh (2002) found that: (i) size tended to play an important role in influencing OBS activities, and (ii) the higher was the levels of capital and liquid assets, lower was the banks' incentive to engage in OBS activities. They found it consistent with the hedging theory which contended that the risk aversion might be an important determinant of banks not getting engaged in off-balance sheet activities.

In exploring the relationship between portfolio risk and capital and its interrelationship with operating efficiency, Das (2002) emphasised on the interrelationship between capital, non-performing loans and productivity. Using data on public sector banks (PSBs) for the period 1995-96 through 2000-2001, he found capital, risk and productivity change to be intertwined, with each reinforcing the other. The results implied that inadequately capitalised banks had lower productivity and are subject to a higher degree of regulatory pressure than adequately capitalised ones.

Ghosh *et al.* (2003) used a dynamic multivariate panel regression model for 27 public sector banks over the period 1997 through 1999, where the independent variables included, among others, profits, deposits, and off-balance sheet activities. They found no conclusive evidence of risk aversion among them. Capital requirements do not seem to have affected bank behaviour over and above the influence of the banks' own internally generated targets.

Ghosh, Nachane and Ray (2004) looked into the behaviour of CAR of public sector banks over 1996–2002 and found that bank-specific factors like return on equity were relevant for bank capital behaviour. They also found some circumstantial evidence that Indian public sector banks were risk averse.

More recently, using a panel of 51 scheduled commercial banks (excluding regional rural banks and foreign banks)[9] based on a quarterly confidential supervisory data on balance sheet of banks for the period 1997: Q1 through 2002: Q2, Pandit *et al.* (2006) tested the veracity of credit channel for Indian banks.[10] The loan equation in their model was modelled in terms of a monetary policy indicator (CRR), total investments in government and other approved securities, aggregate of deposits and borrowings (as a proxy for total sources of funds), capital adequacy ratio and asset size. They found that bank lending seemed to be statistically significant to changes in the contemporaneous (but not the lagged) indicator of monetary policy. The same estimates also revealed that there seemed to be a positive relationship between total lending and total funds and a negative association between lending and investments. Thus, banks

9. The sample comprised 27 public sector banks, 16 old private sector banks and 8 new private sector banks.

10. As these data were proprietary in nature (being made available by the Off-Site Monitoring and Surveillance Division of the RBI) we could not use this data base for the empirical estimation.

tended to cut back lending and adjust their funds in response to a policy shock. Interestingly a contractionary monetary policy in their model tended to force even adequately capitalised banks to cut back on lending. They cited two possible reasons for such a behaviour: (a) the relative attractiveness of investments *vis-à-vis* loans (in terms of risk weights), and (b) characterisation of the sample period by relatively low economic activity. Second, the results also indicated that prudential norms, as proxied by banks' capital adequacy ratios, tended to exert a significant influence on bank lending. Furthermore, their analysis demonstrated that big and small banks also differed in respect to their response to given monetary policy shocks.

6.3 A Description of the Panel and Some Stylised Facts

6.3.1 A Description of the Panel

In order to gauge the veracity of the relationship between bank lending, monetary stance, liquidity and bank size for both public and private banks in recent years, the data are collected from various issues of the RBI publication, *Statistical Tables Relating to Banks in India* giving all the annual audited balance sheets of scheduled commercial banks. The number of scheduled commercial banks (excluding regional rural banks) each year has varied and ranged from 90 to 100 during the period. From this population we constructed a balanced panel of 74 banks for the nine-year period 1995-96 through 2003-04.[11] These 74 banks covered all categories of banks, *viz.*, public, private and foreign.

The construction of the balanced panel primarily entailed exclusion of the winded-up banks (mainly in the private and foreign categories), which ceased their operation during the period. As the instances of mergers and acquisitions as well as closures of banks were limited during the period under study, the coverage of the panel had been large and exceeded 90 per cent of the aggregate asset for all the years under consideration.

11. We have chosen to focus our attention to 1995-96 due to the introduction of various measures particularly those related to CRAR. Joshi and Little (1996) pointed out that these capital adequacy norms reached their full force in 1995-1996.

Annex Table A-6.1 reports the list of banks included in the panel. Some sample statistics of the panel, both in aggregative terms as well as in terms of ownership, are reported in Table 6.1.

Table 6.1

Sample Statistics of the Panel of 74 Banks

(Rs. Crore)

Variable	*Mean*	*Std. Dev.*	*Minimum*	*Maximum*	*Skewness*	*Kurtosis*
(1)	(2)	(3)	(4)	(5)	(6)	(7)
Capital	239	486.0	1	4574	4.3	25.3
Deposits	11793	26806.7	1	318619	7.0	63.4
Borrowings	700	2794.7	1	49219	11.8	169.8
Assets	14721	34482.2	27	407815	7.1	63.8
Liquidity	1785	5021.7	1	60709	7.9	73.5
Investment	5540	13877.9	2	185676	8.3	88.8
Advances	6146	13564.6	1	157934	6.2	50.3

Note: Period: 1994-95 through 2003-04.

Table 6.2

Percentile Distribution of Key Banking Variables

(Rs. Crore)

Variable	*Top 10%*	*Top 20%*	*Bottom 20%*	*Bottom 10%*
(1)	(2)	(3)	(4)	(5)
Capital	578	331	12	1
Deposits	27152	16028	631	222
Borrowings	1320	554	33	9
Assets	31802	19468	872	400
Liquidity	1737	960	27	7
Investment	400	153	1	1
Advances	12375	7650	260	115

Note: Period: 1994-95 through 2003-04.

How far are the bank groups homogenous in character? Towards this end Table 6.2 reports the top 10 per cent and bottom 10 per cent of each banking variable. The heterogeneity in the sample is quite high. After all, while the Indian banking sector clearly has some big banks in the public sector like State Bank of India, Bank of Baroda or

Punjab National Bank coupled with at least three big foreign banks (*viz.*, Citi Bank, Standard Chartered Bank, and HSBC), and the ICICI Bank in the private sector category, there are a number of banks which are quite small.

6.3.2 Some Stylised Facts

Since impact of size, liquidity and capital on bank credit is central to the chapter, let us have a look into the broad trends in these variables. As far as Indian banks are concerned it is increasingly perceived that size does matter. Thus, in the context of this chapter we need to ask whether the three attributes go hand in hand or not? That is to say, are the large banks also the banks with more capital or

Table 6.3

Share of Top (As per Asset Size) Five Banks

(Per cent)

Year	*Top Five Banks*	*Assets*	*Capital*	*Liquidity*
(1)	(2)	(3)	(4)	(5)
1994-95	State Bank of India, Bank of Baroda, Bank of India, Punjab National Bank, Canara Bank	47.4	25.9	47.8
1995-96	State Bank of India, Bank of Baroda, Bank of India, Punjab National Bank, Canara Bank	47.2	15.9	47.2
1996-97	State Bank of India, Bank of India, Bank of Baroda, Canara Bank, Punjab National Bank	46.6	14.3	51.2
1997-98	State Bank of India, Bank of India, Bank of Baroda, Canara Bank, Punjab National Bank	46.3	12.4	49.7
1998-99	State Bank of India, Bank of India, Bank of Baroda, Canara Bank, Punjab National Bank	46.2	13.6	55.0
1999-00	State Bank of India, Bank of Baroda, Bank of India, Canara Bank, Punjab National Bank	45.0	13.2	50.8
2000-01	State Bank of India, Canara Bank, Punjab National Bank, Bank of Baroda, Bank of India	45.0	12.8	53.2
2001-02	State Bank of India, ICICI Bank, Punjab National Bank, Canara Bank, Bank of Baroda	44.3	13.8	59.1
2002-03	State Bank of India, ICICI Bank, Punjab National Bank, Canara Bank, Bank of India	43.3	13.2	51.7
2003-04	State Bank of India, ICICI Bank, Punjab National Bank, Canara Bank, Bank of Baroda	42.1	11.8	45.0

liquidity? In order to answer this question, Table 6.3 presents the share of five top banks (in terms of their asset) in aggregate assets, capital and liquidity. A number of stylised facts emerge from Table 6.3.

First, there has been a steady decline in the share of the top five banks—from 47 per cent in 1994-95 to 42 per cent in 2003-04.[12] Second, since 2001-02, emergence of the ICICI Bank, a private sector bank in the second position is another important feature. Third, share of capital of these top five banks is much less than their share in assets. Fourth, share of liquidity of the top five banks, however, matches broadly with the share of assets of these banks.

Capital and liquidity, in absolute terms, may not make much sense; hence for the sake of comparability they were taken as a proportion of aggregate assets, and an attempt was made to examine the ranking of the banks in terms of capital-assets ratio. Table 6.4 below reports capital-asset ratios of the top ten banks (ranked in terms of capital-assets ratios). Interestingly, one hardly found any of the top banks (in terms of their assets) in the list—at least for the later years. The list typically included a number of foreign banks, which must have had regulatory capital from their head office either for prudential reasons or for some specific credit or for branch expansion. The list also included some of the somewhat weak banks wherein capital had been infused in a specific year. It, therefore, appeared that a large bank in size (in terms of assets) was not necessarily large in its capital base (in terms of capital-assets ratio).

Before we proceed further a digression on the capital adequacy ratio of the Indian banking sector is in order. As far as Indian banks are concerned the question of building up adequate capital had not received much attention in the initial years of nationalisation.[13] Since

12. Koeva (2003) and Mohan (2006a) arrived at similar findings based on asset-based and deposits-based Herfindhal Index.

13. Nachane (1999) noted that in the pre-nationalisation phase of Indian banking, capital standards attracted a modicum of attention from the Reserve Bank of India. The declining ratio of capital (paid-up capital plus reserves) to total deposits from 9 per cent in 1950 to 4 per cent in 1960 for Indian banks, had prompted the RBI to advise banks to aim at a ratio of 6 per cent, through compulsory transfers of 20 per cent of declared profits to reserves. He went on further to add that, "Nationalisation however ushered in a sense of complacency on the issue of capitalisation and the capital to deposit ratio for public sector banks seems to have fallen to fairly low levels (less than 2 per cent) in the early 1980s."

Table 6.4

Un-weighted Capital-Asset Ratios of Top (As per Un-weighted Capital-Asset Ratios) 10 Banks

(in Per cent)

Bank	*1995-96*	*Bank*	*1996-97*	*Bank*	*1997-98*
(1)	*(2)*	*(3)*	*(4)*	*(5)*	*(6)*
State Bank of Mauritius	75.90	State Bank of Mauritius	68.82	State Bank of Mauritius	42.56
ING Bank	73.81	ING Bank	56.14	DBS Bank	32.47
Centurion Bank	28.45	DBS Bank	31.00	ING Bank	27.83
DBS Bank	24.41	United Bank of India	13.43	Indian Bank	12.36
Bank of Punjab	22.48	HDFC Bank	11.02	United Bank of India	11.89
HDFC Bank	20.16	UCO Bank	10.49	UCO Bank	11.11
ICICI Bank	12.96	Bank of Punjab	9.96	HDFC Bank	10.60
United Bank of India	12.70	Punjab & Sind Bank	9.30	Mashreq Bank	10.09
UCO Bank	10.71	Bank of Maharashtra	8.54	Deutsche Bank	8.92
Bank of Maharashtra	9.60	ICICI Bank	8.42	Punjab & Sind Bank	7.82
Bank	*1998-99*	*Bank*	*1999-00*	*Bank*	*2000-01*
(7)	*(8)*	*(9)*	*(10)*	*(11)*	*(12)*
ING Bank	34.21	State Bank of Mauritius	19.90	Oman International Bank	19.24
State Bank of Mauritius	26.18	DBS Bank	15.53	State Bank of Mauritius	18.78
DBS Bank	22.83	Oman International Bank	15.33	ING Bank	15.86
Indian Bank	11.67	ING Bank	12.28	DBS Bank	10.99
UCO Bank	10.91	Bank of Tokyo Mitsubishi	11.42	Bank of Tokyo Mitsubishi	10.56
United Bank of India	10.52	Indian Bank	10.64	Indian Bank	9.40
Mashreq Bank	8.94	UCO Bank	9.61	Societe Generale	9.31
Societe Generale	8.47	United Bank of India	9.28	Mashreq Bank	9.06
Bank of Nova Scotia	8.37	Societe Generale	9.10	United Bank of India	8.43
Bank of Tokyo Mitsubishi	8.17	Mashreq Bank	8.96	UCO Bank	8.29

Contd...

...contd...

Bank	*2001-02*	*Bank*	*2002-03*	*Bank*	*2003-04*
(13)	*(14)*	*(15)*	*(16)*	*(17)*	*(18)*
Barclays Bank	33.17	Barclays Bank	35.64	ING Bank	66.02
Oman International Bank	22.27	ING Bank	29.69	DBS Bank	30.38
State Bank of Mauritius	21.50	Oman International Bank	25.65	Oman International Bank	27.79
Indian Bank	12.57	Societe Generale	24.33	Societe Generale	19.62
ING Bank	12.55	State Bank of Mauritius	20.70	State Bank of Mauritius	19.12
Societe Generale	10.97	DBS Bank	14.88	Barclays Bank	19.04
DBS Bank	9.36	Mashreq Bank	13.11	Mashreq Bank	13.95
Mashreq Bank	9.34	Indian Bank	12.93	Credit Lyonnais	13.21
Bank of Bahrain and Kuwait	8.39	Credit Lyonnais	12.72	Indian Bank	11.68
Credit Lyonnais	8.16	Bank of Tokyo Mitsubishi	9.33	Bank of Bahrain and Kuwait	8.44

bulk of the banks was owned by the Government, they were considered immune to any failure. Nevertheless, it may be noted that as early as 1961 the RBI had advised banks to aim at a ratio of 6 per cent capital and reserves to total deposits (Jagirdar, 1996).[14] However, the question of provisioning did not arise for the commercial banks due to a number of factors. First, as per the then accounting practice, income of the commercial banks was recognised on an accrual basis as against actual recovery of cash. Second, the system of classifying advances as per health codes was quite subjective. It was only after the introduction of prudential and accounting norms in 1992-93 following the Narashimham Committee's recommendations, the losses showed up clearly in the bank's balance sheet.[15]

How do we see the relation between the three variables then? Table 6.5 to this effect reports the year-wise rank correlation of the 74 banks of the panel as per the three attributes of size, capital and liquidity. The correlations are typically low, insignificant and negative (with the exception of the positive correlation coefficient between capital and

14. Jagirdar (1996) noted that this ratio had declined from 9 per cent in 1950 to 4 per cent in 1960 and to 1.5 per cent in 1978 (for public sector banks).

15. Annex Table A-6.2 reports the frequency distribution of banks as per CRAR.

liquidity in some years). Thus, *a priori* one would expect that these three attributes would be reasonably independent and just high magnitude of one may not able to capture the information content of other attributes.

Table 6.5

Rank Correlation of the Three Criteria

Year	*Assets & Capital*	*Capital & Liquidity*	*Assets & Liquidity*
(1)	(2)	(3)	(4)
1994-95	-0.03	-0.08	-0.08
1995-96	-0.08	-0.07	-0.12
1996-97	-0.06	-0.23	0.04
1997-98	-0.10	-0.34	-0.14
1998-99	-0.17	-0.33	-0.03
1999-00	-0.20	-0.28	-0.02
2000-01	-0.23	0.00	-0.25
2001-02	-0.31	0.09	0.15
2002-03	-0.38	0.00	0.12
2003-04	-0.40	0.09	0.09

Note: While assets are in terms of absolute numbers, capital and liquidity have been taken as ratios of assets of the respective banks.

6.4 Empirical Methodology and the Model

6.4.1 Empirical Methodology

Panel data refer to a pooled time series and cross-section data. The basic framework for estimating panel regressions is a model of the following form (Baltagi, 2001; Green, 2003):

$$y_{it} = \mathbf{X}'_{it}\boldsymbol{\beta} + z'_i\boldsymbol{\alpha} + \boldsymbol{\varepsilon}_{it} \quad (6.1a)$$

where, y_{it} be the dependent variable, and $\mathbf{X}_{it}$ be the regressor matrix, not including a constant term, and i (individual) = 1, ... , N, and T (time) = 1, ... ,T. The individual effect is $\mathbf{z}'_i\boldsymbol{\alpha}$ where $\mathbf{z}_i$ is a constant term and a set of individual or group specific characteristics.

There are two basic models of panel data, *viz.,* (a) Fixed Effect and (b) Random Effect Model. In the Fixed Effect (FE) model, the intercept in the regression is allowed to differ among individuals in recognition of the fact that each individual (unit) may have characteristics of their own. Formally, if it is unobserved but correlated with then the least square estimator of it is biased and inconsistent (due to omitted variable), then the Fixed effect model is written as:

(6.1b) $$y_{it} = X'_{it}\beta + \alpha_i + \varepsilon_{it}$$

where, $\alpha_i = z_i'\alpha$ is representative of all the observable effects.

Random Effect (RE) models assume that the intercept of an individual unit is a random drawing from a much larger population with a constant mean value. The RE model is written as:

(6.1c) $$y_{it} = X'_{it}\beta + \alpha + u_i + \varepsilon_{it}$$

The model is estimated using Generalised Least Square (GLS) approach.

A practical issue to the researcher is to determine which model to choose. If N is large and T is small and if the assumptions underlying random effects hold, then the random effect model would give more efficient estimators. Nevertheless, the choice of FE *versus* RE is determined though the Hausman test; this is distributed chi-squared asymptotic around the null hypothesis that Random Effect is appropriate. As per this test (Hausman, 1978), the null hypothesis is that the FE and RE do not differ substantially and the test statistic is distributed asymptotically chi-squared. FE is consistent under both the null and the alternative hypothesis. RE is consistent under the null and inconsistent under the alternative hypothesis. We can test the appropriateness of RE using critical values.

6.4.2 The Model

To test whether banks react differently to monetary policy shocks, a loan equation was estimated in terms of monetary stance as well as three explicit features of banks *viz.*, size, liquidity, and capital. These three features were allowed to interact with the monetary policy indicator, in terms of cross-product terms.

The baseline equation was that of lending, wherein credit growth was regressed on monetary policy stance variables, and on its interaction with three bank-specific characteristics (size, liquidity and capitalisation). The regression also included inflation (π) and GDP growth (y) to control for demand effects. The introduction of these two variables allowed one to capture cyclical movements and serves to isolate the monetary policy component of interest rate changes.

Thus, the specification of the model is as follows[16]:

$$\Delta \ln B_{it} = \alpha_i + \beta \Delta MS_t + \gamma_o S_{i,t} + \gamma_1 S_{,i,t-1} \Delta MS_t + \delta_0 Liq_{i,t} + \delta_1 Liq_{i,t} \Delta MS_t + \lambda_0 Cap_{i,t} + \lambda_1 Cap_{i,t} \Delta MS_t + \theta_0 \pi_t + \theta_1 y_t \quad (6.2)$$

with i=1, …., N and t = 1, …, T, and where N is the number of banks (74 in our sample) and T is the numbers of years.

The variables in the model are as follows: B_{it} is loans, S_{it} is the size, Cap_{it} is the capitalisation, Liq_{it} is the liquidity of the bank i; y_t is the real GDP growth; π_t is inflation rate and MS_t is the monetary stance, which, as earlier, is taken to be the CRR. While assets are taken as proxy for the size of a bank, both liquidity and capital has been expressed as a proportion of aggregate asset of the particular bank.

The definition of size, liquidity, and capitalisation are as follows:

$$\text{Size} = S_{it} = \ln(\text{Assets})_{it} \quad (6.2a)$$

$$\text{Liquidity} = Liq_{it} = \frac{\text{Money at Call}_{it} + \text{Cash in Hand}_{it}}{\text{Assets}_{it}} \quad (6.2b)$$

$$\text{Capitalisation} = Cap_{it} = \frac{\text{Capital}_{it}}{\text{Assets}_{it}} \quad (6.2c)$$

Since we have taken first difference and experimented also with lagged values, the final sample is confined to the eight year span of 1996-97 through 2003-04.

6.5 Empirical Results

6.5.1 Base-line Model

The base-line results from the estimated equation (6.2) using the full sample of all banks are in Table 6.6. The results from the random

16. The variables, being either in growth rates or ratios, are expected to be free from any time trends. An ideal way to treat such problems was to undertake the panel unit root tests. Nevertheless, even if N is large since T is small (*viz.*, eight years), such tests could not be performed in the present context.

effects models are reported in Table 6.6 below. Interestingly, the coefficient of the stance variable in the loan equation is negative but insignificant at conventional levels, implying that at an aggregative level an increase in CRR leads to a reduction in loan disbursal. The coefficients of both size as well as 'size • stance' are both positive and significant, implying thereby, the larger the bank, the more is its capability to avoid the impact of a contractionary monetary policy. The coefficients of both liquidity as well as capitalisation (both independently and as their interaction with stance variable) are positive and significant (with the exception of 'liquidity • stance' variable, which is insignificant), implying that banks with a higher liquidity ratio and/or capitalisation are better able to buffer their lending from changes in monetary policy. Both growth and inflation seem to have exerted positive impact on the loan disbursement.

Table 6.6

Loan Equation for All Banks

Variable	*Coefficient*	*t-statistic*
(1)	*(2)*	*(3)*
Stance	-0.0576	-0.95
Size	0.0694	5.02 *
Size • Stance	0.0111	1.60 ***
Liquidity	0.5060	2.48 *
Liquidity • Stance	0.0290	0.37
Capitalisation	0.2262	1.90 ***
Capitalisation • Stance	0.0601	2.50 *
Inflation	0.0235	2.15 **
Growth	0.0218	1.90 **
Constant	-0.7338	-4.81 *
Adj. R-squared	0.167	
DW	1.187	
Hausman Chi-squared	16.523	
Model	Random Effects	

Note: (1) Period of estimation: 1996-97 through 2003-04.

(2) *, **, and *** indicate significance at 1 per cent, 5 per cent and 10 per cent, respectively.

(3) The t-statistics are derived from heteroscedasticity-consistent standard errors.

Given this base-line result, the validity of this model is specifically examined with certain features of three attributes, *viz.*, size, liquidity and capitalisation. In particular, the attention is focussed around the first (Q1) and third (Q3) quartiles for these three attributes. Illustratively, if the Q1 value (i.e., bottom 25 per cent) for asset size was a_0, and Q3 value (i.e., top 75 per cent) for asset size was a_1, then equation (6.2) is rerun for all observations for which $S_{it} < a_0$ ('small' banks), and for which $S_{it} > a_1$ ('large' banks) separately. Inspection is made as to how far does the lending behaviour for small sized banks would differ from large sized banks? The same exercise is repeated for other two attributes as well (*viz.*, liquidity/capitalisation).

6.5.2 *Results from Specific Attributes of Size, Liquidity and Capitalisation*

Large *versus* Small Banks

As far as size is concerned, from the given sample, the Q1 and Q3 values for assets are arrived at 7.1578 and 9.6352, respectively. As stated all banks for which S_{it} is less than 7.1578 are termed as 'small banks', and all banks for which S_{it} is more than 9.6352 are termed as 'large banks.' The results of equation (6.2) separately for large and small banks are given below in Table 6.7.

Interestingly, while the coefficient for monetary stance variable for the large banks is positive, the same for small banks are negative—indicting that large banks are able to insulate their loan portfolio from the impact of a contractionary monetary policy. However, considering the fact that the coefficient for stance variable for the small banks is not significant at conventional levels, the strength of the above regularity is not enough. Furthermore, the size variable is positive and significant for both the groups.

Liquid *versus* Less Liquid Banks

Similar exercise was done for liquid banks (i.e., all banks with $Liq_{it} > 0.1701$) and less liquid banks (i.e., all banks with $Liq_{it} < 0.0740$). Results are reported in Table 6.8. Interestingly, while for both groups of banks the stance variable is positive and significant, its magnitude is far higher for less liquid banks than the liquid banks, indicating that the 'less liquid' banks were to be affected 'more' by monetary policy actions.

Table 6.7

Loan Equation for Large versus Small Banks

	Large Banks		Small Banks	
Variable	*Coefficient*	*t-statistic*	*Coefficient*	*t-statistic*
(1)	(2)	(3)	(4)	(5)
Stance	0.4882	2.45 *	-0.0685	-0.16
Size	0.0519	1.93 ***	0.7001	1.95 ***
Size • Stance	-0.0499	-2.62 *	0.0510	0.72
Liquidity	1.0298	2.99 *	0.2737	0.42
Liquidity • Stance	-0.0492	-0.47	-0.1451	-0.48
Capitalisation	-0.0338	-0.05	0.3030	0.34
Capitalisation • Stance	0.0597	0.19	-0.1266	-0.65
Inflation	-0.0158	-1.32	0.1841	3.10 *
Growth	-0.0382	-2.75 *	0.1703	1.78 *
Constant	0.8578	2.09 *		
Adj. R-squared	0.154		0.172	
DW	1.317		1.479	
Hausman Chi-squared	7.143		3.603	
Model	Random Effect		Fixed Effect	

Note: (1) Period of estimation: 1996-97 through 2003-04.
(2) *, **, and *** indicate significance at 1 per cent, 5 per cent and 10 per cent, respectively.
(3) The t-statistics are derived from heteroscedasticity-consistent standard errors.

Well-Capitalised *versus* Under-Capitalised Banks

Similarly, well-capitalised banks are defined as those in the top 75 per cent, i.e., with $Cap_{it} > 0.0445$, and under-capitalised banks in the bottom 25 per cent, i.e., with $Cap_{it} < 0.0040$. The estimated loan equations for both these two types of banks are reported in Table 6.9. The size variable is positive for both the bank groups. It is interesting to note that while the stance variable for the well-capitalised is positive and significant, the same for the under-capitalised banks is negative and significant. Thus, capital could have acted as a buffer to counter contractionary monetary policy.

Table 6.8

Loan Equation for Liquid versus Less Liquid Banks

	Liquid Banks		*Less Liquid Banks*	
Variable	*Coefficient*	*t-statistic*	*Coefficient*	*t-statistic*
(1)	*(2)*	*(3)*	*(4)*	*(5)*
Stance	0.1557	1.93 *	0.3571	2.62 *
Size	0.0726	3.27 *	0.0275	0.96
Size • Stance	0.0233	2.72 *	-0.0071	-0.40
Liquidity	0.5273	1.67 ***	-0.7625	-1.12
Liquidity • Stance	0.1615	1.83 ***	-1.3931	-2.98 *
Capitalisation	-0.8617	-2.34 *	0.9335	1.96 **
Capitalisation • Stance	-0.4233	-3.25 **	0.9083	2.67 *
Inflation	0.0089	0.46	0.1125	3.57 *
Growth	0.0613	2.02 **	0.0867	2.48 *
Constant	-0.9635	-3.27 *	-0.7986	-1.95 **
Adj. R-squared	0.154		0.171	
DW	1.681		1.412	
Hausman Chi-squared	248.080		18.119	
Model	Random Effect		Random Effect	

Note: (1) Period of estimation: 1996-97 through 2003-04.
(2) *, **, and *** indicate significance at 1 per cent, 5 per cent and 10 per cent, respectively.
(3) The t-statistics are derived from heteroscedasticity-consistent standard errors.

The results presented so far indicated that out of the three attributes, capitalisation could have exerted the most significant influence on the loan behaviour of the commercial banks. While size and liquidity might have played some role in this story, it was capitalisation that was by far the most important factor.

Is there an Ownership Effect?

The last chapter tried to seek answer to the question whether different types of banks react differently to the monetary policy actions. In a similar spirit the base-line loan equation was run separately for different types of banks, *viz.*, (a) SBI and associates,

(b) nationalised banks, (c) new private banks, (d) old private banks, and (e) foreign banks. The results are reported in Table 6.10. Interestingly while the stance coefficient had turned out to be negative for SBI and associates and old private sector banks, for nationalised banks, new private banks and foreign banks these were found to be positive.

How far are these results robust? The next section, towards this end, relaxes some of the postulates of our analysis.

Table 6.9

Loan Equation for Well-capitalised versus Undercapitalised Banks

	Well-Capitalised Banks		*Under-Capitalised Banks*	
Variable	*Coefficient*	*t-statistic*	*Coefficient*	*t-statistic*
(1)	(2)	(3)	(4)	(5)
Stance	0.1570	1.82 ***	-0.1162	-2.00 **
Size	0.0928	1.96 **	0.0382	2.74 *
Size • Stance	0.0024	0.10	0.0126	1.99 **
Liquidity	0.2345	0.31	-0.0163	-0.07
Liquidity • Stance	-0.1871	-0.49	0.1487	1.82 ***
Capitalisation	0.6381	1.87 ***	-19.8726	-1.74 ***
Capitalisation • Stance	0.0639	0.23	-8.2207	-1.42
Inflation	0.1130	2.83 *	-0.0024	-0.25
Growth	0.0910	2.27 **	0.0214	1.90 **
Constant	-1.7017	-3.73 *	-0.2662	-1.70 ***
Adj. R-squared	0.195		0.142	
DW	1.144		1.821	
Hausman Chi-squared	8.411		28.862	
Model	Random Effect		Random Effect	

Note: (1) Period of estimation: 1996-97 through 2003-04.

(2) *, **, and *** indicate significance at 1 per cent, 5 per cent and 10 per cent, respectively.

(3) The t-statistics are derived from heteroscedasticity-consistent standard errors.

Table 6.10

Loan Equations for Different Types of Banks

Variable	*SBI & Associates*		*Nationalised Banks*		*New Private Banks*		*Old Private Banks*		*Foreign Banks*	
	Coefft	*t-statistic*	*Coefft*	*t-statistic*	*Coefft*	*t-statistic*	*Coefft*	*t-statistic*	*Coefft*	*t-statistic*
(1)	(2)	(3)	(4)	(5)	(6)	(7)	(8)	(9)	(10)	(11)
Stance	-0.063	-1.33	0.328	3.62	1.528	4.63	-0.082	-1.61	0.042	0.23
Size	0.001	0.07	-0.031	-1.36	0.083	1.28	0.019	1.5	0.121	2.74
Size • Stance	0.004	0.89	-0.031	-3.47	-0.162	-4.11	0.010	1.57	0.007	0.27
Liquidity	0.218	1.12	0.376	1.9	1.230	1.64	0.014	0.09	0.727	1.62
Liquidity • Stance	0.077	1.84	-0.045	-0.91	-0.250	-0.62	0.085	1.43	.063	0.3
Capitalisation	0.143	0.19	0.027	0.09	6.099	6.4	2.991	1.52	0.265	0.55
Capitalisation • Stance	0.214	0.68	0.029	0.23	0.781	0.88	1.807	1.53	-0.064	-0.29
Inflation	-0.017	-2.51	-0.006	-0.91	0.054	1.71	-0.011	-1.55	0.079	2.4
Growth	-0.014	-1.73	-0.005	-0.67	0.110	2.97	0.010	1.35	0.051	1.48
Constant	0.266	1.93	0.482	1.87	-1.607	-2.3	-0.001	-0.01	-1.555	-3.64
Adj R squared	0.049		0.106		0.555		0.066		0.077	
DW	1.760		1.057		1.965		1.246		1.198	
Hausman Chi Square	21.968		29.745		13.925		11.207		17.189	

Note: (1) Period of estimation: 1996-97 through 2003-04.
(2) The t-statistics are derived from heteroscedasticity-consistent standard errors.
(3) All equations are from random effects model.

6.6 Some Robustness Tests

6.6.1 Results with Alternative Liquidity Variable

To begin, the definition of liquidity is relaxed to include investments by commercial banks, i.e.,

$$(6.2b)' \qquad Liq2_{it} = Liq_{it} + \frac{Investments_{it}}{Assets_{it}}$$

Equation (6.2) was re-estimated with Liq2 and results are reported in Table 6.11.

Table 6.11

Loan Equation with Broad Liquidity

Variable	*Coefficient*	*t-statistic*
(1)	*(2)*	*(3)*
Stance	-0.0249	-0.24
Size	0.2250	2.31 **
Size • Stance	0.0117	0.98
Liquidity	0.9355	1.08
Liquidity • Stance	-0.0140	-0.37
Capitalisation	0.7885	1.23
Capitalisation • Stance	0.0847	0.39
Inflation	0.0520	2.63 *
Growth	0.0702	2.57 *
Adj.R-squared	0.2446	
DW	1.4148	
Hausman Chi-squared	4.4598	
Model	Fixed Effects	

Note: (1) Period of estimation: 1996-97 through 2003-04.
(2) *, **, and *** indicate significance at 1 per cent, 5 per cent and 10 per cent, respectively.
(3) The t-statistics are derived from heteroscedasticity-consistent standard errors.

A broader measure of liquidity is clearly insignificant both independently as well as in product terms. Considering the fact that during most of the period under consideration banks used to hold their securities portfolio under "held to maturity", inclusion of investment in the liquidity aggregates may not be entirely appropriate and hence these results may not have serious implications.

6.6.2 Results with Alternative Stance Variable

As in the earlier chapter we have experimented with an alternative measure of stance variable, *viz.*, growth of reserve money (GRM). The results for the aggregative credit equation with GRM as the stance variable are reported in Table 6.12. The stance variable is clearly not of the correct sign and is insignificant too. In fact, excepting the size and the control variables such as inflation and growth all other variables have turned out to be insignificant.

Table 6.12

Loan Equation with an Alternative Stance Variable

Variable	*Coefficient*	*t-statistic*
(1)	(2)	(3)
Stance	-0.0247	-0.93
Size	0.1689	2.19 *
Size • Stance	0.0037	1.24
Liquidity	0.3216	0.74
Liquidity • Stance	0.0366	1.29
Capitalisation	0.7096	1.07
Capitalisation • Stance	-0.0195	-0.42
Inflation	0.0228	2.12 *
Growth	0.0503	2.08 *
Adj. R-squared	0.195	
DW	1.431	
Hausman Chi-squared	7.053	
Model	Fixed Effects	

Note: (1) Period of estimation: 1996-97 through 2003-04.
(2) *, **, and *** indicate significance at 1 per cent, 5 per cent and 10 per cent, respectively.
(3) The t-statistics are derived from heteroscedasticity-consistent standard errors.

6.6.3 Results with Normalised Variables

In a similar framework, estimating credit equations for Italy, Gambacorta (2005) normalised all three criteria (i.e., size, liquidity and capitalisation) with respect to their average across all the banks in the respective sample, in order to get indicators that sum to zero over all observations. This means that for the baseline regression model, the average of the interaction terms is also zero, and the parameters are directly interpretable as the monetary policy effect for the average bank. The size indicator has been normalised not just with respect to the mean over the whole sample period but also with respect to each single period. This removes unwanted trends in size (namely, due to the fact that size is measured in nominal terms). The veracity of the basic model was checked with respect to these normalisations. The definitions are as follows:

(6.3a) $$S'_{it} = \ln A_{it} - \frac{1}{N}\sum_{i=1}^{N} \ln A_{it}$$

(6.3b) $$Liq'_{it} = \frac{L_{it}}{A_{it}} - \frac{1}{T}\sum_{t=1}^{T}\left[\frac{1}{N}\sum_{i=1}^{N}\left(L_{it}/A_{it}\right)\right]$$

(6.3c) $$Cap'_{it} = \frac{K_{it}}{A_{it}} - \frac{1}{T}\sum_{t=1}^{T}\left[\frac{1}{N}\sum_{i=1}^{N}\left(K_{it}/A_{it}\right)\right]$$

where A_{it}, L_{it} and K_{it} are assets, liability and capital of the ith bank, respectively.

The loan equation with these normalised variables is reported in Table 6.13.

Table 6.13

Loan Equation with Normalised Variables

Variable	*Coefficient*	*t-statistic*
(1)	*(2)*	*(3)*
Stance	-0.0011	-0.05
Size	0.2869	2.24 *
Size • Stance	0.0102	1.81 **
Liquidity	0.2638	1.53 ***
Liquidity • Stance	0.0904	0.33
Capitalisation	0.6439	1.97 **
Capitalisation • Stance	0.0101	1.05
Inflation	0.0127	1.90 **
Growth	0.0046	2.39 *
Adj R-squared	0.198	
DW	1.459	
Hausman Chi-squared	4.973	
Model	Fixed Effects	

Note: (1) Period of estimation: 1996-97 through 2003-04.

(2) *, **, and *** indicate significance at 1 per cent, 5 per cent and 10 per cent, respectively.

(3) The t-statistics are derived from heteroscedasticity-consistent standard errors.

The results are found to be similar with our aggregative results reported earlier. However, most of the cross product terms, though are in line with expected sign have turned out to be insignificant.

6.6.4 Results with Interest Rates

So far no interest rate was included in the basic loan equation. In order to check the sensitiveness of the results with respect to interest rates, we have run the basic loan equation with the first difference in loan rate (Table 6.14). With loan rate being insignificant, the results are broadly similar to the basic loan equation.

Table 6.14

Loan Equation for All Banks with Interest Rate

Variable	*Coefficient*	*t-statistic*
(1)	(2)	(3)
Stance	-0.0565	-0.93
Size	0.0695	5.02 *
Size • Stance	0.0117	1.67 ***
Liquidity	0.5093	2.50 *
Liquidity • Stance	0.0242	0.31
Capitalisation	0.2414	1.96 ***
Capitalisation • Stance	0.0648	2.53 *
Inflation	0.0264	2.30 **
Growth	0.0258	2.07 **
Interest Rate	0.0191	0.83
Constant	-0.7532	-4.88 *
Adj. R-squared	0.167	
DW	1.149	
Hausman Chi-squared	16.274	
Model	Fixed Effects	

Note: (1) Period of estimation: 1996-97 through 2003-04.

(2) *, **, and *** indicate significance at 1 per cent, 5 per cent and 10 per cent, respectively.

(3) The t-statistics are derived from heteroscedasticity-consistent standard errors.

6.7 Conclusion

This chapter tried to see the implications of existence of cross-sectional differences in determining bank credit behaviour. The results, derived from a comprehensive panel of Indian banks, seemed to have suggested that heterogeneity in the monetary policy pass-through existed and after a monetary restriction banks reduced lending. In determining the nature of this relationship, three crucial variables had been emphasised, *viz.*, size, liquidity and capital. It was found that it was the capital that tended to exert the most significant impact in determining the relationship. In other words, monetary policy seemed to be most effective for the capital constrained banks in the sense that it was their advances that bore the brunt of a contractionary monetary policy. Considering the fact that the small public and private banks sector were mostly capital constrained, monetary policy seemed to be most effective for this group of banks. Foreign banks, on the other hand, were hardly capital constrained, irrespective of their size, and hence were able to bypass to some extent the impact of the contractionary monetary policy—same was true for both large public and new private sector banks as well.

Annex Table A-6.1

List of Banks Included in the Sample

No.	*Bank Name*
(1)	*(2)*
	I. State Bank of India & Associates
1.	State Bank of India
2.	State Bank of Bikaner & Jaipur
3.	State Bank of Hyderabad
4.	State Bank of Mysore
5.	State Bank of Patiala
6.	State Bank of Saurashtra
7.	State Bank of Travancore
8.	State Bank of Indore
	II. Nationalised Banks
9.	Bank of Baroda
10.	Allahabad Bank
11.	Bank of India
12.	Bank of Maharashtra
13.	Canara Bank
14.	Dena Bank
15.	Indian Bank
16.	Indian Overseas Bank
17.	Central Bank Of India
18.	Union Bank Of India
19.	Punjab National Bank
20.	United Bank Of India
21.	UCO Bank
22.	Syndicate Bank
23.	Andhra Bank
24.	Corporation Bank
25.	Oriental Bank Of Commerce
26.	Vijaya Bank
27.	Punjab & Sind Bank
	III. New Private Banks
28.	Centurion Bank
29.	UTI Bank
30.	IndusInd Bank
31.	ICICI Bank
32.	Global Trust Bank
33.	HDFC Bank
34.	Bank of Punjab

Contd...

...contd. ...

(1)	(2)
	IV. Old Private Banks
35.	Bank Of Rajasthan
36.	Catholic Syrian Bank
37.	City Union Bank
38.	Karur Vysya Bank
39.	Lakshmi Vilas Bank
40.	Ratnakar Bank
41.	Sangli Bank
42.	Tamilnad Mercantile Bank
43.	Federal Bank
44.	Karnataka Bank
45.	Nainital Bank
46.	Bharat Overseas Bank
47.	South Indian Bank
48.	Lord Krishna Bank
49.	Vysya Bank
50.	Jammu & Kashmir Bank
51.	United Western Bank
52.	Dhanalakshmi Bank
53.	Ganesh Bank of Kurundwad
	V. Foreign Banks
54.	ABN AMRO Bank
55.	American Express Bank
56.	Bank of America
57.	Bank of Tokyo
58.	BNP Paribas
59.	Standard Chartered Bank
60.	DBS Bank
61.	Citibank
62.	HSBC
63.	Sonali Bank
64.	Deutsche Bank
65.	Abu-Dhabi Commercial Bank
66.	Mashreq Bank
67.	Bank of Nova Scotia
68.	Societe Generale
69.	Oman International Bank
70.	Bank of Bahrain & Kuwait
71.	Credit Lyonnais
72.	Barclays Bank
73.	ING Bank
74.	State Bank of Mauritius

Annex Table A-6.2

Distribution of Scheduled Commercial Banks by Capital Adequacy Ratio

(Number of Banks)

Year	Bank Group	State Bank Group	Nationalised Banks	Old Private Sector Banks	New Private Sector Banks	Foreign Banks in India	Scheduled Commercial Banks
(1)	(2)	(3)	(4)	(5)	(6)	(7)	(8)
1995-96	Below 4%	-	5	3	-	-	**8**
	Between 4% -8%	-	3	3	-	3	**9**
	Between 8% -10%	6	7	7	1	12	**33**
	Above 10%	2	4	12	8	16	**42**
1996-97	Below 4%	-	2	3	-	-	**5**
	Between 4% -8%	-	-	1	-	-	**1**
	Between 8% -10%	3	6	8	-	13	**30**
	Above 10%	5	11	13	9	26	**64**
1997-98	Below 4%	-	1	2	-	-	**3**
	Between 4% -8%	-	-	2	-	-	**2**
	Between 8% -10%	1	6	6	2	12	**27**
	Above 10%	7	12	15	7	30	**71**
1998-99	Below 4%	-	1	2	-	1	**4**
	Between 4% -8%	-	-	2	-	-	**2**
	Between 8% -10%	-	4	3	2	14	**23**
	Above 10%	8	14	18	7	29	**76**

Contd...

...contd...

(1)	(2)	(3)	(4)	(5)	(6)	(7)	(8)
1999-00	Below 4%	-	1	2	-	-	**3**
	Between 4% -8%	-	-	2	-	-	**2**
	Between 8% -10%	-	4	2	1	5	**12**
	Above 10%	8	14	18	7	37	**84**
2000-01	Below 4%	-	1	2	-	-	**3**
	Between 4% -8%	-	1	1	-	-	**2**
	Between 8% -10%	-	2	4	1	4	**11**
	Above 10%	8	15	16	7	38	**84**
2001-02	Below 4%	-	1	-	-	-	**1**
	Between 4% -8%	-	1	-	1	-	**2**
	Between 8% -10%	-	2	2	1	2	**7**
	Above 10%	8	15	19	6	33	**81**
2002-03	Below 4%	-	-	-	2	-	**2**
	Between 4% -8%	-	-	-	-	-	-
	Between 8% -10%	-	1	2	1	-	**4**
	Above 10%	8	18	19	6	36	**87**
2003-04	Below 4%	-	-		1	-	**1**
	Between 4% -8%	-	-		1	-	**1**
	Between 8% -10%	-	1			-	**1**
	Above 10%	8	18	20	8	33	**87**

Note: Scheduled commercial banks (SCBs) had to comply with minimum capital to risk-weighted assets ratio (CRAR) of 8 per cent up to end-March 1999 and 9 per cent from end-March 2000.

7

Conclusion and the Way Forward

7.1 An Overview

How do commercial banks react in response to central bank's monetary policy actions? The question is crucial to understand the nature of the monetary transmission process and operation of monetary policy. Broadly speaking, the present book seeks to answer this question within the framework of credit channel of monetary transmission. In doing so, the following inter-related but distinct issues have been looked into: (a) messages from the theoretical literature on extended IS-LM model with banks, (b) trends in Indian macro-economy and regulatory regime, and (c) econometric assessment of commercial banks' response to central bank's monetary policy actions.

In specific terms, against the backdrop of the emergence of theoretical literature on credit channel and role of banks in monetary policy (Chapter 2) and regulatory and monetary policy environment within the broad framework of the financial sector reforms process in India (Chapter 3), the present book makes an attempt to look into the response of the commercial banks to central bank's policy behaviour. This is done at an aggregative level (Chapter 4) and at a disaggregative level (Chapters 5 and 6).

What has been the major finding of the book? At the risk of broad generalisation, the findings indicate that while monetary policy actions do influence commercial bank behaviour, not all the banks respond uniformly. In particular, attributes like ownership, size, liquidity of balance sheet, or capitalisation play important roles in determining the nature of response. In specific terms the commercial banks have the capability to cushion off its portfolio, at least partially from the impact of a contractionary monetary policy, depending on these attributes.

7.2 Broad contours

As already emphasised, the book in some sense has explored the impact of central bank's policy actions on commercial banks behaviour at three planes, *viz.*, theory, stylised facts, and empirical regularities in the form of econometric evidence. In this concluding chapter it may be worthwhile to recapitulate them.

7.2.1 Theoretical Developments

While surveying the IS-LM-type models with a specific role for banks, two specific models, *viz.*, the Bernanke-Blinder (1988) model and Greenwald-Stiglitz (1990) model have been examined. The major issues that would emerge from the consideration of the extended IS-LM model are four-fold.

First, as money is fungible, mere incorporation of bank loans in the banks' and firms' balance sheets does not add an independent role for commercial banks in transmitting monetary policy actions. Second, the market segmentation between loans and securities is often ensured from information asymmetry based explanations for speciality of banks and bank loans and existence of bank-dependent borrowers. Third, given the assumption of specialty of bank loans, it is possible to reconstruct the standard IS-LM model, with bank loans (as another asset for banks and as another source of financing for corporates). In these models there is an independent credit channel and a consequent role of commercial banks in transmission of monetary policy actions. Fourth, while existence of newer financial instruments like commercial papers (CPs) or certificates of deposits (CDs), as prime examples of non-intermediated borrowing, may weaken the speciality of bank credit, as long as some degree of speciality of bank exists, the independent role of banks in transmitting monetary policy actions is not ruled out.

7.2.2 Stylised Facts for India

In discerning the major stylised facts of the Indian economy during 1991-92 through 2003-04, three distinct issues were highlighted: (a) growth and inflation experience, (b) the RBI's select policy actions (both qualitative and quantitative), and (c) major trends in the commercial bank balance sheet and profit and loss accounts. It was noted that the period witnessed a significant higher growth and lower inflation than what has been achieved in the past. The period also saw initiation of the financial sector liberalisation process on the one hand and imposition of prudential regulation on the other. Dismantling the administered interest rate regime, giving more operational autonomy to the banks to choose their deposit and lending rates, infusing competitive forces through liberal entry of foreign banks and new private banks have been the hallmark of the financial sector reform process. A set of micro-prudential measures (capital adequacy requirements, income recognition, asset classification and provisioning norms for loans, exposure norms, accounting norms) was also stipulated.

A number of interesting trends in the commercial banks balance sheet were noticeable during this period. With the sharp reduction in CRR, there was a gradual decline in the share of balances held with the RBI. Notwithstanding the reduction in CRR and SLR, bank credit did not increase significantly; on the contrary, banks holding of government securities witnessed a significant increase. The declining interest rate scenario in the backdrop of a weakening of credit demand could be behind such a behaviour of commercial banks.

Thus, as far as the relation between central bank's policy actions and commercial banks' balance sheet is concerned, two broad stylised facts emerged. First, while in general monetary policy was non-contractionary in nature, there were episodes where the Reserve Bank adopted a contractionary stance. Second, there were two major forces the balance sheet of the commercial banks: (a) reductions in statutory requirement, and (b) introduction of capital related regulation.

7.2.3 Econometric Evidence

Aggregative Behaviour

Looking into the aggregative evidence of impact of RBI's policy actions (Chapter 3) on three major variables of commercial banks, *viz.*, deposits, credits and investment, and concentrating primarily on the impulses of a unit standard deviation shock in CRR the following broad trends emerge. First, as a result of a shock in CRR, there was a mild rise in the aggregate deposits of the commercial banks in the first month, which started decreasing from the second month and reached a plateau by the end of the second year. Second, a downward trend was noticeable in the behaviour of aggregate investment nearly up to three years. Third, aggregate bank credit on the contrary, is shown to have followed a sharp upward path as a result of the CRR shock in the first few months before reaching a plateau at the end of the first year.

These broad trends were found to be fairly robust with respect to various extensions of the original model. Illustratively, alternative VAR models were run with credit and investment together, as well as with quarterly GDP (as against the monthly index of industrial production in the original specification). Additional variables (such as interest rates) and alternative orderings were also tried. Besides, the proportion of forecast error variance decomposition (FEVD) of the balance sheet variable that was explained by CRR indicated that while CRR tended to explain a large part of FEVD of Investment, for credit and deposits it did not matter much.

Thus, as far as the impact of a contractionary monetary policy is concerned, there seems to be a mild perverse impact on bank advances, in the sense that a positive shock in CRR actually ends up with 'higher' bank advances in the initial period. This is fairly uniform and robust across various specifications of the models.

Ownership of Banks and the Impact of Monetary Policy

An attempt was made to examine the hypothesis: Is the pattern of commercials banks' response to central bank's policy (as found in Chapter 3) is fairly uniform across different bank groups (Chapter 4). In this context, deposits behaviour was found to be reasonably invariant across bank groups, on the contrary, the advances behaviour of different types of banks revealed some diverging patterns. In fact, in case of a CRR shock, advances of nationalised and foreign banks actually exhibited an increasing pattern during the 12 months horizon. In case of the SBI group, the impulses get flattened after an initial increase in the first month. In case of private banks the impulse is an initial downturn followed by a flattening. Thus, the behaviour of private banks seems to be somewhat different from other banks. In general, the investment behaviour of the impulse responses exhibited a downward trend.

As earlier, the robustness of the results was checked. In looking at the sensitiveness of the VARs with respect to ordering, the correlation between the balance sheet variable and CRR was found to be low, indicating that the impulse responses are unlikely to be influenced by the ordering of the variables. Results were also found to be reasonably invariant with respect to the VAR model with first differenced variables as well as with alternative monetary stance variable (*viz.*, growth of reserve money). The broad trends were valid for a shorter period as well (1996-97 through 2003-04, i.e., since the imposition of various prudential measures like CRAR).

While there is some limited support in favour of differential impact of monetary policy on different types of banks (based on ownership), the evidence is at best weak. There could be various explanations for the weak evidence presented in this chapter. After all, ownership cannot be a proxy for different attributes of a bank which gives it some wherewithal to partially bypass the impact of monetary policy.

Bank Credit Behaviour and the Influence of Size, Capital and Liquidity

Within the database of a panel of balance sheets of commercial banks, the impact of different attributes on the credit behaviour with respect to a panel of commercial banks (from 1994-95 to 2003-04) was taken up next. In the baseline model credit growth is sought to be explained in terms of monetary policy stance and its interaction with three bank-specific characteristics (size, liquidity and capitalisation), apart from inflation and GDP growth (to control for demand effects). Various cross product terms were included to account for the interdependence between the variables. The estimated panel regression revealed that at an aggregative level an increase in CRR led to a reduction in loan disbursal. While both growth and inflation seem to have exerted positive impact on the loan disbursement, the coefficients of both size as well as 'size • stance' revealed that the larger the bank, the more is its capability to insulate its portfolio from the impact of a contractionary monetary policy. Furthermore, the coefficients of both liquidity as well as capitalisation implied that banks with a higher liquidity ratio and/or capitalisation are better able to buffer their lending from changes in monetary policy.

Given this base-line result, the validity of this model specifically with reference to the three attributes, *viz.*, size, liquidity and capitalisation was examined. In particular, the results were separately checked for the first (Q1) and third (Q3) quartiles for these three attributes. The results indicated that out of the three attributes it was capitalisation that could have exerted significant influence on the loan behaviour of the commercial banks.

The robustness tests were run with respect to three exercises, *viz.*, (a) with alternative liquidity variable (i.e., including investment), (b) with alternative monetary stance variable (i.e., growth of reserve money), and (c) normalised size, capitalisation and liquidity variable wherein these variables are normalised with respect to their average across all the banks in the respective samples. The results were broadly in consonance with those presented earlier.

As capital exerted the most significant impact in determining the relationship, monetary policy seemed to be the most effective for the capital constrained banks in the sense that their advances bore the brunt of a contractionary monetary policy. Considering the fact that the small public and private banks sector are mostly capital constrained, monetary policy seems to be most effective for this group of banks. Foreign banks, on the other hand, are hardly capital constrained, irrespective of their size, and hence are able to bypass to some extent the impact of the contractionary monetary policy. The same is true for large public and private sector banks as well.

7.3 Policy Implications and Futuristic Scenario

What are the policy implications of these results? How far are these empirical regularities valid for the Indian banking sector for years to come? As these questions lie in the realm of an uncertain future, the forthcoming analysis becomes somewhat in the nature of crystal ball gazing.

In a nutshell, the results presented so far indicate that while the central bank does influence the portfolio behaviour of commercial banks, the impact is not uniform across banks of differential characteristics. Bigger and well-capitalised banks are able to withstand, 'albeit' partially, the impact of a contractionary monetary policy stance. How far would these results remain valid in the days to come? Will there be more of large banks as against small banks? Will there be more of foreign banks as against domestic banks? These questions will have important ramifications not only on the structure of the Indian banking system but also on the nature of monetary transmission.

7.3.1 Consolidation in Indian Banking

An important consideration in this respect will be the extent of consolidation of the Indian banking sector. It is widely acknowledged that the key drivers of the banking sector in the future will be, 'Competition, Consolidation and Convergence.'[1] A relevant question in this context is: Is India going to have larger banks in future? A review of the international banking scenario reveals that consolidation has been a dominant feature of the banking sector in most countries over the past decade and most countries have higher levels of concentration in their banking industry than India. In fact, none of the Indian banks are among the top 20 in the world. India's largest bank, the State Bank of India, according to the *Banker* Magazine, ranks 82 in terms of business worldwide. The largest banks in terms of asset size are now over a trillion dollars and some like Citi Bank, JP Morgan Chase, HSBC and Bank of America have a market capitalisation of over $150 billion.[2] In contrast, the market capitalisation of the entire Indian banking sector is about $40-45 billion, which would make the entire banking sector rank after the 30 largest banks in the world.[3]

The future in this respect is likely to be significantly influenced by the relevant policies, as articulated in two important RBI documents released on February 28, 2005, *viz.*, (a) *Roadmap for Presence of Foreign Banks in India*, and (b) *Guidelines on Ownership and Governance in Private Sector banks.*

---

1. Finance Minister P. Chidambaram mentioned this in his Speech for the Union Budget for 2004-05.
2. This is despite the fact that the US had one of the most fragmented systems because of stringent regulations preventing consolidation. Over the past decade the market share of the top five banks has, however, risen to about 45 per cent today from about 26 per cent in the 1990s.
3. Asia saw much greater government activism in consolidation in recent years. Illustratively, Malaysia reduced the number of banks from 55 to 10. Taiwan aimed to bring down the number of state banks from 12 to six in 2006. Singapore government guided the system down to three players with DBS being supported to become a regional leader. Similar initiatives are in place in Indonesia, South Korea and Japan. The four big Chinese banks are over $400 billion in assets size (Sinha, 2005).

The Roadmap for Presence of Foreign Banks focused on the future of Indian banks into two phases:

- First Phase: March 2005 to March 2009, when foreign banks will be permitted to establish presence by way of setting up a wholly owned banking subsidiary or conversion of the existing branches into a wholly owned banking subsidiary.
- Second Phase: April 2009 - onwards, when after a review of the experience gained a view would be taken concerning extension of national treatment to wholly owned banking subsidiary, dilution of stake and permitting mergers/acquisitions of any private sector banks in India by a foreign bank.

The Guidelines on Ownership and Governance for Private Banks reinforces the draft policy framework for ownership and governance in private sector banks of July 2, 2004. These guidelines emphasised desirability of diversified ownership in banks, 'fit and proper' status of important shareholders, directors and the CEO and the need for a minimum capital/net worth criteria. In effect, the guidelines provide for higher levels of shareholding, inter alia, for ensuring restructuring and consolidation simultaneous with compliance of fit and proper criteria.

What will be the implication of these policies on the future of banking system in India? Through the new road map on banking reforms, the aim is to perhaps enable the smaller private banks to get in shape before the floodgates to the impending Mergers and Acquisitions (M&A) are opened. In fact, domestically, the policy regime was in favour of consolidation in respect of a number of old private banks, many of which have been constrained by the paucity of capital.

In sum, the evidence is a pointer to the fact that the forces of consolidation will be operative in India in the years ahead, and in all likelihood the banking industry will have fewer (and perhaps bigger) players, akin to the one envisaged in the Narasimham Report. In the context of the results presented in this book, this consolidated banking sector is expected to considerably pose challenges to the transmission of central banks policy on the commercial banks.

Interestingly, a consolidated banking sector is not the only future scenario for India. In a futuristic study, McKinsey (2005) uncovers 'three potential scenarios' that could emerge in the banking sector by

2010 (after the entry of a large number of foreign players), based on the interplay between policy and regulatory interventions and management strategies:

- The first is a 'high performing' scenario, where policy makers intervene only to the extent required to ensure system stability and protection of consumers' interest, and bank managements step up the drive for far-reaching change.
- In the second 'evolving' scenario, policy makers adopt a pro-market stance but are cautious on pushing reform. The share of the banking sector value added would be 4.7 per cent of GDP in such a case.
- In the third 'stagnating' scenario policy makers intervene to set restrictive conditions and management is unable to execute changes to deliver value to shareholders or customers. Here, the share of the banking sector value added would be only 3.3 per cent of GDP.

How far and in what degrees would these scenarios get unfolded is a matter of conjecture at present. The bottomline nonetheless remains that the market concentration in the banking industry is perhaps going to increase and with that the power of the commercial banks to insulate their portfolio, at least partially, from the impact of a contractionary monetary policy.

7.3.2 Changes in Operating Procedure of Monetary Policy

As the present book primarily used CRR as a policy instrument, a question arises: What happens when the central bank switches to indirect instruments of monetary policy? The question is relevant in view of the fact that as the RBI currently uses repo operations to conduct monetary policy, how far will the conclusions be valid in the context of the changed operating procedure of monetary policy?[4]

4. Due to paucity of data, repo/reverse repo operations could not be used as a monetary policy measure. After all, that the liquidity adjustment facility (LAF) was introduced much later; in April 1999, an Interim LAF (ILAF) was introduced pending further upgradation in technology and legal/procedural changes to facilitate electronic transfer and settlement. Besides, bank specific bidding structure for repo and reverse repo operations are not available in the public domain.

Before attempting any answer, a review of operations under Liquidity Adjustment Facility (LAF) may be in order.[5] Pursuant to the recommendations of the Narasimham Committee on Banking Reforms, the RBI decided, in principle, to introduce a Liquidity Adjustment Facility (LAF) operated through repo and reverse repo in order to set a corridor for money market interest rates. Accordingly, in April 1999, an Interim LAF (ILAF) was introduced pending further upgradation in technology and legal/procedural changes to facilitate electronic transfer and settlement. The IALF was operated through a combination of repo, export credit refinance, collateralised lending facilities (CLF) and open market operations. ILAF provided a mechanism for injection and absorption of liquidity available to banks and Primary Dealers (PDs) to overcome mismatches in supply and demand from time to time. In view of the experience gained in operating the ILAF, a full-fledged LAF was introduced in stages subsequently.[6]

Some minimum liquidity support to PDs, however, continued but at an interest rate linked to the variable rates as obtained in the daily repo auctions. With full computerisation of Public Debt Office (PDO) of the RBI and introduction of Real Time Gross Settlement (RTGS) System, repo operation through electronic transfers was envisaged for the third stage. In the final stage, LAF operations at different timings of the same day were introduced.

In order to make the market more sensitive to trades while bidding, multiple price auction was implemented effective from May 8, 2001 in place of the discriminatory price based auction for repos. 14-day reverse repo was introduced from November 5, 2001. For a brief period, reverse repo for 28 days was also conducted during October 20-24, 2003. The minimum bid size for LAF was reduced from Rs. 10 crore to Rs. 5 crore from May 8, 2001. From March 29, 2004, 7-day fixed rate reverse repo auctions were conducted on a daily basis. In order to rationalise the existing structure of provision of liquidity facility from the RBI, the entire amount of export credit refinance to

5. See Mohan (2006b) for a detailed discussion on LAF operations in India.

6. In the first stage, with effect from June 5, 2000, the additional CLF and level II support to PDs was replaced by variable rate repo auctions with same day settlement. In the second stage, CLF and level I liquidity support was replaced by variable rate repo auctions.

banks and liquidity support to PDs was made available at a single rate, at the repo rate from March 29, 2004. Effective November 1, 2004, LAF is being operated with overnight fixed rate repo and reverse repo, replacing auctions of 7-day and 14-day repo and reverse repos.

In the wake of forex inflows and absence of appropriate instrument for absorption of liquidity of permanent nature, LAF was increasingly used for the purpose of sterilisation, which in a way clouded the policy signaling role of LAF rates. Indeed, the RBI Internal Group on LAF (2003c) observed that 'it would be desirable to de-emphasise the passive sterilisation attribute of the LAF repo facility so that it could emerge as the exclusive policy signaling rate.' The subsequent operationalisation of the market stabilisation scheme to absorb liquidity of a more enduring nature from April 2004 has now considerably reduced the burden of sterilisation on the LAF window.

As already indicated, bank-specific details of LAF bidding are not available—thus, there is no way to categorically affirm which type of banks—big or small, well-capitalised or under-capitalised—are the dominant players in this market. Nevertheless, reports in the print media and casual commentaries indicate that since LAF facility is available against Government securities, banks which are rich in their investment portfolio will approach the LAF window. Interestingly, as a part of their liquidity management strategy, banks have three windows available: (a) the collateralised borrowing and lending obligations (CBLO) facility from the Clearing Corporation of India (CCIL), (b) market repo, and (c) repo from the RBI. In general, large ones are found to rely more on the various segments of the money market—RBI repo, market repo, CBLO and call—for the purpose of borrowing.

What happens in such a scenario when a contractionary monetary policy is implemented through a rise in repo and reverse repo rates? Given the fixed repo auctions, banks with larger kitty of Government securities will be able to tide over the liquidity shortages either through repo or through Collateralised Borrowing and Lending Obligation (CBLO) routes. Thus, broadly speaking, banks with larger holding of G-Sec will be able to cushion their balance sheet from the central bank's policy action.

7.3.3 Newer Norms of Bank Capital

One of the finings of the book is that the more capitalised banks are in better position to withstand a contractionary monetary policy. The new Capital Accord or Basel II in this context deserves special mention. The *New Capital Adequacy Framework*, proposed in June 1999, rests on three major elements or 'pillars': (i) minimum capital requirements, based on weights intended to be more closely aligned to economic risks than in the 1988 Accord, (ii) supervisory review, which set basic standards for bank supervision to minimise regulatory arbitrage and (iii) market discipline, which spells out greater levels of disclosure and standards of transparency by the banking system (BIS, 2003; BIS, 2004)

The first pillar of minimum capital requirements is more relevant in the context of the present book. As per the January 2001 Consultative Paper, banks can choose from either of the following three evolutionary variants to measure risks, *viz.*, (a) a basic standardised model (modified version of the existing approach), (b) an internal rating based (IRB) foundation model, and (c) an advanced IRB model.

While the basic standardised model is heavily dependent on the ratings of the external rating agencies like Moody's or Standard and Poor's, the key requirement for the foundation or advanced IRB model is the development of the bank's own internal rating system. Furthermore, as Basel II makes a distinction between credit risk, market risk and operational risk, regulatory capital is the sum of capital requirements on account of each of these three risks. The definition of capital in the New Basel Capital Accord has been retained unchanged from that of the original Accord.

What has been the reaction of the Indian regulators? While the RBI agreed with the view that the focus of the New Accord might be primarily on internationally active banks, it contended that after a period of time, all 'significant' banks would be expected to adhere to it and further pointed out that that the 'standardised approach' might not suit the needs of the smaller banks. As a consequence, the RBI suggested a 'simplified standardised approach' for those banks that are not internationally active. The RBI defined these 'internationally active banks' as banks with cross-boarder business exceeding 20 or 25 per cent of their total business (RBI, 2003a). 'Significant banks', on the other hand, have been defined as those banks with complex structures and whose market share in the total assets of the domestic banking system exceeds one per cent.

In particular, it has been pointed out that the adoption of the New Accord in its present format could result in a significant increase in the capital charge for banks. After all, although capital requirements for credit risk may go down due to adoption of more risk sensitive models—such an advantage will be more than offset by additional capital charges for operational risk and increased capital allotment for market risk (Leeladhar, 2005). These could make capital constraints more binding, making the transmission of the central bank's policy actions more effective on commercial banks.

7.4 Scope of Further Research

A number of important research issues have been neglected in the present book. Some of the limitations of the book have already been elaborated in the earlier section. These emanate from the fact that India is quite in a transition state as far as banking structure and monetary policy operating procedure are concerned. Some comments about the possible validity of our broad conclusions have already been made in the context of repos and reverse repos as the major weapons of monetary policy, as well as ensuing trends in bank consolidation. Any quantitative estimates in this regard, however, could not be provided here.

Another important issue that has not been touched upon is the impact of monetary policy on the co-operative banking sector. If attributes like size, capitalisation or liquidity are important considerations in the determination of the central bank's policy actions on commercial bank's behaviour, then many of the co-operative banks, by virtue of their small size and low capital base, are likely to be more susceptible to the central bank's monetary policy actions.

Yet another issue is the role of capital flows. Given the fact that banks have of late been increasingly tapping the international capital market, it is likely that capital constraint could get eased in the days to come. It remains to be seen as to how far the story presented here gets modified in presence of large capital inflows.

The present book is about the banks and monetary policy actions. A distinct but related issue is: how does the central bank affect the ultimate borrowers, *viz.*, corporates? The usual balance sheet variant of the credit channel of monetary transmission looks into this question. This issue is beyond the scope of the present book.

References

Acharya, S. (2002). "Macroeconomic Management in the Nineties", *Economic and Political Weekly* 37(16): 1515-38.

Acharya, S. and S. Madhur (1983). "Informal Credit and Black Money: Do They Frustrate Monetary Policy?", *Economic and Political Weekly* 18: 1751-56.

Arena, Marcos, C.M. Reinhart, and F. Vazques (2006). "The Lending Channel in Emerging Economics: Are Foreign Banks Different?", *NBER Working Paper* No. W12340.

Agung, Juda (1998). "Financial Deregulation and Bank Lending Channel in Developing Countries: The Case of Indonesia", *Asian Economic Journal* 12(3): 273-94.

Ahluwalia, Montek S. (2002). "Economic Reforms in India: Has Gradualism Worked?", *Journal of Economic Perspectives* 16(3): 67-88.

Ajit, D. and R.D. Banger (1997). "Banks in Financial Intermediation: Performance and Issues", *RBI Occasional Papers* 18(2&3): 303-49.

Alger, Guillermo and Ingela Alger (1999). "Liquid Assets in Banks: Theory and Practice", *Working Paper.* Boston College.

Altunbas, Y., Evans, Lynne & Molyneux, Philip (2001). "Bank Ownership and Efficiency", *Journal of Money, Credit and Banking* 33(4): 926-54.

Altunbas, Y., O. Fazylow, P. Molyneux (2002). "Evidence on the Bank Lending Channel in Europe", *Journal of Banking and Finance* 26(11): 2093-110.

Angeloni, I., A.K. Kashyap, B. Mojon (2003). *Monetary Policy Transmission in the Euro Area.* Cambridge: Cambridge University Press.

Altunbas, Yener and de Bondt, Gabe and Marqués-Ibánez, David (2004). "Bank Capital, Bank Lending, and Monetary Policy in the Euro Area", *Kredit and Kapital* 4: 1-17.

Ashcraft, A.B. (2001). "New Evidence on the Lending Channel", *Federal Reserve Bank of New York Staff Reports* No. 136.

Balakrishnan, Pulapre (2005). "Macroeconomic Policy and Economic Growth in the 1990s", *Economic and Political Weekly* 40(36): 3969-77.

Baltagi, B. (2001). *Econometric Analysis of Panel Data (2nd Edition).* Chichester: John Wiley and Sons.

Baltensperger, E. (1989). "Credit", in Eatwell *et. al* (eds.), *The New Palgrave Money.* pp.97-102. London: Macmillan.

Banerjee, Abhijit V., Shawn Cole, and Esther Duflo (2004). "Banking Reform in India", *India Policy Forum # 1*. Brookings Institution. (available at *http://econ-www.mit.edu*).

Bank of England (2000). *Economic Models at the Bank of England, September 2000 Update.* London: Bank of England.

Bank of Korea (1998). "Korea's Experience of the Monetary Transmission Mechanism", in Transmission of Monetary Policy in Emerging Market Economies, *BIS Policy Papers* No.3: 140-54.

Bank for International Settlement (BIS) (1999). "Capital Requirements and Bank Behavior: The Impact of the Basel Accord", *Working Paper* No.1. April.

———. (2003): *The New Basel Capital Accord.* Basel: BIS.

———. (2004): *Basel II: International Convergence of Capital Measurement and Capital Standards: A Revised Framework.* June. Basel: BIS.

Beauliue J.J, and J.A. Miron (1993). "Seasonal Unit Roots in Aggregate U.S. Data", *Journal of Econometrics* 55(1&2): 305-28.

Bernanke, Ben (1983). "Non-Monetary Effects of Financial Crisis in the Propagation of Great Depression", *American Economic Review* 73(3): 257-76.

———. (1986). "Alternative Explanations of Money-Income Correlations", *Carnegie Rochester Conference Series on Public Policy* No.25. pp.49-100.

———. (1993). "Credit in the Macroeconomy", *Federal Reserve Bank of New York Quarterly Review* 18: 50-70.

Bernanke, Ben, and Alan S. Blinder (1988). "Credit, Money, and Aggregate Demand", *American Economic Review* 78(2): 435-39.

———. (1992). "The Federal Funds Rate and Channels of Monetary Transmission", *American Economic Review* 82(4): 901-21.

Bernanke, Ben, and C. Lown (1992). "The Credit Crunch", *Brookings Papers on Economic Activity* No.2: 205-39.

Bernanke, Ben, and M. Gertler (1987). "Banking and Macroeconomics Equilibrium", in W.A. Barnett and K.J. Singleton (eds.): *New Approaches to Monetary Economics.* pp.89-111. Cambridge (UK): Cambridge University Press.

———. (1989). "Agency Cost, Net Worth and Business Fluctuations", *American Economic Review* 79(1): 14-31.

Bernanke, Ben and I. Mihov (1998). "Measuring Monetary Policy", *Quarterly Journal of Economics* 113(3): 869-902.

Bhaumik, Sumon and Paramita Mukherjee (2003). "The Indian Banking Industry: A Commentary", in Parathasarathi Banerjee and Frank-Jurgen Richter (eds.), *Economic Institutions in India.* New York: Palgrave Macmillan.

Bhaumik, Sumon and Jenifer Piesse (2004). "Are Foreign Banks Bad for Development Even if they are Efficient? Evidence from the Indian Banking Industry", University of Michigan (William Davidson Institute) *Working Paper* No. 619.

Bhaumik, Sumon and Ralitza Dimova (2004). "How Important is Ownership in a Market with Level Playing Field? The Indian Banking Sector Revisited", *Journal of Comparative Economics* 32(1): 165-80.

Blanchard, O. and D. Quah (1989). "The Dynamic Effects of Aggregate Demand and Supply Disturbances", *American Economic Review* 79(4): 1146-64.

Blanchard, Oliver (1995). "Why does Money affect Output: A Survey", in B.M. Friedman and F.H. Hahn (eds.), *Handbook of Monetary Economics* Vol.II. Amsterdam: North Holland. pp.779-835.

Boschen, John F. and Len O. Mills (1995). "The Relation between Money Market and Narrative Indicators of Monetary Policy," *Economic Inquiry* 33(1): 24-45.

Brainard, W. and J. Tobin (1968). "Pitfalls in Financial Model Building", *American Economic Review* 58(2): 99-122.

Brunner, Karl, and Allan H. Meltzer (1972). "Money, Debt and Economic Activity", *Journal of Political Economy* 80(5): 951-77.

———. (1993). *Money and Income: Issues in Monetary Analysis.* Cambridge: Cambridge University Press.

Burgess, Robin and Rohini Pande (2005). "Do Rural Banks Matter? Evidence from the Indian Social Banking Experiment", *American Economic Review* 95(3): 780-95.

Calomiris, Charles W., C.P. Himmelberg, Paul Wachtel (1995). "Commercial Paper, Corporate Finance, and the Business Cycle: A Microeconomic Perspective", *Carnegie Rochester Series on Public Policy* No.42: 203-50.

Canova, Fabio (1995). "The Economics of VAR Models", in Kevin D. Hoover (ed.), *Macroeconometrics: Developments, Tensions and Prospects.* Boston: Kluwer.

Chambers, Marcus J. (2001). "Cointegration and Sampling Frequency", *Economics Discussion Papers* 531. University of Essex, Department of Economics.

Christiano, L. and J.M. Eichenbaum (1992). "Identification and Liquidity Effects of Monetary Policy shocks", in A. Cukierman, Z. Hercowitz and L. Leiderman (eds.), *Political Economy, Growth and Business Cycles.* Cambridge: MIT Press. pp.335-370.

Christiano, L., J.M. Eichenbaum and C.L. Evans (1996). "The Effects of Monetary Policy Shocks: Evidence from the Flow of Funds", *Review of Economics and Statistics* 78(1): 16-34.

———. (1999): "Monetary Policy Shocks: What Have we Learned and to What End?", in John B. Taylor and M. Woodford (eds.), *Handbook of Macroeconomics,* Volume 1A. Amsterdam: Elsevier. pp.65-148.

Das, Abhiman (2002). "Risk and Productivity Change of Public Sector Banks", *Economic and Political Weekly* 37(5): 437-48.

Dale, Spencer and Andrew G. Haldane (1995). "Interest Rates and the Channels of Monetary Transmission: Some Sectoral Estimates", *European Economic Review* 39(9): 1611-26.

Desai, Ashok V. (2001). "A Decade of Reforms", *Economic and Political Weekly* 36(20): 4627-30. December 15.

de Bondt, G.J. (1998). "Credit Channel in Europe: Bank Level Panel Data Analysis", *Research Memorandum* No.WO&E nr 543/9813. Amsterdam: De Nederlandsche Bank.

———. (1999). "Banks and Monetary Transmission in Europe: Empirical Evidence, *BNL Quarterly Review* No.209: 149-68.

———. (2000). *Financial Structure and Monetary Transmission in Europe.* Cheltenham (UK): Edward Elgar.

Diamond, D.W. and P. Dybvig (1983). "Bank Runs, Deposit Insurance and Liquidity", *Journal of Political Economy* 91(3): 401-19.

Dimsdale, Nicholas (1994). "Banks, Capital Markets and Monetary Transmission Mechanism", *Oxford Review of Economic Policy* 10(4): 305-60.

D'Souza, Errol (2000). "Prudential Regulation in Indian Banking", *Economic and Political Weekly* 35(5): 287-95.

Eichenbaum, Martin and Kenneth J. Singleton (1986). "Do Equilibrium Real Business Cycle Theories Explain Postwar U.S. Business Cycles?", *NBER Macroeconomics Annual.* Boston: NBER. pp.91-135.

Ehrmann, Michael, Leonardo Gambacorta, Jorge Martínez-Pages, Patrick Sevestre & Andreas Worms (2003). "Financial Systems Stems and the Role of Banks in Monetary Policy Transmission in the Euro Area", in I. Angeloni, A. Kashyap and B. Mojon (eds.), *Monetary Policy Transmission in the Euro Area.* Cambridge: Cambridge University Press. pp.235-269.

Engle, Robert F. and C.W.J. Granger (1987). "Cointegration and Error-Correction: Representation, Estimation, and Testing", *Econometrica* 55(2): 251-76.

Ericsson, N.R., D.F. Hendry and H.A. Tran (1994). "Cointegration, Seasonality, Encompassing and the Demand for Money in the United Kingdom", in C.P. Hargreaves (ed.), *Non-stationary Time Series Analysis and Cointegration.* Oxford: Oxford University Press.

Favero, C.A., L. Flabbi, F. Giavazzi (1999). "The Transmission Mechanism of Monetary Policy in Europe: Evidence from Banks' Balance Sheets", CEPR *Discussion Paper* No. 2303.

Fevaro, Carlo A. (2001). *Applied Macroeconomics,* Oxford: Oxford University Press.

Farinha, L. and C. Robalo Marques (2001). "The Bank Lending Channel of Monetary Policy: Identification and Estimation using Portuguese Micro Bank Data", *European Central Bank Working Paper* No.102.

Fuller, W.A. (1976). *Introduction to Statistical Time Series.* New York: Wiley.

Gambacorta, L. (2005). "Inside the Bank Lending Channel", *European Economic Review* 49(7): 1737-59.

Ghosh, Saibal, D.M. Nachane, Aditya Narain and Satyananda Sahoo (2003). "Capital Requirement and Bank Behaviour: An Empirical Analysis of Indian Public Sector Banks", *Journal of International Development* 15(2): 145-56.

Ghosh, Saibal, D.M. Nachane and Partha Ray (2004). "Behaviour of Bank Capital: Issues and Evidence from India", *Economic and Political Weekly* 39(12): 1291-98.

Ghysels, Eric (1993). "Seasonality and Econometric Models", *Journal of Econometrics* 55(1&2): 1-8.

Ghysels, Eric, C.W.J. Granger and Pierre L. Siklos (1995). "Is Seasonal Adjustment a Linear or Non-Linear Data Filtering Process?", *University of Montreal Scientific Series* 95s-19.

Government of India (1998). *Report of the Committee on Banking Sector Reforms* (Chairman: M Narasimham). New Delhi: Government of India.

Green, W.H. (2003). *Econometric Analysis.* Singapore: Pearson Education.

Greenwald, B. and J. Stiglitz (1988). "Information, Finance Constraint and Economic Activity", in Meir Kohn and S.C. Tsiang (eds.), *Finance Constraints, Expectations and Economic Activity.* London: Oxford University Press. pp.141-165.

———. (1990). "Macroeconomic Models with Equity and Credit Rationing", in R. Gleen Hubbard (ed.), *Asymmetric Information, Corporate Finance and Investment.* Chicago: University of Chicago Press. pp.15-42.

———. (1993). "Financial Markets Imperfections and Business Cycles", *Quarterly Journal of Economics* 108(1): 77-114.

Greenwald, B., J. Stiglitz and A. Weiss (1984). "Informational Imperfections in the Capital Market and Macroeconomic Fluctuations", *American Economic Review* 74(2): 194-99.

Hamilton, J. (1992): *Time Series Analysis.* Princeton: Princeton University Press.

Hausman, J.A. (1978). "Specification Tests in Econometrics", *Econometrica* 46(6): 1251-71.

Hein, Scott E. and Jose Mercado-Mendez (1992). "The Credit View, Financial Announcements and Interest Rate Responses", *Journal of Banking and Finance* 16(4): 743-56. August.

Holmström, B., and J. Tirole (1998). "Private and Public Supply of Liquidity", *Journal of Political Economy* 106(1): 1-40.

Hubbard, R. Gleen (1994). "Is there a Credit Channel for Monetary Policy?", *NBER Working Paper* No. 4977.

Hylleberg, S., R. Engle, C.W.J Granger and B.S. Yoo (1990). "Seasonal Integration and Cointegration", *Journal of Econometrics* 44(1&2): 215-38.

Jadhav, Narendra (1994). *Monetary Economics for India.* New Delhi: Macmillan India.

Jadhav, Narendra, Partha Ray, D. Bose and Indranil Sen Gupta (2005). "Financial Sector Reform and Balance Sheet of the RBI", *Economic and Political Weekly* XL(3): 1142-50.

Jagirdar, Brinda (1996). "Capital Adequacy and Competition", in *Proceedings of the Bank Economists' Conference.* pp.97-104.

Johansen, Søren and Ernst Schaumburg (1999). "Likelihood Analysis of Seasonal Cointegration", *Journal of Econometrics* 88(2): 301-39.

Joshi, Vijay and I.M.D. Little (1994). *Indian—Macroeconomics and Political Economy, 1964-1991.* New Delhi: Oxford University Press.

———. (1996). *Indian Economic Reforms: 1991-2001.* New Delhi: Oxford University Press.

Kakes, Jan (2000). *Monetary Transmission in Europe—The Role of Financial Markets and Credit.* Cheltenham (U.K.): Edward Elgar.

Kashyap, A.C. and J.C. Stein (1994). "Monetary Policy and Bank Lending", in N. Gregory Mankiw (ed.), *Monetary Policy.* Chicago: University of Chicago Press. pp.221-56.

———. (1995). "Impact of Monetary Policy on Bank Balance Sheets", *Carnegie Rochester Series on Public Policy* 42: 151-95.

———. (1997). "The Role of Banks in Monetary Policy: A Survey with Implications for the European Monetary Union", *Federal Reserve Bank of Chicago Economic Perspectives.* September/October. pp.2-18.

———. (2000). "What Do A Million Observations on Banks Say About The Transmission of Monetary Policy", *American Economic Review* 90(3): 407-28.

Kashyap, Anil, Jeremy C. Stein and D.W. Wilcox (1993). "Monetary Policy and Credit Conditions: Evidence from Composition of External Finance", *American Economic Review* 83(1): 78-98.

Kashyap, Anil, Raghuram Rajan, and Jeremy C. Stein (2002). "Banks as Liquidity Provider: An Explanation for the Coexistence of Lending and Deposit-Taking", *Journal of Finance* 57(1): 33-74.

Keeton, William R. (1992). "Monetary Policy Implications of Bank Security Holdings and Large CDs", Federal Reserve Bank of Kansas City, *Research Working Paper* No. RWP 92-08.

Khusro, A.M. (1996). *Monetary and Banking Econometrics.* New Delhi: New Age International.

Kishan, R. and T. Opiela (2000). "Bank Size, Bank Capital, and the Bank Lending Channel", *Journal of Money, Credit and Banking* 32(1): 121-40.

Koeva, Petya (2003). "The Performance of Indian Banks during Financial Liberalization", *IMF Working Paper* WP/03/150.

Koop, G., M.H. Pesaran and S.M. Potter (1996). "Impulse Response Analysis in Non-linear Multivariate Models", *Journal of Econometrics* 74(1): 119-47.

Kumbhakar, Subal and Subrata Sarkar (2003). "Deregulation, Ownership Change and Efficiency in Indian Banking: An Application of Stochastic Frontier Analysis", *Journal of Money, Credit and Banking* 35(3): 403-24.

Leeladhar, V. (2005). "Basel II Accord and Its Implications", *RBI Bulletin*, April. pp.321-325.

Litterman, R.B. and L. Weiss (1985). "Money, Real Interest Rates, and Output: A Reinterpretation of Post-war U.S. Data", *Econometrica* 53(1): 129-56.

Lutkepohl, Helmut (1991). *Introduction to Multiple Time Series Analysis.* Berlin: Springer-Verlag.

Lutkepohl, Helmut, and H.E. Reimers (1992). "Impulse Response Analysis of Co-integrated Systems", *Journal of Economic Dynamics and Control* 16(1): 53-78.

McMillin, Douglas W. (1996). "Monetary Policy and Bank Portfolio", *Journal of Economics and Business* 48(4): 313-35.

McKinsey & Company (2005). *Indian Banking 2010: Towards a High Performing Sector.* Mumbai: McKinsey & Company.

Mishkin, F. (1995). "Symposium on the Monetary Transmission Mechanism," *Journal of Economic Perspectives* 9(4): 3-10.

Miron, Jeffrey A. and Christina D. Romer and David N. Weil (1994). "Historical Perspectives on the Monetary Transmission Mechanism", in N. Gregory Mankiw (ed.), *Monetary Policy.* Chicago: University of Chicago Press for NBER. pp.263-306

Modiglinai, F. and Lucas D. Papademos (1980). "The Structure of Financial Markets and the Monetary Mechanism", in *Controlling Monetary Aggregates III.* Boston: Federal Reserve Bank of Boston. pp.111-155.

———. (1987). "Money, Credit, and the Monetary Mechanism" in M. De Cecco and J.P. Fitussi (eds.), *Monetary Theory and Economic Institutions.* London: Macmillan Press. pp.121-160.

———. (1990). "The Supply of Money and the Control of Nominal Income", in B.M. Friedman and F.H. Hahn (eds.), *Handbook of Monetary Economics* Vol.1. Amsterdam: North-Holland. pp.399-494.

Mohan, Rakesh (2002). "Transforming Indian Banking: In Search of a Better Tomorrow", Valedictory address at the *Twenty-Fourth Bank Economists' Conference*, Bangalore. printed in *Reserve Bank of India Bulletin*, January 2003.

———. (2005). "Financial Sector Reforms in India: Policies and Performance Analysis", *Economic and Political Weekly* 40(12): 1106-19.

———. (2006a). "Reforms, Productivity and Efficiency in Banking: The Indian Experience", Address at the Pakistan Institute of Development Economists, *RBI Bulletin*, March.

———. (2006b). "Coping with Liquidity Management in India: A Practitioner's View", *RBI Bulletin*, April.

———. (2006c). "Economic Reforms in India: Where are We and Where do We Go?", *RBI Bulletin*, December.

Mojon, Benoît and Gert Peersman (2003). "A VAR Description of the Effects of Monetary Policy in the Individual Countries of the Euro Area", in I. Angeloni, A. Kashyap and B. Mojon (eds.), *Monetary Policy Transmission in the Euro Area.* Cambridge: Cambridge University Press. pp.56-74

Mukhopadhyay, Hiranya (1999). "Monetary Transmission Mechanism: The Credit Channel Hypothesis Revisited", *International Journal of Development Banking* 17(2): 47-58.

Myers, S. and N. Majluf (1984). "Corporate Financing and Investment Decisions when Firms have Information that Investors do not have", *Journal of Financial Economics* 13(2): 187-221.

Nachane, D.M. (1999). "Capital Adequacy Ratios—An Agnostic Viewpoint", *Economic and Political Weekly* 34(1&2).

———. (2006). *Econometrics*. Delhi: Oxford University Press.

Nachane, D.M. and R. Lakshmi (2000). "Have the Monetary Policy Lags chnaged in the Post-Liberalisation Period?", Paper presented at 36th *Annual Conference of the Indian Econometric Society* at Indore.

Nachane, D.M. and Saibal Ghosh (2002). "Determinants of Off-Balance Sheet Activities: An Empirical Analysis of Public Sector Banks", *Economic and Political Weekly* 37(5): 421-28.

Nachane, D.M., P. Ray and S. Ghosh (2005). "The New Basel Capital Accord: Rationale, Design and Tentative Implications for India" in K. Parikh and R. Radhakrishna (eds.), *India Development Report 2004-05*. Delhi: Oxford University Press. pp.171-190.

Nag, A.K., and Abhiman Das (2002). "Credit Growth and Response to Capital Requirement: Evidence from Indian Public Sector Banks", *Economic and Political Weekly* 37(32): 3361-68.

Okun, A.M. (1981): *Prices and Quantities*. Oxford: Basil Blackwell.

Pandit, B.L., Ajit Mittal, Mohua Roy, and Saibal Ghosh (2006). "Transmission of Monetary Policy and the Bank Lending Channel: Analysis and Evidence for India", *DRG Study* No. 25. Mumbai: Reserve Bank of India.

Parikh, Ashok (1994). "An Approach to Monetary Targeting in India", *Development Research Group Study* No. 9. Mumbai: Reserve Bank of India.

Patinkin, Don (1965). *Money, Interest and Prices* 2nd ed. New York: Harper Row.

Peek, Joe and Eric S. Rosengren (1995a). "The Capital Crunch: Neither a Borrower nor a Lender Be", *Journal of Money, Credit and Banking* 19(1): 679-92.

———. (1995b). "Bank Lending and Transmission of Monetary Policy", in Joe Peek and Eric S. Rosenburg (eds.), *Is Bank Lending Important for Monetary Policy?. Federal Reserve Bank of Boston Conference Series* No. 39. Boston: Federal Reserve Bank of Boston. pp.46-68

Pesaran, M.H., and B. Pesaran (1997). *Working with Microfit 4.0: Interactive Economic Analysis*. Oxford: Oxford University Press.

Pesaran, M.H. and Y. Shin (1998). "Generalized Impulse Response Analysis in Linear Multivariate Models", *Economic Letters* 58(1): 17-29.

Pill, H. (1997). "Bank Behaviour and Monetary Policy in a Small Open Economy: The Case of Spain". Harvard Business School. *(mimeo)*.

Pyle, D. (1971). "On the Theory of Financial Intermediation", *Journal of Finance* 26(3): 737-47.

Ram Mohan, T.T. (2003). "Long-run Performance of Public and Private Sector Bank Stocks", *Economic and Political Weekly* 38(8): 785-88.

Rangarajan, C. (1998). *Indian Economy: Essays on Money and Finance*. New Delhi: EBS Publishers.

Reddy, Y.V. (1999). "Monetary Policy Operating Procedures in India", in *Monetary Policy Operating Procedures in Emerging Market Economies, BIS Policy Papers* No. 5. Basel: Bank for International Settlement.

———. (2003). *Economic Policy in India: Managing Change.* New Delhi: UBSPD Publishers.

———. (2005). "Banking Sector Reforms in India: An Overview", Address at the Institute of Bankers of Pakistan, Karachi on May 18, 2005. *RBI Bulletin.*

Reserve Bank of India (1985). *Report of the Committee to Review the Functioning of the Monetary System* (Chairman: Prof Sukhamoy Chakravarty). Mumbai: Reserve Bank of India.

———. (1987). *Report of the Working Group on the Money Market.* (Chairman: N. Vaghul). Mumbai: Reserve Bank of India.

———. (1992). Report of the Committee on the Financial System, (Chairman: M. Narasimham), Mumbai: Reserve Bank of India.

———. (2001). *Report on Currency and Finance, 1999-2000.* Mumbai: Reserve Bank of India.

———. (2002). *Report on Currency and Finance, 2000-01.* Mumbai: Reserve Bank of India.

———. (2003a). *Report on Currency and Finance, 2001-02.* Mumbai: Reserve Bank of India.

———. (2003b). *Report of the Working Group on Instruments of Sterilisation* (Chairperson: Usha Thorat). Mumbai: Reserve Bank of India.

______. (2003c). *Report of the Internal Group on Liquidity Adjustment Facility.* Mumbai: Reserve Bank of India.

———. *Handbook of Statistics on the Indian Economy.* Mumbai: Reserve Bank of India.

Romer, Christina D. and David H. Romer (1990). "New Evidence on the Monetary Policy Transmission Mechanism", *Brookings Papers on Economic Activity* No. 1: 149-213.

———. (1993). "Credit Channel or Credit Actions? An Interpretation of the Post-war Transmission Mechanism", in *Changing Capital Markets: Implications for Monetary Policy,* Kansas City: Federal Reserve Bank of Kansas City. pp.71-116.

Runkle, David E. (1987). "Vector Autoregressions and Reality", *Journal of Business and Economic Statistics* 5(4): 437-42.

Santos, J.A.C. (2000). "Bank Capital Regulation in Contemporary Banking Theory: A Review of Literature", *BIS Working Paper* No. 90.

Sarkar, Jayati (1999). "India's Banking Sector: Current Status, Emerging Challenges, and Policy Imperatives in a Globalized Environment", in James Hansen and Sanjay Kathuria (eds.), *India: A Financial Sector for the Twenty First Century.* New Delhi: Oxford University Press.

———. (2004). "The Banking Industry", in Subir Gokarn, Anindya Sen and Rajendra Vaidya (eds.), *The Structure of Indian Industry.* New Delhi: Oxford University Press.

Sarkar, Jayati, Subrata Sarkar and Sumon K. Bhowmik (1998). "Does Ownership Always Matter?—Evidence from the Indian Banking Industry", *Journal of Comparative Economics* 26(2): 262-281.

Sen, Kunal, T. Roy, R. Krishanan and A. Mundlay (1996). "A Flow of Funds Model for India and its Uses", *Journal of Policy Modelling* 18(5): 469-94.

Sims, C.A. (1974). "Seasonality in Regression", *Journal of American Statistical Association* 69: 616-27.

———. (1980). "Macroeconomics and Reality", *Econometrica* 48(1): 1-48.

———. (1992). "Interpreting Macroeconomic Time Series Facts: The Effects of Monetary Policy", *European Economic Review* 36(5): 975-1011.

Sims, C.A. and H. Uhlig (1991). "Understanding Unit Rooters: A Helicopter Tour", *Econometrica* 59(6): 1591-99.

Sims, C.A., J.H. Stock and M. Watson (1990). "Inference in Some Linear Time Series Models with Some Unit Roots", *Econometrica* 58(1): 113-44.

Singh, K. and K.P. Kalirajan (2003). "An Empirical Analysis of Monetary Transmission in India", in K. Kalirajan and U. Shankar (eds.), *Economic Reforms and the Liberalisation of the Indian Economy.* Cheltenham (U.K.): Edward Elgar. pp.275-308

Sinha, J. (2005). "India Needs Bigger Banks", *Business Standard.* October 03.

Söderlind, Paul (1999). *Lectures on Macroeconomics and Monetary Policy.* Stockholm School of Economics. Available at *http://www.hhs.se/personal/psoderlind.*

Stein, J.C. (1998). "An Adverse Selection Model of Bank Asset and Liability Management with Implications for the Transmission of Monetary Policy", *RAND Journal of Economics* 29(3): 466-86.

Strongin, S. (1995). "The identification of Monetary Policy Disturbances: Explaining the Liquidity Puzzle", *Journal of Monetary Economics* 35(3): 463-97.

Stiglitz, J. and A. Weiss (1981). "Credit Rationing in Markets with Imperfect Information", *American Economic Review* 71(3): 393-410.

Stiglitz, J. and B. Greenwald (1992). "Toward a Reformulation of Monetary Theory: Competitive Banking", *NBER Working Paper* No. 4117.

———. (2003). *Towards a New Paradigm in Monetary Economics.* Cambridge: Cambridge University Press.

Stock, J.H. and M.W. Watson (2001). "Vector Autoregression", *Journal of Economic Perspectives* (4): 101-15.

Tobin, James (1969). "A General Equilibrium Approach to Monetary Theory", *Journal of Money, Credit and Banking* 1(1): 15-29.

Todd, Richard (1990). Vector Autoregression Evidence on Monetarism: Another Look at the Robustness Debate, *Federal Reserve Bank of Minneapolis Quarterly Review,* Spring.

Wallis, K.F. (1974). "Seasonal Adjustment and Relation between Variables", *Journal of American Statistical Association* 69: 18-31.

Vasudevan, A. (2002). "Evolving Monetary Policy in India: Some Perspectives", *Economic and Political Weekly* 37(11): 1055-1061.

———. (2003). *Central Banking in Emerging Market Economies.* New Delhi: Academic Foundation.

Vazquez, F. (2001): "Bank Lending and Monetary Conditions in Developing Countries: International Evidence on Lending Channel", *Working Paper.* University Maryland.

Index

D